# EDITH WHARTON AND THE UNSATISFACTORY MAN

# EDITH WHARTON AND THE UNSATISFACTORY MAN

by

David Holbrook

*Emeritus Fellow, Downing College, Cambridge*

VISION PRESS · LONDON
ST. MARTIN'S PRESS · NEW YORK

#225/0303

Vision Press Ltd.
c/o Vine House Distribution
Waldenbury, North Common
Chailey, E. Sussex BN8 4DR

and

St. Martin's Press, Inc.
175 Fifth Avenue
New York
N.Y. 10010

ISBN (UK) 0 85478 137 4
ISBN (US) 0 312 03565 9

British Library Cataloguing-in-Publication Data

Holbrook, David, 1923–
Edith Wharton and the unsatisfactory man. (Critical studies series)
1. Fiction in English. American writers. Wharton, Edith, 1862–1937.
I. Title II. Series
813.52

Library of Congress Cataloging-in-Publication Data

Holbrook, David.
Edith Wharton and the unsatisfactory man/ by David Holbrook.
(Critical studies series)
ISBN 0-312-03565-9
1. Wharton, Edith, 1862–1937—Criticism and interpretation.
2. Wharton, Edith, 1862–1937—Characters—Men. 3. Men in literature. I. Title. II. Series.
PS3545.H16Z665 1991
813'52—dc20 90-19431
CIP


First published in the U.S.A. 1991



Printed and bound in Great Britain by
Billing & Sons, Worcester.
Typeset by Galleon Photosetting,
Ipswich, Suffolk.
MCMLXLI

# Contents

# Introduction

Edith Wharton bridges the nineteenth century and the twentieth; she was brought up in old New York, in an environment where a young woman was trained for a marriage in which social relationships and inheritance were an integral part of the scene. If women were educated, it should be 'in order to be to the man all he needs', and to act as a 'moral lever' in the home. Edith believed her life had been ruined by her mother's failure to enlighten her as to what was going to happen on her wedding night: this seemed to her all part of an 'innocence'—meaning ignorance and submission—imposed on woman. During her life this structure and pattern were broken and, like D. H. Lawrence, she set out to follow the idea of woman becoming independent, seeking her own fulfilment and authenticity. But she was aware that in her own case she had been crippled by her upbringing and by the social manipulations that brought her into marriage. So, she is of special interest to today's feminist writers.

There is, however, another element in these matters, that of human consciousness, and it is not insignificant that another observer of the scene, Sigmund Freud, developed his insights from treating hysteric symptoms in women of the bourgeoisie in Vienna, more or less at the same time. His achievement was phenomenological. Freud found that these symptoms had a meaning, and so set off the great development of phenomenology in psychoanalysis: attention to the meanings of consciousness.

It is my intention to try to apply these deeper insights here, in hoping to contribute to a better understanding of Edith Wharton's novels, and her achievement. For she lived through cataclysmic events—the Great War of 1914–18, for example, a catastrophe from which consciousness is still trying to recover—and while dealing with the realities of suffering, maintained her attention as an artist to the deepest and most central problems of being, in men and women, as a novelist. She wrote from the depths of her own being, at best, and involved herself closely in her characters who must be seen, at times, as enactments of aspects of herself, and dramatisations of elements of her own make-up.

While most of her novels have at their core a preoccupation with sexuality, this is dealt with as lying at the centre of a need for good relationship and meaning. In the grave atmosphere of the psychotherapeutic consulting-room the therapist learns that what each human being needs is a love relationship in which he or she can find his uniqueness and so find a confirmation of his being; this is perhaps as near as we can get to anything that we can call meaning. In Edith Wharton's novels her characters, like herself, are in pursuit of this mode of relationship, love in which the real self can meet another and find that 'creative reflection' in which (as Martin Buber put it) 'the heavenly bread of self-being is passed.' With some, like Ethan Frome or Lily Bart, this quest is a life-or-death struggle; but the truth is that none of her characters are ever allowed to find fulfilment. They settle for other, inauthentic, forms of relationship, which have their own meaning, but the 'meeting of true minds' seems to elude them, as it eluded her.

A phrase intrudes here, from Viktor Frankl: 'a thoroughly decadent sensualism'—which suggests perhaps the worst (existential) danger in the modern world of sexual freedom. In *The Children* it is clear that Edith Wharton regards the antics of the parents with a deep moral loathing, as much as Henry James shows his loathing in *What Maisie Knew.* Around this theme in Edith Wharton there is a personal problem: she herself had an adulterous affair with a Morton Fullerton, who one commentator has called an 'experienced seducer'. In this affair she found sensual happiness, and she wrote a rapturous Whitmanesque poem about one night—the last night—she spent with this lover. Yet Fullerton obviously lacked the stamina for a committed relationship and was also, it would seem, bisexual: he could only sustain his love for a woman for about three years, and he maintained several relationships at once, while also having sexual relationships with men. After a while Edith Wharton obviously radically revised her picture of him. Her deepest friendships actually were with *bachelor* men like Henry James and Walter Berry, and it could even be argued that some of these men seemed to be homosexual. So, we have to ask ourselves, what kind of woman has an inclination to form relationships with men who are unable or unlikely to commit themselves to her as man to woman—as, evidently, she would like to have had them do?

The answer, I believe, is a woman who has a strong attachment to her father, and who has had traumatic experiences in her introduction to sexual relationships. A woman, we may perhaps add, who has such fantasies of an incestuous relationship with her father that it haunts her all her life, or who was actually abused by her father. She is haunted by a sense that there is something inherently menacing—even filled with horror—in sexual intercourse, and that the sexual experience of passion will inevitably burn itself out: '*That the veil of passion must wear through was life's unescapable lesson,* but if no deeper understanding underlay it, what was left?' (*GA*, p. 345; my italics).

This comes at the end of *The Gods Arrive,* which is the last complete novel Edith Wharton wrote. Of Vance's relationship with Halo this character reflects, 'their last weeks at Oubli seemed to have made it clear that their experiment had reached its term:' The word 'term' should be noted: Edith Wharton's last poem to Morton Fullerton was called *Terminus* and they met at a significant moment in a railway terminus hotel; she seemed to have a proclivity for a sexual affair whose end was inherent in its beginning. Edith Wharton herself failed to make a lasting relationship, and this was felt deeply by her, as we may discover from her work, in all its bearing on her philosophy of being.

Questioned by his grandmother, Mrs. Scrimser, in *The Gods Arrive,* Vance declares:

> . . . It's a whole complex of things—it's me as the lord made me, I suppose: a bunch of ill-assorted odds and ends. I couldn't make any woman happy—so what's the use of worrying about it. (*GA*, p. 375)

Mrs. Scrimser replies: '. . . as if being happy was the

whole story! It's only the preface: any woman worth her salt'll tell you that.' When he declares himself not to be worth any woman's salt, she replies: '. . . Don't you go running yourself down, either. It's the quickest short cut to losing your self-respect. And all your fine writing won't help if you haven't got that' (*GA*, p. 375). Edith Wharton was such a consummate artist because, despite her literary success, she went on writing to sustain not only her self-respect, but also her sense of meaningful identity in the face of her emotional shortcomings and the exigencies and chances of her life.

Mrs. Scrimser has an especial call on our attention, for the whole of the two last novels, *Hudson River Bracketted* and *The Gods Arrive,* are haunted by Vance's traumatic recollection of Mr. Scrimser's behaviour. He was clearly a promiscuous man, deeply disloyal to Vance's grandmother. Vance is seduced by Floss Delaney, but he has been haunted all his life by Floss Delaney's betrayal, when he was a boy, at the beginning of the first novel:

> The light was failing fast and Vance was a good hundred yards from the river; but in the thicker dusk, and at a greater distance, he would have known the quick movements, the light outline, of the girl slipping through the trees toward Mr. Scrimser . . . He saw—or thought he saw—the two figures come together in the dimness, just where, so often, he had caught Floss Delaney to his first embrace. . . . (*HRB*, p. 23)

The pain is excrutiating:

> He had never been able to imagine what excrutiating physical pain was like, the kind you felt when you were smashed under a train, or torn by a whirling engine in a factory—but he knew, he found out in the glare of that blinding instant, that when the soul is smitten deeply enough it seems to become one with the body, to share all the body's capacity for suffering a distinct and different anguish in each nerve and muscle. (*HRB*, p. 23)

The intensity of this experience, combined with the fact that Vance is fascinated by Floss Delaney later in his life, and goes back to her (although she is a cold, cruel adventuress) suggests a complex and ambiguous ambivalence in Edith Wharton. The intensity of the writing here seems to go with a certain compulsion, to dwell on and to revert to an early passion known to be deadly, which is a theme often found in her novels. For despite his horror at her original duplicity, Floss remains a source of inspiration for Vance.

> Certain obscure fibres in both their natures seemed inextricably tangled. There was a dumb subterranean power in her that corresponded with his own sense of the forces by which his inventive faculty was fed. (*GA*, p. 385)

Floss Delaney is far from being a true literary companion for Vance: she says, 'I wish your new novel wasn't so dreadfully long . . . I've tried to read it but I can't. . . .' But his obsession with her is only broken after being told by her that she has used a man's letters to blackmail a family in business competition with her, the Shuntses, into buying her out at her own price. At this triumph, 'there was a veiled radiance in her face which he had seen in it only once or twice, in moments of passionate surrender.' (The scene is examined below, p. 160.)

In his tormented reflection on his disillusionment, Vance dreams of two women:

> Two women peopled these agitated vigils; the one that his soul rejected and his body yearned for, the other who had once seemed the answer to all he asked of life, but who had now faded to a reproach and a torment. The whole question of woman was the age-long obstacle to peace of spirit. . . . All he wanted was to be himself, solely and totally himself, *not tangled up in the old deadly nets of passion and emotion.* (*GA*, p. 415; my italics)

I shall deal with these two novels later, but I want here to try to distil Edith Wharton's latest wisdom in them: does she agree with her character Frenside?

> *Dichterliebe*, eh! Well, you're probably right. Most artists are incurably polygamous. When they're not it's because they die young—and their books generally do. But I don't know that their loving so lavishly matters as much itself, as what it makes of them. . . . (*GA*, p. 433)

At the end of the novel, however, Vance is rescued by Halo from the collapse of his belief in human nature, and is accepted by her as a 'child'. 'But then I shall have two children to take care of instead of one!' (*GA*, p. 439). It may be seen as a beginning to recognize the degree of infantile dependence in the adult sexual relationship, but to accept the other partner as a 'child' is no solution. In this tendency we may glimpse the limitations of Edith Wharton's view of sexual relationships.

For there is an ambiguity in Edith Wharton's novels, between the adult relationship that often seems unappealing and the relationship as to a child that seems inviting and mysterious—as in *The Children.* In *Summer* the relationship between the girl and her lover seems full of dangers from which the safe marriage of convenience with lawyer Loyall seems to be a haven. In *Ethan Frome* the relationship with Mattie is full of childish elements. Darrow in *The Reef* continually calls Sophy Viner 'child'. Halo takes Vance back as a child.

By contrast with this eagerness to become preoccupied with the 'child' relationship, the adult relationship seems deadly—as between Selden and Lily Bart, or Newland Archer and Ellen Olenska. These relationships are not fulfilled, and behind the hesitancy of the men seems to lie a horror of what Halo calls 'the other thing': sexual meeting. Here there is a revealing passage in *Hudson River Brackettted*:

> perhaps his recoil from the idea of combining physical endearments with such a communion was due to Laura Lou's persistent suspicion. *He would have to dissociate sensual passion from all that had debased or cheapened it before it could blend with his vision of this woman who had understood and pitied him.* (*HRB*, p. 354; my italics)

But there is no indication of any element of debasement or cheapening in Vance's sexual life; the comment is an intrusion of the author's feelings, which again occasionally surfaces, that there is something inherently debasing and cheapening in sex itself. Both Vance and Halo reflect continuously on the strange links or disconnections between Vance's creativity and their sexual love; yet he seems to find in Floss Delaney's cruel sensuality something that 'corresponded with his own sense of the forces by which his inventive faculty was fed' (*GA*, p. 345).

If we examine the rôle of sexual relationships in Edith Wharton's novels, the startling fact emerges that there is mostly very little sexual meeting. If as a novelist she sees the quest for fulfilment of being in sexual encounter, then this pursuit is largely frustrated. As one critic has noted, there is a preoccupation with the 'female intruder' who threatens the normal progress of relational development: Sophie Viner, Ellen Olenska, Judith. But often the growth of a love is frustrated by the failing of the man to commit himself or to develop: Newland Archer, Laurence Selden, Martin Boyne, Vance Weston. In one of her most powerful novels, *The Custom of the Country*, significantly, to her heroine, Undine Spragg, sex hardly matters. Undine is bored on honeymoon with Ralph, while in her marriage to de Celles, he soon loses sexual interest in her. Even the sexual adventurer Van Degan, with whom she forms a liaison almost out of inertia, is appalled by his discovery of her hard-hearted indifference to her husband's illness, and fears that she might treat him with similar coldness. By this incident Edith Wharton makes it clear that personal manners, in the widest sense, count for more than sensual indulgence, even to the sexual conquerer. The anguish suffered by Undine's son, towards the end of the novel, emphasizes, in a Jamesian way, the real moral considerations that ought to guide personal commitment in sexual matters.

What is illuminating in Edith Wharton's novels is the light she sheds on the way in which individuals cast fantasies over one another. She herself, of course, must have been involved in such a process, as her lover Morton Fullerton was the kind of man who tended to turn sex into verbal expression, while she herself experienced with him a gradual disillusionment.*

There seems no possibility, in Edith Wharton's perspectives, of reconciliation between the romantic yearning and marriage. Ellen Olenska in *The Age of Innocence* may be a 'guileless temptress', and she is perhaps the most attractive of Edith Wharton's 'female intruders', but she belongs to a fantasy world, and the irony is that Newland Archer himself has taught her that the best values are those based on a realistic appraisal of authenticity. Even his wife May realizes

* Later in life when he sent her a novel and reported that they had read it aloud together, she rejoined wryly: 'I was not the woman with whom you read. . . .'

what he has given up, while Ellen becomes an 'abstraction' to remember, so that, years later, when she might have been available to him, he remains seated on a bench outside her apartment thinking, 'It's more real to me here than if I went up.'

Again, authenticity is baffled by the failure of the man to be full-blooded and committed, while the woman he loves allows herself to be romanticized in an unreal way. I cannot agree with those who, like Carol Wershoven, find that the novel ends in 'a pair of gentle negatives':

> Archer's life not entirely wasted, thanks to his widening perceptions; May's marriage intact if stultifying . . . a free Ellen Olenska, who . . . has lived as an independent woman, safe from her husband. . . . (Wershoven, p. 90)

There may be generosity, tolerance and goodwill in Ellen's renunciation, but if she and Newland were in love, while the marriage was 'stultifying', what satisfaction could there be in the failure of authenticity and the man's final determination to live in memories of his fantasy—even though we may suspect it was, indeed, too late to take up the woman who had once offered him the clue to a higher meaning?

What is puzzling is the way in which critics of Edith Wharton elevate some of her women figures to a high value, and speak of their 'innocence' as being 'positive and enduring': Charles Doyle, for instance, calls Ellen Olenska a 'guileless temptress' ('Emblems of Innocence: Imagery Patterns in Wharton's *The Age of Innocence*', Xavier University Studies, 10 (1971), pp. 19–25). Carol Wershoven finds Judith, Sophy and Ellen possess a 'kind of innocence that is positive and endearing' (*The Female Intruder,* p. 120), while Geoffrey Walton calls Judith 'an older version of Maisie who, in spite of it all, preserves a basic innocence of intention and sense of responsibility' (*Edith Wharton,* p. 152). This concept of 'innocence' seems to be related to a certain idealized view of childhood, but is surely unreal in the light of Freudian realism about the child's awareness of sexuality? It therefore seems to indicate a certain inclination on Edith Wharton's part to deny in woman the capacities for sexuality and the forfeiture of innocence that such awareness must bring. One might even go so far as to say that she is trying to preserve the unspeakable quality of her child relationship to her father, in order to present this innocence as a valid mode of existence. There would seem to lie behind this tendency a number of existential questions in Edith Wharton's own life. She felt unable to discover who she was because of the ignorance imposed on her by her mother and by her attachment to her father, either through her intense fantasies or because he abused her. Later, she discovered her sexual self through her adulterous *affaire* with Morton Fullerton after a marriage which offered no such fulfilment and ceased to be sexual. Thus, she has herself a predeliction for the woman who is a sexual adventuress, while feeling that sex is dangerous and deathly. In the title of her novel *The Age of Innocence* the word 'innocence' is heavily ironic: yet there is a deeper ambiguity around the word for her, as she continues to yearn from a certain child-like disingenuousness (like Judith's) that has none of the dangers and obligations of mature sexuality. Edith Wharton's problem is not quite that of bringing together the ideal and the libidinal, however. In her triangular relationships there is often a mature woman on the one hand, and a child-woman on the other, competing for the same man. As others have noticed, she seems often to find cross-generational liaisons, even incestuous ones, more exciting, while the young 'female intruder' seems to have the livelier appeal.

In trying to understand these inclinations I believe the 'Palmato' fragment of pornography she wrote is most revealing. This fragment is given in Appendix C of R. W. B. Lewis's *Biography of Edith Wharton,* together with the extraordinary story of its discovery. Lewis points out that Edith Wharton could never have hoped to have these pages published, so why did she write it and keep it among her papers? As C. G. Wolff makes clear, 'Her final illness was a merciful and slow heart failure and she had plenty of opportunity' to destroy the piece—but she left it. Wolff declares that 'something in her seems to have whispered: 'Let them discover that I, too, have lived.' But this seems a strange interpretation, when the piece seems to have been written out to realize the horror behind the projected short story *Beatrice Palmato,* in which man and wife are faced with the horror of incest and her guilt destroys the woman.

The story to which the passage relates is hardly one of sexual fulfilment! It is a story of some terrible legacy which lies behind a marriage:

> . . . many mysterious things in their married life—the sense of some hidden power controlling her, and perpetually coming between them, and of some strange initiation, some profound moral perversion of which he had always been afraid to face the thought—all these things became suddenly clear to him, lit up in a glare of horror. (*RWBL*, p. 546)

The mother realizes that, in responding strongly to her husband's embracement of her daughter, she has betrayed her terrible secret and rushes off to kill herself. Cynthia Wolff suggests that Edith Wharton wanted to write out in an articulate form the horror behind her short story, just as Joseph Conrad is reported to have written out that behind *Heart of Darkness.* But the Palmato passage is not offered as a horror at all; in the gloating language of pornography, it dwells on the excited heat of the encounter with relish. Moreover, the intense eroticism of the sexual act is contrasted with the woman protagonist's 'dull misery of her marriage', as she experiences the first open performance of this encounter with her *father.* By contrast, the experience of her husband is described as 'Austin's rough advances', while of her wedding night her father declares: 'The experience is a cruel one—but it has to come once in all women's lives.'

In the way the episode is written, there are a number of strange phrases which are, I believe, most revealing. The father says, for instance, 'let me show you what only you and I have the right to show each other.' The sense that the father has a *right* to abuse his daughter here could well be a slant on her incestuous experience to which Edith Wharton was inclined, because, as a child, she had to 'preserve the good father' in spite of his abuse of her. Then, as the man slips his hand down to her genital, she writes: 'At the same moment the other hand softly separated her legs, and began to slip up the *old path it had so often travelled in darkness*' (my italics). This suggests that the father had often masturbated his daughter in the darkness—and only now is he making love to her in full light, while she can look down on his 'dark silver-sprinkled head'. The loving detail of this conveys a deep erotic proclivity towards the father.

Then the father 'presses into her hand the strong fiery muscle that they used, in their old joke, to call his third hand'. The familiarity behind this conveys an experience of long-standing intimacy, which the details of the story do not require. It is the first time she has seen his penis. The passage has greater importance, and reveals more, than R. W. B. Lewis or Cynthia Wolff find in it. Such mementos left behind by an author often have considerable unconscious significance. George Macdonald, for instance, left in his desk a lock of his mother's hair and a letter she wrote to speak of the horrors he went through when she suddenly weaned him, and this was the focal interest of the whole of his creative life.

Here, I believe, we may make a phenomenological interpretation, and suggest a key importance to this Palmato fragment. It is intensely clitoral, and masturbatory, and could be the product of a childish fantasy. But there are those references to a private intimacy, and old habits or procedures, together with the reference to 'rights' which could be the product of being fixated on an incestuous father who abused the daughter. The name 'Palmato', meaning 'the felt one' seems also important, as is the indirect reference to Beatrice Cenci. We shall never know, of course, whether the abuse was actual: Lewis and Wolff seem to believe that it was all fantasy. Edith Wharton, according to Wolff, was a 'little girl' with a 'powerful emotional hunger'; she carried this intense need into her attachment to her father, and the consequent crisis was incompletely resolved.

> A woman who has had such a past can never completely eradicate its effects . . . just as the little girl's unresolved feelings about her father might affect all subsequent sexual relationships, so the same persistent ghost of oedipal uncertainty might resonate in any *cross-generational* relationship. An adult rôle that could be construed as an individuation to rehearse the feelings of an 'amorous child' would be made more difficult by the relics of past conflicts; and so would any demand to assume the rôle of 'parent'. (Wolff, p. 379)

The Palmato episode, says Wolff, 'provides an *aperçu* into the well-springs of the girl's fantasy life' and, she declares, 'is a rather striking insight into the way Edith Wharton conceptualised love and sexuality'. Indeed, this may be so, for what it reveals is that Edith Wharton tended to invert normal perspectives, to idolize incestuous sex and to declare it superior to a husband's 'rough advances'. At the same time, putting the passage within the context of the short story that ends in madness and death, we can see why Edith Wharton felt there to lurk such a horror behind sex.

As Wolff admits, Edith Wharton does find incest 'irresistably attractive'. But Wolff goes on to claim that it is only the bans of society that make incest a horror. Can we believe this, after all we have learnt about child abuse? Surely the idolization—as in the pornographic passage—is an attempt to hide the horror, in trying to preserve a false solution to the problem? Edith Wharton's affection for her father, says Wolff, was 'so great that it fixed upon her father with voracious and terrifying intensity'. The power of this hunger and attachment generated the strange phrases which I indicate above, about the father's 'rights', the secret of the 'third hand' and the 'old path', and the hand fetishism. Wolff refers to the account in *A Backward Glance* of the little girl's attitude to her father: her hand 'in the large safe hollow of her father's bare hand; her tall handsome father, who was so warm-blooded that in the coldest weather he always went out without gloves'. She also connects the same 'Palmato' with the fetishistic reference to the 'third hand' and points out that in several of Edith Wharton's love scenes, as in *Summer* and 'Terminus', lovers are 'palm to palm'.

We have seen that Cynthia Wolff and Lewis discuss Edith Wharton's motives in leaving this passage for her biographers. Would she not have indicated more clearly that there was no biographical element in this, to protect her father's memory? Or did she mean it as a clue to a traumatic experience that wrecked her life?

In her study of Edith Wharton's psychological make-up, *A Feast of Words,* Cynthia Wolff speaks of 'the problems that had impeded her earlier life' (p. 380). She carried throughout her life 'certain emotional habits': 'an inevitable residuum from those early traumas remained to complicate the dilemmas of adult life' (Wolff, p. 379). She also speaks in a footnote of '*the initial failure of trust'*; the language of *hunger*, she points out, turns up in the late books, in Kate Clephane (*The Mother's Recompense*), the elder Manfords (in *Twilight Sleep*) and Martin Boyne (in *The Children*).

She goes on to discuss the theme of incest; in these later works incest is seen 'from the vantage of the parent—not the child'. In a footnote she adds that the one exception is the episode in *Hudson River Bracketted* 'when Vance catches sight of his leering grandfather scuttling into the bushes with the town tramp (whom Vance himself has earlier bedded)' (p. 435). What Cynthia Wolff does not say, however, is that in *The Gods Arrive* Vance is totally bowled over by this same 'tramp', Floss Delaney, who becomes a fascinating ideal for him, and for a time completely destroys his more authentic relationship with Halo.

I should like to pick up the word 'trauma' in Cynthia Wolff's book. She speaks earlier of Edith Wharton's emotional starvation by her mother, and the way in which her intense imaginative hunger fixated on her father: 'his little girl contrived to pour all of her passionate imagination into some representation of him that satisfied the emotional storms within her' (Wolff, p. 19). And she quotes Edith Wharton herself:

> I have wondered since what stifled cravings had once germinated in him, and what manner of man he was really meant to be. That he was a lonely one, haunted by something always unexpressed and unattained, I am sure. (Wolff, p. 19)

Cynthia Wolff goes on:

> he walked with his daughter often of an afternoon. His warm presence, like the encompassing touch of his warm hand, must have been a powerful emotional magnet, drawing to it all the child's unsatisfied cravings. (Wolff, p. 19)

It could be, of course, that she was such an imaginative child that her fantasies, compensating for a deficiency of warmth from her mother, came to be projected over her father, and the intensity of these was enough to disturb radically her emotional life. But can a child be traumatized by her own fantasies? It seems unlikely. So much of Edith Wharton's writing seems to belong to those processes by which a child must preserve the 'good' father; so much does she idolize incest, that I believe we must consider whether, in fact, her father did abuse her. She often refers to problems so unspeakable that people flinch from even daring to refer to them. Now that child abuse is recognized to occur at all levels of society, can we not examine the possibility that such an experience both twisted her view of sexuality, and even that, like Vance's obsession with Floss Delaney's cross-generational experience of Grandfather Scrimser, it was a mainspring of her art?

# 1

# *The House of Mirth*

*The House of Mirth* was Edith Wharton's first major success and her first work of serious and original examination of the contemporary scene. It deals with some seventeen months in the life of Lily Bart, a beautiful girl who is penniless, but who is fascinated by high life, fashion and manic behaviour. She becomes a hanger-on, in New York society and the American life of the French Riviera, and finds herself enmeshed in and seriously compromised by scandalous situations—while, because of her need for funds to sustain herself in this life, she falls into further entanglements and moral decline. She has a sharper conscience than those with whom she consorts, but is unable to maintain any degree of moral superiority—though she does not become really corrupt or degraded. She is the epitome of the kind of woman that society demands; indeed, in a sense, she is the product of that society. She is continually exerting her 'independence', but then becomes ensnared in scandal that is not of her own making: for instance, she goes with a friend, Laurence Selden, to 'the Benedick', a set of bachelor apartments, but no one will afterwards believe she did not go there for a sexual rendezvous with him; she takes money from Gus Trenor, who offers to gain dividends for her, but finds herself in debt to him and seriously compromised in advances he makes to her.

Selden—the hero of the novel—regards her from a distance, but is attracted to her; he even believes himself in love with her. But even though he is the one person who might offer an alternative to her parasitic life, in which she is seeking a rich husband, he fails her. He has ideals, of what he calls 'the republic of the spirit', but he turns out to be too careful, too liable to try to make her, in her beauty, into a 'work of art', while protecting himself by remaining aloof, and only too ready to believe the worst of her.

Edith Wharton's earlier titles for the novel relate it to society's idea of what a woman should be. The first title was 'A Moment's Ornament', the second 'The Year of the Rose': women were expected to be ornaments, whose existence was fragile and momentary. 'The House of Mirth' comes as a phrase from *Ecclesiastes*: 'the heart of fools is in the house of mirth'—a phrase which rings with the bitterness and irony with which Edith Wharton wrote the novel.

Lily is a subtle and endearing character. R. W. B. Lewis suggests her closeness to the author herself, pointing out that 'Lily' was a name used by Edith in her early days. Lily regards herself as unfitted by her society and misunderstood by it: but there is no alternative, and, of course, she dies. She dies, moreover, in such a way as to be just out of touch with the man who could have saved her.

He, like so many of the men in Edith Wharton's own life—Walter Berry, Egerton Winthrop, Eliot Gregory—is unsatisfactory; none of them had sufficient blood in their veins. But besides this, we need to say, I believe, that Edith Wharton, because of her strong attachment to her father, saw men in general as being non-commital, self-protective, unresponsive to women, even possibly homosexual (though Selden has already had an adulterous affair with Bertha Dorsett, for which, unlike Darrow, he is apparently pardoned). Selden may be taken, as R. W. B. Lewis says, as 'an emblem of masculinity in Edith's world'—but he may also be seen as an indication of her own inclination to seek out the unsatisfactory man for herself—the man who (like Morton Fullerton) has the end of an affair in mind, even as he embarks upon it.

*The House of Mirth* is a tragic novel, deeply involved with Edith Wharton's own predicament. She, too, had to endure the triviality and nastiness of the New York rich; she, too, must have yearned for a man to rescue her. Yet she never knew a man who would say, with passionate conviction, 'I love you—we must marry.' (This novel was written before her *affaire* with Fullerton.) It is a study of compromise—of the woman who cannot give up her attachment to wealth and luxury, and of the man who loves her but who is baffled by suspicion and thwarted by circumstances. As he is alone with the body of Lily in the extraordinary last chapter, Laurence Selden finds a positive gain, in the thought of his love for Lily. Now she is dead, stripped of her mortal longings, he can penetrate her secrets, and find the authentic Lily whom he genuinely loved. That two such individuals can only meet when one of them has died, largely through the inanition of the one who survives, is a grim message.

Here, perhaps, we need to examine the unconscious meanings, not least because the note of that last chapter is so positive. It is as if Edith Wharton is saying, once one were dead, one could be known and appreciated, one could be really *loved*—as if this were true of herself.

The morning is bright ('The next morning rose mild and bright, with a promise of summer in the air'); Selden has at last found 'the word he meant to say to her, and it could not wait another moment to be said'.

> It was strange that it had not come to his lips sooner—that he had let her pass from him the evening before without being able to speak it. But what did that matter? It was not a word for twilight, but for the morning. (*HM*, p. 509)*

Gerry Farish opens the door, and 'the trembling hand she laid on him seemed instantly to close about his heart.'

He finds Lily dead in the sunlight:

> Though the blind was down, the irresistible sunlight poured a tempered golden flood into the room, and in its light Selden saw a narrow bed along the wall, and on the bed, the semblance of Lily Bart. (*HM*, p. 510)

The consciousness has departed; what has he to do with the remains?

* References are to the Macmillan 1905 edition.

> That it was her real self, every pulse in him ardently denied. Her real self had lain warm on his heart but a few hours earlier—what had he to do with this estranged and tranquil face which, for the first time, neither paled nor brightened at his coming. (*HM*, p. 510)

He feels, however, that the 'real Lily' was still there, 'close to him, yet invisible and inaccessible'. 'There had never been more than a little impalpable barrier between them—and yet he had suffered it to keep them apart' (*HM*, p. 511).

Gerty leaves him alone with the body, 'and as she spoke a light broke through Selden's strong misery, and he saw deep into the hidden things of love.' He looks round her room, and finds two letters—one to a bank, and another to Gus Trenor. Why has she written to Trenor? 'The thought unhallowed the memory of that last hour, made a mock of the word he had come to speak, and defiled even the reconciling silence upon which it fell' (*HM*, p. 513).

He thrusts the letter to Trenor from him. Among her papers, he finds one which he sent her the day after the Brys's entertainment: 'When may I come to you?' These words overwhelm him with a realization of his cowardice *'which had driven her from him at the very moment of attainment'*. And he is reminded that even now, all his old doubts have started to life again, at the mere sight of Trenor's name.

From her other records, he deduces that yes she had taken money from Gus Trenor, but that the obligation had become intolerable to her, and she had used Mrs. Penistone's legacy of $10,000 to repay her debt to Trenor, although the act had left her 'face to face with bare unmitigated poverty'.

She had kissed him the night before, on his forehead, and he could now read into that 'all that his heart craved to find there: he could even draw from it courage not to accuse himself for having failed to reach the height of his opportunity.'

> He saw that all the conditions of life had conspired to keep them apart; since his very detachment from the external influences which swayed her had increased his spiritual fastidiousness, and made it more difficult for him to live and

> love uncritically. But at least he *had* loved her—had been willing to stake his future on his faith in her—and if the moment had been fated to pass from them before they could seize it, he saw now that, for both, it had been saved whole out of the ruin of their lives. (*HM*, p. 516)

It has to be said, this is a very wordy, and a rather subtly 'documented' end!

> It was this moment of love, this fleeting victory over themselves, which had kept them from atrophy and extinction; which, in her, had reached out to him in every struggle against the influence of her surroundings, and in him, had kept alive the faith that drew him penitent and reconciled to her side.
>
> He knelt by the bed and bent over her, draining their last moment to its lees; and in the silence there passed between them the word which made all clear.
>
> THE END
>
> (*HM*, p. 516)

The words describe a state of reconciliation, love, faith and hope—and this is a triumph of authenticity and reality over chaos; but Lily is dead all the same, and there is a sense in which our response is, 'They could only find one another in death' and 'Only such a radical transformation as death could heal the barriers of triviality and suspicion between these protagonists.' So, in the novel's 'upshot' are we to take it that Edith Wharton is telling us that her femininity can only fulfil itself in death, while the maleness she knows is unsatisfactory until it encounters the challenge of death—whereupon it is too late, and becomes the final impotence? The word 'impotence' entirely describes the failure of Selden, and even his final intercourse with Lily. It is, at the unconscious level, as if Edith Wharton is saying that she could never find, in herself or a man, the possibility of love before death removes the yearning forever. Perhaps we may interpret this novel thus: for a girl whose all-possessing love has been for her father, love-in-death is the only solution, since the father belongs to a past generation and is dead anyway?

Lily Bart has an addiction to luxury, to high living and high spending; yet her ambitions here all go wrong. As she examines the wedding presents at the Van Osburgh household,

> The glow of the stones warmed Lily's veins like wine. More completely than any other expression of wealth they symbolised the life she longed to lead, the life of fastidious aloofness and refinement in which every detail should have the finish of a jewel, and the whole form a harmonious setting to her own jewel-like rareness. (*HM*, p. 140)

But even on the next page, as she learns that Percy Gryce is to marry Evie Van Osburgh, 'Lily's passing light-heartedness sank beneath a renewed sense of failure.' Her attempts to turn her life into a harmonious work of art signally fail, and she sinks down and down, both in her own estimation, and that of the world.

The reasons for this decline are twofold: the corrupting influence of the milieu in which she exists, and her own fall into inauthenticity. The nature of the environment is made clear from time to time, with profound irony. She aspires to marry Percy Gryce—who is rich, but 'handsome in a didactic way—he looked like a clever pupil's drawing from a plaster cast.' He has a close affinity with his fiancée:

> . . . the two had the same prejudices and ideals, and the same quality of making other standards non-existent by ignoring them. This attribute was common to most of Lily's set: they had a force of negation which eliminated everything beyond their own range of perception. (*HM*, p. 74)

Yet even so Lily can fantasize a marriage to this same Gryce:

> The certainty that she could marry Peter Gryce when she pleased had lifted a heavy load from her mind . . . she would be able to arrange her life as she pleased, to soar into that empyrean of security where creditors cannot penetrate . . . she would be free for ever from the shifts, the expedients, the humiliations of the relatively poor. . . . (*HM*, p. 75)

She feels that 'so to identify herself with her husband's vanity that to gratify her wishes would be to him the most exquisite form of self-indulgence'. And the basis of her fantasized power is her beauty:

> Her beauty itself was not the mere ephemeral possession it might have been in the hands of inexperience: her skill in enhancing it, the care she took of it, the use she made of it, seemed to give it a kind of permanence. (*HM*, p. 76)

She is shown using her beauty, to manipulate Gus Trenor and Rosedale—with fatal results. In her fantasies of power through the employment of her beauty, Lily owes a great deal to Gwendolen Harleth.

The one great challenge to her fallacies of power and luxury is Laurence Selden. She has known Selden for eight years, 'had found him more agreeable than most men, and had vaguely wished that he possessed the other qualities needful to fix her attention'—Selden is not rich. But

> Miss Bart was a keen reader of her own heart, and she saw that her sudden preoccupation with Selden was due to the fact that his presence shed new light on her surroundings . . . he had preserved a certain social detachment, a happy air of viewing the show objectively, of having points of contact outside the great gilt cage in which they were all huddled. . . . (*HM*, pp. 83–4)

Selden had never forgotten the way out of this cage. Looking at the others at table, Lily thinks 'what a long stretch of vacuity! How dreary and trivial these people were . . .' (*HM*, p. 84).

Selden has had some entanglement with Bertha Dorset, though the extent and the timing of this is never made quite clear. However, Lily has a number of *tête-à-tête* encounters with Selden, and in these she develops a very special relationship with him. In Chapter VI they have a walk all to themselves, in an idyllic setting. They rest and 'he had no wish to make her talk: her quick-breathing silence seemed a part of the general hush and harmony of things.' In his mind there is only a lazy sense of pleasure, but in hers 'There were . . . at the moment two beings, one drawing deep breaths of freedom and exhilaration, the other gasping for air in a little black prison-house of fears' (*HM*, p. 99). She feels ' a sense of buoyancy which seemed to lift and swing her above the sun-suffused world at her feet. *Was it love,* she wondered' (*HM*, p. 99; my italics).

'Lily has no definite experience by which to test the quality of her feelings.'

> She could put her finger on every link of the chain that was drawing them together. . . . She admired him most of all, perhaps, for being able to convey as distinct a sense of superiority as the richest man she had ever met. (*HM*, p. 100)

He tells her she is a 'splendid spectacle', and that her 'genius lies in converting impulses into intentions':

> 'My genius?' she echoed with a sudden note of weariness. 'Is there any final test of genius but success? And I certainly haven't succeeded.'
>
> Selden pushed his hat back and took a side-glance at her, 'success—what is success? I shall be interested to have your definition.'
>
> 'Success?' she hesitated. 'Why, to get as much as one can out of life, I suppose. . . .'
>
> . . .
>
> 'My idea of success,' he said, 'is personal freedom.'
>
> 'Freedom? Freedom from worries?'
>
> 'From everything—from money, from poverty, from ease and anxiety. *To keep a kind of republic of the spirit.*' (*HM*, p. 104; my italics)

She finds such seriousness odd; there has been no one to tell her about the republic of the spirit. She says she has seen into this republic, at dinner. . . . Selden is fascinated by her short-coming: 'The hint of this weakness had become the most interesting thing about her.' There follows a somewhat wordy conversation about 'society', money and 'the decorative side of life', but at the end of it he implies to her that after struggling to get the things she is trying to get, she will not like them.

> 'Well—have you never forseen it for yourself.'
>
> The slow colour rose to her cheek, not a blush of excitement but drawn from the deep wells of feeling; it was as if the effort of her spirit had produced it.
>
> 'Often and often,' she said. 'But it looks so much darker when you show it to me.'

By degrees, she grows more serious. ' ''Why do you do this to me?'' she cried. ''Why do you make the things I have chosen seem hateful to me, if you have nothing to give me instead?'' ' (*HM*, p. 110). Here they have touched on the underlying area of *authenticity of being*:

> an indwelling voice in each called to the other across unsounded depths of feeling.
>
> 'No, I have nothing to give you instead,' he said, sitting up and turning so that he faced her. 'If I had, it should be yours, you know.'
>
> She received this abrupt declaration in a way even stranger than the manner of its makeup: she dropped her face on her hands and he saw that for a moment she wept. (*HM*, p. 110)

It is perhaps their closest moment, until Lily is dead; he pulls down her hands and says to himself that 'even her weeping was an art.'

She accuses him of belittling her, by being so sure the things he derides are the only things she cares for. The exchange becomes very Jamesian at this point and difficult to follow:

> 'Ah,' she cried, 'for all your fine phrases you're really as great a coward as I am, for you wouldn't have made one of them if you hadn't been so sure of my answer.' (*HM*, p. 111)

But she clarifies everything by suddenly asking—'Do you want to marry me?'

> He broke into a laugh.
>
> 'No, I don't want to—but perhaps I should if you did.'
>
> 'That's what I told you—you're so sure of me that you can amuse yourself with experiments.' She drew back the hand he had regained and sat looking at him sadly. (*HM*, p. 112)

It needs to be said that in this tragic study, with its fugitive resort to Jamesian modes, there is a signal lack of passion, in both characters. Selden is too willing to seize any indication that Lily does not belong to 'the republic of the spirit' and to withdraw himself. Of course, Selden is unsatisfactory in this way, lacking the capacity for immediacy of sensual commitment, but Lily, too, has a distaste for masculine assertiveness, which is manifest in her use of the word 'repugnant', for instance, to describe the presence of Gus Trenor. In the meeting of two such protagonists, one might even say, death is the only possible outcome.

Yet this episode is full of promise, and provides the hinge on which the action of the rest of the novel depends.

> 'I am not making experiments,' he returned, 'or if I am, it is not on you but myself. I don't know what effect they are going to have on me—but if marrying you is one of them, I will take the risk.'
>
> She smiled faintly. 'It would be a great risk, certainly—I have never concealed from you how great.'
>
> 'Ah, it's you who are the coward,' he exclaimed.
>
> She had risen, and he stood facing her with his eyes on hers. The soft isolation of the falling day enveloped them: they seemed lifted into a finer air. All the exquisite influences of the hour trembled in their veins, and drew them to each other as the loosened leaves were drawn to the earth.
>
> 'It's you who are the coward,' he repeated, catching her hands in his.
>
> She leaned on him for a moment, as if with a drop of tired wings: he felt as though her heart were beating rather with the stress of a long flight than from the thrill of new distances. Then, drawing back with a little smile of warning—'I shall look hideous in dowdy clothes: but I contain my own hates,' she declared.
>
> They stood silent for a while after this, smiling at each other like adventurous children who have climbed to a forbidden height from which they discover a new world. (*HM*, p. 113)

She asks him, on their way back, 'were you serious?' and he turns this off with a remark about risks; but somehow the images of 'adventurous children' and the neat wordiness of their commitment give the lie to the growth of the relationship. We cannot find in the encounter the passionate possessiveness that represents a really new stage in the lives of two people.

Lily's mistake is to suppose she can 'handle' Gus Trenor and 'keep the obligation on his side'. Perhaps, in her attitudes to the cost of things, she derives something from Harold Skimpole? Certainly, she is extremely naïve, and falls completely for Gus Trenor's pretence that the large sums of money he gives her are dividends on her own savings. They are in fact absurd bribes, in return for which he expects favours. In a grotesque scene, in which Trenor has tricked Lily into visiting his house while his wife is away, he makes it plain that what he would like from her is some display of affection:

> . . . I don't doubt you've accepted as much before—and chucked the other chaps as you'd like to chuck me. I don't care how you settled your score with them—if you fooled 'em I'm that much to the good . . . you know I'm mad about you . . . damn the money, there's plenty more of it. . . . (*HM*, p. 229)

What Lily experiences is a 'sea of humiliation', so awful that 'the moral shame was one with the physical dread', and 'the words were worse than the touch'; for what she learns from Trenor is not only that he has been paying her, but that her reputation has become such that she is generally suspected of getting money from men by giving favours.

As she leaves his house, she 'even observed a man's figure—was there something half-familiar in its outline?'—which, as she enters the hansom, turns from the opposite corner and vanishes in the obscurity of the side street. Lily is overcome by the sense of being observed and she feels terribly alone; she has agreed to meet Selden next day at 4 p.m., and he does not come. He has embarked on a sea voyage, as she later finds out, in order to forget her, having assumed she is compromised. Instead, she encounters Rosedale, to whom she offers a reply to an earlier offer of marriage, only to be rejected. Rosedale reveals himself to be a really cynical manipulator: later he taunts her over her reference to her 'dressmaker'—by which foolish denial she tries to hide the fact that she had visited Selden in his rooms at the Benedick. And in the end he suggests that she should use the letters she bought from a cleaner there to bring Bertha Dorset round to her side:

> He would marry her tomorrow if she could regain Bertha Dorset's friendship: and to induce the open resumption of her friendship . . . she had only to put to the lady the latent menace contained in the packet so miraculously delivered into her hands. . . . (*HM*, p. 404)

Rosedale supposes her reluctance is due to her knowledge that the incriminating letters are addressed to Selden. But Lily has come to perceive that Rosedale's calculations include a suspicion that she might deceive him, too.

This exchange with Rosedale comes after another long and complex episode, in which Mrs. Dorset invites Lily to go on a cruise, during which trip she is supposed to keep George Dorset engaged, allowing Mrs. Dorset to make a 'sentimental experiment' with young Ned Silverton. In the end, the episode ends badly, with Mrs. Dorset, as it were, expelling Lily from their yacht.

During all these entanglements, Selden remains aloof, except for a momentary involvement in the Dorset affair, and we see very little of him. Meanwhile, Lily experiences a continual process of disillusionment, ruin and frustration. Her impulse to marry someone who is capable of sustaining her in luxury leads to continual encounters. These become 'tales'—gossip to make the situation ever more complex and disastrous. Rosedale, for instance, has changed his view of her:

> 'You mean to say that I'm not as desirable a match as you thought me?'
>
> 'Yes; that's what I do mean,' he answered resolutely. 'I won't go into what's happened. I don't believe the stories about you—I don't *want* to believe them. But they're there, and my not believing them isn't going to alter the situation.' (*HM*, p. 399)

These stories haunt Mrs. Penistone, so that six weeks before she dies she alters her will, to disinherit Lily, and remove forever all chance of the woman escaping the moral consequences of the depravity of the 'set' to which she belongs.

Selden sees this:

> She was on the edge of something—that was the impression left with her. He seemed to see her poised on the brink of a chasm, with one graceful foot advanced to assert her unconsciousness that the ground was failing her. (*HM*, pp. 299–300)

Her 'art' has become a facility to deal with a vile world—and it has failed. 'To Selden it seemed like that moment of pause and arrest when the warm fluidity of youth is chilled into its final shape. . .' (*HM*), p. 298).

Previous to her encounter with Gus Trenor, Selden had found Lily as strikingly different from the rest of womankind.

> It had always seemed to Selden that experience offered a great deal besides the sentimental adventure, *yet he could vividly conceive of a love which should broaden and deepen till it became the central fact of life.* (*HM*, p. 240; my italics)

This, one could say, is a central theme of the book, as it could be said to be a central theme of Edith Wharton's life. But she goes on:

> What he could not accept, in his own case, was the makeshift alternative of a relation that should be less than this: that should leave some portions of his nature unsatisfied, while it put an undue strain on others. He would not, in other words, yield to the growth of an affection which might appeal to pity yet leave the understanding untouched: sympathy should no more delude him than a trick of the eyes, the grace of helplessness than a curve of the cheek. (*HM*, p. 241)

But now, a little 'but' passes like a sponge over his vows: he is in 'the state of imprisoned self-absorption that the first surrender to love produces', and he provides the text, '*Blessed are the pure in heart, for they shall see God*' (*HM*, p. 241). But it is only a moment after this that he is sickened by the reflection that Gus Trenor's name had been associated with Lily's.

Selden has fallen in love in part by seeing Lily at a *tableau vivant*. His response to Lily has a cultured or literary quality: he tends to have a visionary response to her; he is one who yields to 'vision-making influences as completely as a child to the spell of a fairy-tale' (p. 176). 'He seemed to see before him the real Lily Bart'—but he is aware of the gloating and coarse comments of members of her entourage, and he is appalled that 'these are the standards by which she was fated to be judged.'

They meet at the De Brys', for yet another magical moment, and there is what seems a significant exchange:

> Suddenly she raised her eyes with the beseeching earnestness of a child. You never speak to me—you think hard things of me,' she murmured.
>
> 'I think of you at any rate, God knows!' he said. . . . 'You promised once to help me.' . . .
>
> 'The only way I can help you is by loving you,' Selden said in a low voice. . . .
>
> . . .
>
> She made no reply, but her face turned to him with the soft motion of a flower. His arm met it slowly, and their lips touched. (*HM*, p. 216)

But she cries, 'Ah, love me, love me—but don't tell me so!' What is in the letters Lily buys from Mrs. Dorset?

> The letter before her was short, but its few words, which had leapt into her brain before she was conscious of reading them, told a long history—a history over which, for the last four years, the friends of the writer had smiled and shrugged. . . . Now the other side presented itself to Lily, the volcanic nether side of the surface over which conjecture and innuendo glide so lightly till the first fissure turns their whisper to a shriek. (*HM*, p. 162)

> Selden was inextricably involved in their fate. *Men do not, at worst,* suffer much from exposure; and in this instance the meaning of the letters . . . had revealed also that they were appeals—repeated and therefore probably unanswered—for the renewal of a tie which time had evidently relaxed. (*HM*, p. 164)

Selden, Lily feels, 'would wish the letters rescued'. The man, it seems, is to be pardoned and excused for a *mesalliance;* the woman must be doomed by even the suspicion of one.

The final exchange between Selden and Lily comes in

Chapter XII. She tells him she has left Mrs. Hatch's, because he told her to.

> She saw that her presence was becoming an embarrassment to him. Such a situation can be saved only by an immediate outrush of feeling; *and on Selden's side the determining impulse was still lacking*. (*HM*, p. 480; my italics)

So, to Lily, 'the sense of loneliness returned with *redoubled force as she saw herself for ever shut out from Selden's innermost self*' (my italics). She tells him she needed the help of his belief in her. She speaks of the 'Lily Bart he knew'—'I am going to leave her here.' The moment has gone, when he did love her briefly, 'and it helped me'. He tells her, 'You can never go out of my life', yet he continually seems unwilling to grasp the obligations this should bring.

She drops the packet in the fire, kisses him, goes out, and encounters one Nellie Crane. This girl has been seduced by a man who had promised to marry her, but has abandoned her. Her George came round and asked her to marry him:

> At first I thought I couldn't . . . because . . . I knew he knew about me . . . I could never have told another man, and I'd never have married without telling; but if George cared for me enough to have me as I was—I didn't see why I shouldn't begin over again—and I did. (*HM*, p. 494)

To Lily, this working girl seems 'to have reached the central truth of existence'. Her husband's faith in her had made her renewal possible:

> Well—Selden had twice been ready to stake his faith on Lily Bart; but the third trial had been too severe for his endurance. *The very quality of his love had made it the more impossible to recall to life*. If it had been a simple instinct of blood, the power of her beauty might have revived it. But the fact that it struck deeper, that it was inextricably wound up with inherited habits of thought and feeling, made it impossible to restore to growth as a deep-rooted plant torn from its bed. Selden had given her of his best; but he was as incapable as herself of an uncritical return to former states of feeling. (*HM*, p. 501; my italics)

The episode with Nellie's child is now seen as being of great significance; the end of Lily is revealed as being a form of schizoid suicide. She becomes conscious that Nellie's infant is 'lying on her arm': 'She settled herself into an easier position, hollowing her arm to follow the round downy head' (*HM*, p. 506). She becomes aware of a concept: 'As she lay there she said to herself that there was something she must tell Selden, some word she had found that should make life clear between them. . .' (*HM*, p. 506). At the end: 'in the silence there passed between them the word which made all clear.' What is the word? It cannot be 'love' as love has been spoken between them already. It can hardly be 'marriage'.

The novel penetrates to the level of 'the republic of the spirit'; yet for both Selden and Lily this realm seems unattainable. Why should it be? Whenever they are closest to one another, they are described as being ineffectual children:

> She looked at him helplessly, like a hurt or frightened child: this real self of hers, which he had the faculty of charming out of the depths, was so little accustomed to go alone! (*HM*, p. 147)

So one may find in the work a pervading theme—a theme found elsewhere in Edith Wharton—which is that of the adult world perceived as a child. The novel makes sense as an adult story, but it seems also to have a deeper unconscious undercurrent, which the last two chapters reveal. There is a particular symbolic value in Lily's feeling, as she lies dying, that she is holding Nellie's baby in her arms. That baby may symbolize the working girl's ability to grasp life and commit herself to love, in the face of circumstances, as Lily cannot. But we may also read it as symbolizing Lily's urge to care, at the very deepest level, for Selden, and for herself—for the unborn child in herself. Neither she nor Selden, although they can meet in love, in a detached fantasy, like children in a dream, can ever cross the gulf, to step into the real world and seek to fulfil the relationship there.

Each lets the other down, at moments of crisis—out of emotional impotence. The fact that the novel has qualities Edith Wharton may have taken from Henry James perhaps helps us to identify this problem; for James himself had serious schizoid difficulties, and is overcome in the end by an obsession with subtlety and reticence, so that his characters suffer from impotence in the face of corruption, as with

Nanda in *The Awkward Age*. Nanda's fate is not tragic like that of Lily Bart. Edith Wharton knows sexual passion as Henry James did not, and her portrayal of the toils of sex is capable of a deeper moral repugnance ('Does one go to Caliban for a judgement on Miranda?'). In the wider frame of the novel, 'the ugliness, the pettiness, the attrition and corrosion of the soul' is what corrupts the possibilities of a meeting between a man and a woman which is of 'the pure in heart'.

The end is subtle in a way that seems to follow inevitably the sense of destiny that overcomes Selden and Lily. Lily receives a legacy that enables her to escape the toils of Gus Trenor, but at that moment she dies from an accident with her sleeping draught. Selden is on his way to propose to her, and finds her dead. As Geoffrey Walton says, it is done with 'perfect tact': 'suicide would have been cheap and sensational, a rescue sentimental.' But the moment when Lily is dying and dreams of the baby has a significance which is phenomenological. There is a sense in which all the grossness represents the real world, while the spiritual relationship between Selden and Lily, and their transcendence at the end, in death, seem to belong to another realm. In this perhaps we may gleam an unconscious hope for a rebirth of the psyche and the achievement of the possibility of fulfilled relationship not possible with one's present 'condition', in the society of time. That is, in the ending of this novel we may find the symbolism of schizoid suicide, expressing the desire to withdraw from the world, even unto death, to begin again.

# 2

# *The Reef*

*The Reef* is, I believe, the greatest of Edith Wharton's novels. From the beginning of this novel, the reader is aware that Edith Wharton is in a sense 'fixing' her hero, George Darrow: she needs a reason for him to fall into a passing affair. He has 'a healthy enjoyment of life' and is 'tolerant of agglutinated humanity' in travel. He has committed himself to a stormy channel crossing, and a trip to Paris and beyond, to join the widow whose acquaintance he has renewed, Mrs. Anna Leath. She has sent a telegram, however, to his Embassy address rather than to his private address, and it is flung into his compartment as his train sets out for Dover. At that moment he had rashly vowed, 'At any rate I won't turn back'—though later he has doubts when he sees 'the fury of the waves outside the harbour'. In this mood he lapses into a momentary *affaire* with a chance acquaintance, Sophy Viner.

There are often strange reasons for certain sexual acts; often they are undertaken out of revenge, like some of those that Oliver Mellors perpetrates (there is no other word for it) on Connie Chatterley. What is fascinating about *The Reef* is that Darrow's catastrophic sexual liaison with Sophy Viner is prompted by exasperation. Our problem with Darrow is that he is a man who, although the most authentic goal of his pursuit of emotional fulfilment is Anna, is fallible enough to fall into an *affaire* out of mere annoyance and frustration. What could be more revealing of an unsatisfactory man than for him to pick up a passing girl and make love to her, on his way to his betrothed, for no better reason than that he is piqued by the latter's request for a brief postponement of their meeting?

The exasperation is clear from the start and heavily underscored by the author, whose novel opens with the words of her telegram: 'Unexpected obstacle. Please don't come till thirtieth.' On her part, it is equally clear that she is emotionally reticent, and there is an undercurrent of reluctance in Anna which speaks of some unconscious perplexity—and it is this which arouses what we can only call Darrow's *rage*. The 'reef', then, is not only Sophy Viner, the object of a promiscuous moment, but Anna's own sensual reluctance.

There is a great deal of anger in the first pages. The noise of the train 'hammered the words of the telegram into George Darrow's ear, *ringing every change of irony* on its commonplace syllables' (my italics). The train rattles them like a discharge of musketry, and they 'drip slowly and coldly into his brain'. The sounds become 'dice in some game of the gods of malice', and they leap out at him as if from the crests of the stormy waves off Dover, which 'stung and blinded him with a *fresh fury of derision*'. What kind of man, we feel, is so disturbed by a polite request for time that he feels so mocked?

He rages inwardly at Anna's 'sweet reasonableness' and her 'usual good reasons'. He wonders whether this reasonableness casts doubt on his belief that there was some exceptional warmth in the greeting she had recently given him after their twelve years apart. He recalls meeting her at an Embassy dinner, at which 'her smile had been like a red rose pinned on her widow's mourning', while he felt he should have known her beautiful face 'as he would have recognised, after half a lifetime, the details of a room *he had played in as a child*'. Once more, Edith Wharton's male protagonist has many characteristics of the child—for Darrow's rage and frustration at this moment are those of an infant who cannot tolerate rejection of any kind.

When he has met Mrs. Leath again, he has appreciated how much she has matured, and he notes how tenderly she speaks of her little girl Effie and her charming clever young stepson Owen Leath. She herself is 'much finer and surer an instrument of expression' than the intent, grave-eyed girl he had originally known.

But now, asked if he is crossing the Channel, he only feels 'the derision of his case'. There is now no reason why he should cross, except to demonstrate his own rather immature will. He reflects on Anna's marriage; he believes her 'reticence' betrays that Leath had not come up to her expectations. He thought she spoke of her husband with 'impersonal seriousness' in words which sounded as if they had been learnt by heart and had become 'slightly dulled by repetition'. In his view, the way she had responded to him, Darrow, had left him with a sense that he 'was a being singled out and privileged, to whom she had entrusted something precious to keep'. (It is noticeable how Jamesian some of the subtle phrases are that are used here to delineate a complex relationship.) A later meeting has deepened the impression, and developed a deeper feeling of communion. She even contrived to make him understand that 'what was inevitably coming was not to come too soon.'

> It was not that she showed any hesitation as to the issue, but rather that she seemed to wish not to miss any stage in the gradual reflowering of their intimacy. (*R*, p. 6)

It is very important to savour the exact flavour of this opening, as it is crucial to the poignant culmination of the story, which, although it is so Jamesian, is done from a female perspective. Anna is a woman, and it is the nature of woman to enjoy letting an experience develop over a long length of time, slowly; her satisfaction, in terms of being, requires this. The trouble with Darrow is that he is not mature enough to enjoy or even tolerate this slow growth—and in this, again, betrays his male immaturity.

He is described as being 'content to wait', but temperamentally her plea for time fills him with exasperation. He recalls a moment in a garden when she was walking towards him: 'something in her eyes said "wait" ': this is her character—he must allow the woman to come to him. When she has to leave at their last meeting to attend to family matters, before he 'had the chance he counted on'—presumably to declare himself to her—he curses himself. But she now seems to be beset by family duties, and he feels she is 'too easily resigned to them'. Even so, they manage to have 'an almost decisive exchange of words'.

But now, in the stormy wind of the Channel, Darrow

seems to hear a mocking echo of her message, 'unexpected obstacle'. He decides it is a mere 'pretext'; any reason seems good enough for postponing him. He grumbles to himself that there was no word of regret or excuse: 'She didn't want him, and had taken the shortest way to tell him so. The "obstacle" was a fib.' '"If I asked her to marry me, she'd have refused in the same language. But thank heaven I haven't!" he reflected' (*R*, p. 9).* He admits 'the sex's traditional right to change' but goes on grumbling about being brought into this storm, pointlessly, and her failure to grasp his private address seems to him to be a 'minor proof of her indifference'. And he even seems to believe it would cause her 'malicious joy' to have him retrace his steps.

All this adds up to an unconscious element in the man who, put off for quite reasonable reasons, feels bitterly rejected, and begins to fantasize a malicious woman who is the Rejecting Mother—obsessed with seeking 'proof of her indifference'—and whom he hates. And it is at this moment that Darrow encounters the 'helpless female arm' of Sophy Viner.

This opening sequence of the novel, then, must be read with care, and so, too, must the final pages of Book I. Here is registered the astonishing response of Darrow to his *affaire* with Sophy. I have suggested that this impulse to take Sophy was an act of rage, but it is, of course, more complex than that. As we shall see, it gives him the reassurance he needs to posture at Sophy as a protector and a sophisticated man-about-Paris. At the end of their few days, he looks dismally round his hotel room, feeling 'the nudge of a transient intimacy'—a most significant phrase. The terms used about his feelings are as strong as those used about his exasperation in the Channel storm: 'It was extraordinary with what a microscopic minuteness of loathing he hated it all.' He hates most the door linking his apartment with Sophy's. He has never been in such an adventure before, but the three days' rain has destroyed the enchantment, and the episode is not 'helped by being thought about'. He has an almost sleep-walking sense of Sophy coming in, and he

* The edition to which references are made is the Macmillan 1913 edition.

becomes aware of her face leaning over him as he pretends to be asleep 'and that in a moment he would have to look up and kiss it'—and in that phrase Edith Wharton conveys that Darrow now realizes that this episode has been totally inauthentic for him—so 'wrong' for him, indeed, that it must destroy his future emotional life completely.

The pages rendering Darrow's disillusion are startling, because Sophy Viner is a lively and attractive girl, and the moment of their encounter seems adventurous and romantic; he is showing her Paris, after all. But the rain brings an unromantic reality into view: Paris now simply looks like 'a black oily huddle', while the room is filled with 'the drab twilight of an underground acquarium'. The emphasis is on *meaninglessness*: in the weather 'there was no variation of rhythm, no lyrical ups and downs', while 'the grey lines streaking the panes were as dense and uniform as a *page of unparagraphed narrative*' (*R*, p. 72; my italics). Darrow sits staring 'with dull acquiescence' into the 'boundless blur of rain' which affects him like 'a vast projection of his own state of mind'. The rain presses upon him the continuous reality of the world, and its unrelating featurelessness seems to echo his own state of depression—as he perceives he has given himself up to inauthenticity.

In the background, I believe we can say, the power of this rendering of disillusion has behind it Edith Wharton's own experience with Morton Fullerton, of whose character (R. W. B. Lewis tells us) she made a profound reappraisal in 1910. (*The Reef* was written at 'a squalid hole', Pouques-les-Eaux, in 1912—it came into print in November.) Lewis says:

> Darrow . . . represents the Edith Wharton of 1912 rather than 1909: the person whom other events—chiefly Teddy's simultaneous and sordid-seeming liaisons—had caused to look back on the London adventure with a good deal of distaste. *It was a revulsion* against her own behaviour. . . . (*R*, p. 327; my italics)

And yet she was very dissatisfied with the novel. Fullerton she now recognized as being 'undependable, weak . . . irresistably attractive'—someone with whom intimate commerce had ceased in the summer of 1910.

Darrow seems to see the hotel room with Edith Wharton's distaste at the temporary nature of the liaison:

> It was exactly ten days since his hurried unpacking had strewn it with the contents of his portmanteaux. His brushes and razors were spread out on the blotched marble of the chest of drawers. A stack of newspapers had accumulated on the centre table under the 'electrolier', and half a dozen paper novels lay on the mantelpiece among cigar-cases and toilet bottles. (*R*, p. 73)

The room has the 'look of being the makeshift setting of *innumerable transient collocations*' (my italics). And there was 'something sardonic, almost sinister', in the appearance of 'having deliberately "made up" for its anonymous part'—with its '*noncommittal*' drabs and browns and chairs and tables as 'impersonal as railway porters'. This room, which the rain forces him to look at, 'seems to have taken complete possession of his mind', 'to be soaking into him like an ugly indelible blot'—with that 'nudge of a transient intimacy'.

There is a great deal of bitterness beneath the power of this prose to create ugliness, which is the ugliness of a wounded consciousness:

> . . . the grimy carpet and wall-paper, the black marble mantel-piece, the clock with a gilt allegory under a dusty bell, the high-bolstered brown-counterpaned bed, the framed card of printed rules under the electric light switch and the door of communication with the next room. *He hated the door most of all. . . .* (*R*, p. 74; my italics)

It is almost as if he is in a brothel. We may learn a great deal here about Edith Wharton's attitudes to her own experience, and to the experiences she delineates in the novel *The Reef*, by comparing the poem she wrote about a last night with her lover Morton Fullerton, spent at the Charing Cross Hotel: 'Terminus'. The title is fascinating and indicates not only that the encounter took place at a railway station, but also that it marked a temporary end to their relationship. It also implies the end of Edith Wharton's idealized view of love, as she, with her novelist's insights, comes closer to the realities of common human sexuality. All the same, it is an adolescent poem, with strange undercurrents of the sordid, which are transmuted into the version of events given in *The Reef*.

The room in which the sexual encounter takes place is 'common-place' with 'its dull impersonal furniture'. A red lamp 'kindles a mystic flame' in the 'swinging mirror'. But what Edith sees in this mirror is

> Faces innumerous and vague of the endless travelling
> automata
> Whirled down the ways of the world like dust-eddies swept
> through a street,
> Faces indifferent or weary, frowns of impatience or pain,

—and then she adds faces with smiles like theirs, as her lover unloosens her dress. But this seems an afterthought: what loving couple would dwell, in a moment of passion, on the 'innumerous . . . automata' who are like 'dust-eddies', with faces showing indifference, weariness, frowns of impatience or pain? And then we come to the bed:

> The low wide bed, as rutted and worn as a high road,
> The bed with its soot-sodden chintz, the grime of its brasses,
> That has born the weight of fagged bodies, dust-stained,
> averted in sleep
> The hurried, the restless, the aimless. . . .

Even though they may be dwelt on, to emphasize the rapture, the images are of death, exhaustion and of aimless automata, with terms like 'fagged' and 'dust-stained' introducing a sense of sordid futility. To this the description of the 'soot-sodden chintz' and 'the grime of the brasses' adds a note of distaste.

Around the lovers is the 'shaking and shrieking of trains' and the 'night-long shudder of traffic', and she imagines some woman 'staggering out into darkness', who thinks she will go forth to 'the fixed rail of habit by the hand of implacable fate'. The impression is of a shattering experience from which the outcome can only be to find conventional life more intolerable. She is bound (she declares) for a town where people look languidly at a train from which, as it halts, one sees the houses turned into *grave-stones*. The streets are grassy paths between the low roofs of the *dead*; at the end, she returns to drink of her lover's lips for 'oblivion'. To take the most forcible words throughout—'dust-eddies', 'dust-stained', 'night-long shudder', 'black rain', 'grave-stones', 'the dead'—the impression is one of futility and death, rather than of love. We have noted the association between sex and death throughout Edith Wharton's work.

What happens when the substance of this poem is transmuted into *The Reef*? Here Darrow, after three days of sexual encounter with Sophy Viner, has been studying a timetable, and we have noted that the chairs and tables are as 'impersonal as railway porters'. 'Through the rain he could just discover the face of a clock in a tall building beyond the railway roofs' (*R*, p. 73). The rain brings things down to a level of mundane reality: the lyrical fantasy of love is absent and the lines of rain on the window, as we have seen, look *like a narrative without form*. It is a common feature of Edith Wharton's novels that the man conceives of the woman as a fantastic story—and, of course, Morton Fullerton had this effect on Edith Wharton: Newland Archer weaves a literary spell around Ellen Olenska; Laurence Selden has a bookish concept of Lily Bart. Both concepts fail in the face of the woman's actual reality. With Darrow now, the 'boundless blur of rain . . . affected him like a vast projection of his own state of mind'.

There are many parallels between the poem and the passages in the novel:

> . . . the glass that has seen
> Faces innumerous and vague of the endless travelling
> automata. . . . ('Terminus')

> There was something sardonic, almost sinister, in its appearance of having deliberately 'made up' for its anonymous part, all in noncommittal drabs and browns, with a carpet and paper that nobody would remember. (*R*, p. 73)

> . . . the commonplace room of the inn, with its dull impersonal furniture. . . . ('Terminus')

When Darrow looks round the room, it

> seemed *to have taken complete possession of his mind,* to be sinking itself into him like an ugly indelible blot. Every detail pressed itself on his notice with the familiarity of an *accidental*

> *confident*: whichever way he turned, *he felt the nudge of a transient intimacy*. (*R*, p. 74; my italics)

The whole essence of both 'Terminus' and this last passage is that nudge of a transient intimacy: the recognition that the sexual intimacy *is* an 'accidental confident' and is neither the focus of love, nor is it a part of a whole complex of committed relationship. Darrow will have to go back to 'a daylight world of recognised activities', yet on this it is difficult for him to fix his thoughts—'the room jerked him back into the circle of its insistent associations.'

> It was extraordinary with what a microscopic minuteness of loathing he hated it all: the grimy carpet and wallpaper. . . . (*R*, p. 74)
>
> . . . the grime of its brasses. . . ('Terminus')
>
> . . . the black marble mantelpiece . . . the high-bolstered brown-counterpaned bed. . . . (*R*, p. 74)
>
> The bed with its soot-sodden chintz. . . . ('Terminus')

Reflecting on his affair with Sophy, he felt that this had been 'enacting itself in some unmapped region outside the pale of the usual'—that is, in a realm coloured by idealization like Morton Fullerton's escapades. 'It was not like anything that had ever happened to him before, or in which he had ever pictured himself as likely to be involved.' He felt he could deal with this, but the rain made all the difference:

> It had thrown the whole picture out of perspective, blotted out the mystery of the remoter planes and the enchantment of the middle distance, and thrust into prominence every commonplace face of the foreground. . . . (*R*, p. 75)

He hears Sophy Viner moving about in the next room. The effect is to make her seem a disembodied alien creature; we hear only noises while he suffers 'a precise photographic picture of that other room' which haunts him:

> He heard another sound, and recognised it as that of a wet umbrella placed in the black marble jamb of the chimney-piece, against the hearth. . . .

> The step crossed the floor again. It was strange how much better he knew it than the person to whom it belonged. (*R*, p. 76)

There is no delight for Darrow in these sounds. His heart does not leap for her: there is no feeling of tenderness, of cherishment or even delight. He does not answer Sophy's knock, and feigns to be asleep.

Sophy brings him a letter from Anna. It falls, and she reaches out to pick it up.

> 'Oh, don't—*don't*,' broke from him, and he bent over and caught the arm. The face above it was close to his.
>
> 'Don't what?'
>
> '—take the trouble,' he stammered. (*R*, p. 77)

He feels trapped, by the sensual needs of the woman:

> Suddenly he felt the pressure of the hand on his shoulder, and became aware that the face was still leaning over him, and that in a moment he would have to lean over and kiss it. . . . (*R*, p. 77)

To do that, it is clear, would be as inauthentic as anything could be; Darrow is trapped in his own adventurism. Edith Wharton here shows her feminine appreciation that Fullerton's love-making was itself impelled by egotism, that his 'technique' was essentially narcissistic.

Those who make Sophy Viner the heroine of *The Reef* must surely have failed to read these paragraphs, in which we find placed the catastrophe that has occurred for Darrow, long before he discovers Sophy in Anna Leath's own household. He has 'taken advantage' of Sophy, and Sophy has collaborated; but sexual union of the kind they have enjoyed—without the idolizations Morton Fullerton might have imbued it with—is utterly inauthentic. Although Sophy later proclaims her love for Darrow, she is not in love with him when she goes to bed with him in Paris. And none of Sophy's subsequent apologies, and her braving it out in the name of woman's right to self-assertion, could alter that. Darrow's response, after his orgy of three days, is one of repugnance, while all the articles in the hotel room speak of emotional death—as much, strangely, as do the articles in 'Terminus'. In the end, in the novel, the sexual adventure destroys authenticity—the possibility of becoming their own selves—in all three protagonists.

Interestingly enough, Edith Wharton takes George Darrow's attitude to sexuality to be that of the *homme moyen sensuel* of the American middle class of the time.

> George Darrow had had a fairly varied experience of feminine types, but the women he had frequented had either been pronouncedly 'ladies' or *they had not*. Grateful to both for ministering to the more complex masculine nature, and disposed to assume that they had been evolved, if not designed, to that end, he had instinctively kept the two groups apart in his mind, avoiding that intermediate society which attempts to conciliate both theories of life. (*R*, p. 25; my italics)

He liked people who went as far as they could in their own kind, liked his 'ladies' to be unashamed of showing exactly what they were. He had known a third type—does the author mean the *demi-mondaine*? Lady Ulrica is mentioned, but 'that experience left him with a contemptuous distaste for the woman who uses the privileges of one class to shelter the customs of the other.'

Edith Wharton writes, of course, as a highly sophisticated member both of American middle- and upper-class society and of the Paris bourgeoisie aware of Bohemian life. Yet her attitudes here are strangely imprisoned within the bourgeois view of sexuality, and she does not present the stereotype with much incisive criticism. The man's world here, like Tolstoy's, is one in which your gentleman accepts on the one hand the meaningful sexual manipulations of 'ladies', also are bound up with marriage, class and property, and on the other the sensual gratification derived from women who are *not ladies*. The *demi-mondaine* type like Lady Ulrica is a menace, because she threatens to undermine the divide. But the 'independent' modern woman, who believes in free love, as Sophy Viner pronounces herself to be, also threatens the system—and, indeed, through her liaison with Darrow she brings about the earthquake that undermines his betrothal to Anna Leath.

Sophy's ease of manner seems to him to show that 'her experience had made her free without hardness and self-assured without assertiveness' (*R*, p. 26).

Sophy is 'clearly an American'. She speaks openly and sometimes, to Darrow embarrassingly; of Lady Ulrica she says, 'She was false from head to foot'—

> Oh, I only mean externally . . . In fact I used to say to Jimmy—just to make him wild—: 'I'll bet you anything you like there's nothing wrong, because I know she'd never dare un-' She broke the word in two. . . . (*R*, p. 17)

—and she blushes. She refers openly to Darrow's visits to Mrs. Murrett's to see Lady Ulrica, and in a Jamesian exchange her frankness is seen to overcome Darrow's qualms:

> 'You don't like my saying that you came for Lady Ulrica?' she asked, leaning over the table to pour herself a second cup of tea.
>
> He liked her quickness, at any rate. 'It's better,' he laughed, 'than your thinking I came for Mrs. Murrett!'
>
> 'Oh, we never thought anybody came for Mrs. Murrett. . . .' (*R*, p. 16)

Sophy has in fact parted from the awful vulgar menage of Mrs. Murrett, forfeiting her salary and leaving her trunk behind: another gesture that endears her to Darrow and makes him want to protect her.

The developing encounter between Darrow and Sophy Viner is written with great subtlety. At first he connects her 'with something uncomfortable and distasteful', with 'boredom and a vague discomfort'—which turns out to be his futile pursuit of Lady Ulrica at Mrs. Murrett's 'awful house in Chelsea'—a pursuit now seen by him as 'insipid' and 'the taste of stale follies'. But Sophy has a growing fascination for him; he studies her face: 'Its fugitive slanting lines, that lent themselves to all manner of tender tilts and foreshortenings, had the freakish grace of some young head of the Italian comedy' (*R*, p. 14). Even her 'doubtful taste' is appealing, at a moment when he feels he is suffering a 'catastrophe' in Anna's rejection, and that she has made him an 'anonymous rag of humanity'; with Sophy to impress, he can feel himself 'a personable young man' again. And from her tasteless references to his antics at Mrs. Murrett's, he comes to the conclusion that 'the girl had stuff in her'—because she had endured so much in Chelsea. She believes in 'luck' and in seizing opportunities as they are offered—it is partly this that *tempts* him—for we must see him as tempted by a fantasy to which Sophy's adventurism lures him. Her philosophy is that '. . . at any moment . . . a turn of the kaleidoscope might suddenly toss a bright spangle into the grey pattern of one's days' (*R*, p. 24) This light-headed philosophy 'was not without charm', and the encounter particularly allures him at a moment when he cannot avoid comparing Sophy with Anna. That he does so, of course, is deeply treacherous to his own love, and his tendency to make such comparisons is part of his unsatisfactoriness; one cannot avoid being aware of his critical views of Anna which reverberate through the novel, as he sinks more and more deeply into duplicity. One of the most poignant aspects of Anna's later suffering is that she becomes bitterly jealous of the romantic sexual experience Sophy enjoyed with her lover in Paris.

Behind the novel lies Edith Wharton's own perplexities, about emotional warmth, and the lack of it, in a properly trained 'lady'. Watching Sophy sleep and wake in the train compartment, Darrow finds a naturalness in her that Anna could not have: 'How differently Anna Leath would have behaved—her adaptability would have been "tact".' To be 'well bred' is to be without spontaneity. Then he reflects bitterly on the reluctance which has left him feeling so rejected and desolate: 'What were all her reticences and evasions but the result of the deadening process of forming a "lady" ' (*R*, p. 28). And we sense behind her reticences an emotional impotence: 'her eyes had made promises which her lips were afraid to keep'—'she was afraid of life.' He reflects with poignancy on the failure of his relationship with Anna:

> If she had been given to him then he would have put warmth in her veins and light in her eyes: *would have made her a woman through and through*. Musing thus, he had the sense of waste that is the bitterest harvest of experience. (*R*, p. 29; my italics)

Anna he sees as 'fated to fade into old age repeating the same gestures . . . never guessing that . . . life rolled away'. It seems deeply disloyal of Darrow to reflect so critically on 'the woman he adored', and we can see that it is this deep dissatisfaction with her that is the real 'reef' on which he founders.

But behind this novel one senses the experience of Edith Wharton herself, just as one senses D. H. Lawrence's problems behind his obsession with awakening women who have never yet known sexual fulfilment. Edith Wharton herself seems not to have become sexually awakened, until her affair with Morton Fullerton; but his sexual capacities were integral with a personal mode of life that had by now become repugnant to her. So, we may say, she has been in one mode herself an Anna Leath, and wants to become a Sophy Viner—but she is also perplexed by the unsatisfactoriness of the man. Darrow alternates between idealization of Anna—'he did not want the woman he adored to think he could forget her for a moment' (*R*, p. 44) —and an excitement about what he can do for Sophy. He finds it 'pleasant to be able to give such pleasure' to such a naïve girl in Paris, and becomes aware of 'the frank greed of her famished youth', a girl who was 'dying . . . for someone before whom she could unfold and shake out to the light her poor little shut-away emotions'; he yearns to 'fill her few free hours to the brim'. She grows 'prettier and more interesting to him, and eventually he becomes actively duplicitous to her—deliberately not posting her letter to the Farlows, whose reply might take her away'. He blunders into this adventure. Meanwhile there are recurrent irritations with Anna, whose failure to reply causes him 'humiliation', and he even compares Sophy with Anna in her approach to writing a letter. In his responses Edith Wharton notes a certain egoism: of Sophy's temperament Darrow thinks, '. . . he felt a fleeting desire to make its chords vibrate for his own amusement. . .' (*R*, p. 50). While in a way his interest is 'fraternal, . . . almost fatherly', he is increasingly impelled by Anna's failure to communicate: 'He felt a blind desire to punish someone else for the pain it caused him' (*R*, p. 54). The element of rage and punitiveness behind Darrow's sexual liaison with Sophy persists at a deep level, and this impels both his wrong-doing (which he confesses to Sophy who at that moment displays 'a small malevolent white mask') and enhances 'the excitement of pursuit'. 'She has a child after all' and so he feels he can take advantage of her; for her part she proclaims 'you've given me the only chance I've had.' (A thin chance, as it turns out.)

Edith Wharton is thus far from idealizing this momentary sexual encounter; as a woman she perceives what is involved. The man is unsatisfactory because, despite his sensitivity and intelligence, he is simply unable to take in the reality of womanliness, in Anna or in Sophy. (His view that he could have brought Anna to complete womanliness is illuminated ironically.) His persistent pique at Anna's reticence has at its heart a resentment of his own failure to respond adequately to her, in the early years. And behind his fascination with Sophy lies an impulse to punish both Anna and Sophy—to *punish woman*, really, for her nature, which is to be involved, and to run deep. The irony, of course, is that (as we later learn) Sophy falls in love with him ('something passed through her eyes', p. 53) and feels that, having had him, she must have him forever.

The unsatisfactoriness of the man here leads to a situation in which he can 'have' neither woman, since by his inauthenticity he has destroyed that absolute commitment to a woman that woman demands, if her life is to be meaningfully enriched.

The impending catastrophe is deepened by Anna's reflections, at the beginning of Book II. Waiting for Darrow's arrival, some four months later, at Givré, Anna is experiencing 'that equipoise of bliss which the fearful human heart scarce dares acknowledge'. She is experiencing 'long slow waves of joy' and reflects that up to now 'a veil had hung between her and life.'

Ironically, she reflects that 'the unusual' in her background 'was regarded as either immoral or ill-bred'. She believes that love will one day release her from her lady-like repression and reserve. She wants love to pervade everything, and she reflects that the young Darrow merely wanted to kiss her while she (as a woman) wanted something with a much wider perspective. She is aware that as a young girl she was cold and a prude, and sensed that she was missing something. Once aware of George Darrow looking in a certain way at a silly girl involved in some scandal, Anna experienced a 'hurricane of jealousy'. But she never managed to meet Darrow's approaches then.

In her marriage, however, she has felt 'another layer of gauze between herself and reality', except in her motherhood of Effie and her affection for Owen Leath her stepson, to whom she is intensely attached. He, on his part, has a profound anxiety about the possibility of her remarriage ('the shade of anxiety which . . . had kept its fixed line between his handsome eyes'). He, of course, is to play a crucial rôle in the drama.

As soon as Darrow appears, however, the duplicity to which he is driven to resort menaces the relationship at once. She may proclaim, 'Between you and me everything matters'—but at once it becomes clear that since he never read her explanatory letter which arrived at the hotel where he was sleeping with Sophy (and which he threw it in the fire unopened), he does not know what the 'obstacles' were at that time—while deeper obstacles now spring up between any authentic intimacy.

The progress of Darrow's dilemma is superbly managed by the novelist. The 'ground bass' of the situation is the contrast between the woman's being and consciousness and that of the man—his being spoiled by his betrayal. Every touch of Anna's hopes for the future is set on edge, our teeth are set on edge, by the memory of Darrow's memory of his exploitation of Sophy and his ultimate disgust at what he has done.

Anna is experiencing 'long slow waves of joy'. She has always hoped that 'love would release her' from the state in which she has often found herself with 'a veil between herself and life'. It has been four months since she first wrote to her lover—the letter he threw unopened into the fire—and he has ignored the second letter; she asks him to 'frankly tell me why'. He replies, with the smooth, bland, duplicity he now has to use:

> I can only repeat what I've just said. I was hurt and unhappy and I doubted you. I suppose if I'd cared less I should have been more confident. I cared so much that I couldn't risk another failure. For you'd made me feel that I'd miserably failed. So I shut my eyes and set my teeth and turned my back. There's the whole pusillanimous truth of it! (*R*, p. 113)

It seems like a 'frank confession' of his immaturity—it is a part truth; but, of course, we know the real reasons for his failure to respond, and so his duplicity is evidently growing to disastrous proportions: ' "Oh, if it's the *whole* truth—!" She let him clasp her' (*R*, p. 113). The word 'clasp' is exact: his physical postures seem mere gestures. And she has a subtle and mysterious woman's perception that this is not all: 'Oven saw you in Paris', she at once says challengingly. He tries to turn her anxiety aside ('In a crush—in a Paris *foyer*? My dear!'. 'I think he said the cloak was pink.' . . . 'Of course it was—they always are!') But, she goes on—chillingly to us— '. . . If I thought that at that moment . . . when you were on your way here, almost—' (*R*, p. 115). He puts a floating end of her scarf to his lips: he cannot, of course, dispel her fears. He affirms, 'That this is no light thing between us . . .', and

> For a long moment they looked at each other without speaking. She saw the dancing spirit in his eyes turn grave and darken to a passionate sternness. He stooped and kissed her, and she sat as if folded in wings. (*R*, p. 115)

—but to us the moment is deeply flawed, and the gestures towards the future ominous. The inauthenticity is intensifying.

On the one hand, Anna is 'spinning luminous webs of feeling' and the countryside seems like an 'enchanted forest'. She experiences 'the security and lightness of happy love' (*R*, p. 121). She wants him to find her as she really is—'her forehead was too high . . . her eyes were not large enough'. She has a triumphant sense that

> *as she was,* with her flattened hair, her tired pallor, her thin sleeves a little tumbled by the weight of her jacket, he would like her even better, feel her nearer, dearer, more desirable, than in all the splendour she might put on for him. (*R*, p. 124; my italics)

She 'feels like a slave, and a goddess, and a girl in her teens'. (We feel behind this urge to be 'found in her true reality', I believe, a yearning of Edith Wharton herself.) They reflect that 'There'll be evenings and evenings', while beneath his physical exultation he feels 'a certain gravity of mood': 'He was a little tired of experimenting on life; he wanted to "take a line", to follow things up, to centralize and concentrate, and produce results. . .' (*R*, p. 127). To be loved by a woman like that made 'all the difference', and as he contemplates his diplomatic career and afterwards, she becomes promisingly part of the meaning of his life; with such a 'comrade' he feels sure of 'doing something'. He is almost complacent about his moral conduct:

> As for the private and personal side of his life, it had come up to the current standards, and if it had dropped, now and then, below a more ideal measure, even those declines had been brief, parathentic, incidental. In the recognized essentials he had always remained strictly within the limits of his scruples. (*R*, p. 128)

In Millicent Bell's *Edith Wharton and Henry James* she speaks of how Darrow is 'made to pay for his moment of indiscretion' by a 'trick of fate'—and goes on to say that Edith Wharton was interested in 'the interior dynamics of her characters' souls'. But the liaison has been more than a 'moment's indiscretion': Darrow goes into it with his eyes open, calculatingly and duplicitously, in exasperation and egoism, and that he can do so reveals a certain obtuseness, a fatal inability to grasp the reality of another person—of two other people—and of himself. Now his confidence in himself and his future rings hollow.

When Sophy Viner appears, what strikes us as ghastly is the deepening duplicity he must use, to preserve his situation. When Anna questions him about the girl, he has to confess he has known her:

> '. . . She was a secretary, or something of the sort, in the background of a house where I used to dine.'
>
> He loathed the slighting indifference of the phrase, but he had uttered it deliberately, and had been secretly practising it all through the interminable hour at the luncheon-table. Now that it was spoken, he shivered at its note of condescension. In such cases one was almost sure to overdo. . . . But Anna seemed to notice nothing unusual. (*R*, pp. 142–43)

They begin to watch one another: he in dread of 'overdoing' it, she with her intuitive perception that there is 'something' between Darrow and Sophy. 'I'm so glad it turns out that you know her.' ' "Know" is rather exaggerated: we used to pass each other on the stairs. . .' (*R*,

p. 143). The reader draws in his breath sharply: the word 'know' takes on its Biblical echoes ('seeing I know not a man'), and the duplicitous blandness of Darrow casts a shadow over the integrity of the relationship which is all to him, while his self-contempt returns: 'His voice sounded to his own ears like an amateur actress in a "light" part' (*R*, p. 147).

Darrow tries to find relief in the open air, but Edith Wharton is all too aware of the agony of consciousness that is beginning in him:

> . . . all the while, behind these voluntarily emphasized sensations, his secret consciousness continued to revolve on a loud wheel of thought. For a time it seemed to be sweeping him through deep gulfs of darkness. . . . He had an almost physical sense of struggling for air, of battling helplessly with material obstructions, as though the russet covert through which he trudged were the heart of a maleficent jungle. . . . (*R*, p. 143)

The 'malificent jungle' is, of course, the primitive reality of his own make-up, which has led to this. It needs to be emphasized, at a time when sexual adventure is taken so lightly, that there is a deep moral perception behind Edith Wharton's exploration of the profound, physically experienced, anguish caused by inauthenticity. Darrow is in this 'complex horror' (*R*, p. 146) because he has failed to find the reality of the girl he has used; at least he realizes 'he must give the girl every chance' (*R*, p. 146), and he thinks now, 'Poor thing . . . poor thing.'

Sophy was happy at Givré: when he asks her 'you *are* happy here?' she replies, 'I *was*.' He does not yet know, but she is engaged to Owen. Darrow offers to help her; but, again, the offer is duplicitous—he wants to get rid of her—and the news of her engagement to Owen blows this into the air. She now threatens to become a permanent feature of his life, and insists on being found as integral with his reality (Man's attitude to woman being traditionally duplicitous: 'Thou hast committed fornication', 'Ay, but that was in another country/ And, besides, the wench is dead').

Sophy is afraid of him, 'sick with fear of him', yet declares she will not be sorry for anything. The discovery that she is so afraid beats him 'down to a lower level', as he becomes increasingly aware of the fateful part he has played in *her* life. And it represents a profound moral awakening in Darrow that he is chastened by his own agony of conscience:

> Till late in the night his thoughts revolved in a turmoil of indecision. His pride was troubled by the discrepancy between what Sophy Viner had been to him and what he had thought of her. . . .

This is 'galling': '. . . The bare truth, indeed, was that *he had hardly thought of her at all,* either at the time or since. . .' (*R*, p. 167; my italics) 'If I'd ever cared a straw for her', he reflects.

In today's fashionable novel, of course, what is triumphant is the endorsement of sexual acts completely and pervertedly dissociated from the person and being. In a coarse Australian novel, *Last Exit to Manley,* a woman is subjected to a sexual act on a beach: 'Don't humanize it!' the man cries, as she tries to speak; and there is novel after novel—they are called 'novels'—in which sex is brutally presented with coldness and distaste, as a mechanical and meaningless process. This can only be achieved at the expense of emotional realism, by separating sex from feeling. The subtle art of a woman writer like Edith Wharton gives the lie to any such schizoid perversion of the truth. Her intelligence and intuition knows the truth about women—and men too—that intimate involvement cannot be divorced from being, and that behaviour which fails to find the other person is deeply wounding and destructive.

Darrow's liaison with Sophy could even be seen to have some kind of vitality in its sensuality—something like that of Antony and Cleopatra, though the couple are not in love, and Darrow's excitement is vengeful and egoistic. But it makes them committed to one another in an extraordinary way, as Darrow finds once he knows Sophy plans to marry Owen. He becomes conscious of 'an obscure indignation against her', and this is set against his previous feelings for her defenceless state, of 'a sympathy profoundly tinged with compunction'. He feels an 'instinctive recoil', as if the relationship would be incestuous; and it brings a 'sudden realisation of his utter helplessness' (*R*, p. 187). He is in a 'black misery of mind'.

The web around Darrow now takes on a Jamesian complexity. Anna, he knows, has a lurking sense of 'something unexpressed and perhaps unexpressible', between the girl and himself. He feels he must go on talking to her, in clandestine meetings, despite the danger. When he escorts her to a safe place in the grounds in the rain, under Anna's umbrella, it reminds him of Paris, and he becomes excited again by her presence, and the response he senses in her blood to him; they are, in a strange sense, married, for he is more married to Sophy than he is engaged to Anna.

What confronts him in Sophy now is the same 'mask of wrath' with which she faced him when he told her how he had tricked her by not posting her letter to the Farlows. She sobs:

> 'Don't suppose I don't know what you must have thought of me!'
>
> The cry struck him to a lower depth of self-abasement. 'My poor child,' he felt like answering, 'the shame of it is that I've never thought of you at all!' But he could only uselessly repeat; 'I'll do anything I can to help you.' (*R*, p. 205)

But when he tries to persuade her that it would be wrong to marry Owen, how duplicitous is he? Is he jealous? Or merely trying to safeguard his own situation? Does he really mean it when he tries to persuade her he is too inexperienced a youth? And that she would 'be wretched if you marry a man you're not in love with' (*R*, p. 206). Sophy protests, 'I'm as happy as if I deserved it'—but later, of course, we are to find that she is now in love with Darrow himself, terrible as this is.

*The Reef* is about the failure of the typical man of Edith Wharton's time to understand woman, and to come up to the requirements of her nature, to her standards of being. While Anna is a woman of subtle and insightful perception—albeit somewhat slow and cold in emotional and sexual response because of her upbringing as a 'lady'—Darrow interprets her sensitive carefulness as a rejection of himself; her tardiness appears to him as a humiliation. In revenge he exerts his capacity for exploitation on Sophy Viner, to punish her for Anna's reticence: that is, he seeks to get his revenge on woman—by treating her as an exciting object, separated from her whole being as a woman. It is made clear in many places that he *does not care for Sophy* ('the shame of it is that I've never thought of you at all' (*R*, p. 205) ). Yet while she can say, 'What have you to do with me?' (*R*, p. 204), he has impressed himself upon her as a lover, as virtually a husband. He is still excited by her sensual presence, even when he is considering her engagement to Owen ('he felt old sleeping instincts stir in him': 'every drop of her blood must be alive to his nearness' (*R*, pp. 199–200) ). Here again, he completely fails to understand what has happened to her, at the level of being. He may ruefully reflect, 'If I'd ever cared a straw for her', but his moral dilemma arises from his failure to understand what sexual experience *means*. He still operates within the traditional separation between 'ladies' and those 'who are not'; Sophy is an independent, free-thinking woman, who lives by great honesty and frankness: 'Don't imagine,' she tells Darrow, 'I'm the least bit sorry for anything.' So, she crosses the barriers and exists in his world as a woman-as-being; Darrow cannot cope with such a creature. She lives from 'valiant common-sense' as the new American woman. Darrow simply tries to live by an out-of-date masculine code. The liaison has left him merely with a sense of 'exasperation' and 'self-contempt': 'it bore on his preconceived ideal of his attitude towards another woman. He had fallen below his own standard of sentimental loyalty' (*R*, p. 152). But we only have to trace the progress of the shattering of Anna's 'spell of divine security' to see how unsatisfactory Darrow's attitudes are, however much he learns insights into the disaster: 'The essential cheapness of the whole affair . . . came home to him with humiliating distinctness. . .' (*R*, p. 168).

By contrast, Anna is a woman whom he tries to find real: 'pride and passion were in conflict—magnificent qualities in a wife', 'she's a woman to be proud of' (*R*, p. 129). The memory of Sophy Viner has no place in his present picture of himself. But in his consideration of Anna he remains egoistical in that masculine way: he thinks, 'It's the best thing that's ever happened to me.' He contemplates 'the miracle of the union', it is true (*R*, p. 131), but is strangely (and masculinely) comic about this:

> . . . he felt a thrill of youthful wonder at the coincidence of their views and their experience, at the way their minds leapt to the same point in the same instant.
>
> 'The old delusion, I suppose,' he smiled to himself, 'will Nature never tire of the trick?'
>
> But he knew it was more than that. There were moments in their talk when he felt, distinctly and unmistakeably, the solid ground of friendship underneath the whirling dance of his sensations. 'How I should like her if I didn't love her!' he summed it up. . . . (*R*, p. 131)

Behind this again I believe we can sense Edith Wharton's experience of Morton Fullerton, who was a literary friend but with whom her friendship extended to 'the whirling dance of . . . sensations'—and yet one she found wanting, because of his duplicity.

The unsatisfactoriness of her own men is transmuted in *The Reef* into a profound and subtle analysis of the needs of woman, for both Sophy and Anna are complex and feeling women: 'women alive'. Henry James was especially fascinated by Anna:

> . . . the woman an exquisite thing, and with her characteristic finest, scarce differentiated notes (that is some of them) sounded with a wonder of delicacy. *I'm not sure her oscillations are not beyond our notation*; yet they are so held in your hand, so felt and known and shown, and everything seems to come of itself. (Letter, December 1912; my italics)

But while the subtle depiction of Anna may be compared with that of Isabel Archer, James could never have 'done' a Sophy Viner. Although Sophy is made by Darrow into an exciting object split off from the whole woman's reality, in the liaison which generates ultimately 'self-contempt' in him, she increasingly gains our sympathy, as the damage done to her life by the inauthenticity of Darrow's exploration becomes apparent. Although I would not want to use the word 'tragic' about her, we do need some such term for her to convey the poignant sense of a life destroyed or, if not destroyed, unutterably blighted, despite the woman's energy and frankness, her openness to experience. Perhaps in all three women, the message is that the danger to the 'modern' independent intelligent woman, 'open' to the world, is the unsatisfactoriness of man—and his failure to begin to understand woman.

In the remainder of Book III things on the surface seem placid. But there are many disturbances beneath. It is to be from the pressure of the reality of the next generation that the central challenge is to come (*cf.* Owen and Sophy: Anna says, 'If *they're* not happy I feel as if we shouldn't be' (*R*, p. 214; my italics) ). Another breath of reality comes with Adelaide Painter, a typical American woman whose judgement they invite (in America, she points out, 'it's enough to know that a girl is pure and lovely'—a comment that rings with irony in this context). During the last chapters of this book it begins to become evident that Sophy is now in love with Darrow: she wears at dinner the dress she had in Paris, and she looks 'so much like her Paris self that Darrow has a double consciousness', and as they go out into the garden she wears her pink Paris cloak—which strikes a chord, as we find later, in Anna's suspicions.

This is the moment when Sophy learns that Darrow is to marry Anna ('You too! I wish you all the luck') and everything seems set for the future; Darrow has to go back to London and then return to marry her before they go off to South America. He becomes fatalistic and gives himself up to the joy of Anna's presence: 'He kept repeating to himself "It's over" as though some monstrous midnight hallucination had been routed' (*R*, p. 222). He contemplates his future and 'yearns for rest, stability, a comfortably organised middle age' (*R*, p. 223). But in this moment of calm Darrow is seen to 'adjust his disguise', and sees others doing the same, and the radical insecurity beneath the situation cannot but surface.

Book IV opens with Anna in bliss: 'bliss has wound itself into every fold of her being', as she relishes 'the deep and tranquil current of her love'. But the Sophy who appears is one in whom the nature of her being, as a woman, exerts herself: she has been crying, and her 'unusual pallor' turns out to be powder, which she has used to try to hide the fact.

She wants to go away, and she appears to Anna 'so small, so slight, so visibly defenceless and undone'—yet in some way 'possessed of a secret she missed' (*R*, p. 235). Anna feels a vague tightening of the heart at the sense that something has happened, and what blows in upon the situation is the reality of the relationship between Owen and Sophy. At the meeting point between them they know that their intimacy has been deeply disturbed by the presence of Darrow, and Owen bursts out into a fury—declaring, 'Ask Darrow!'

It is not that Darrow is against the marriage. It is that Sophy has hated the idea of the marriage since Darrow appeared. The development, this discovery, 'shot its light along dark distances of fear' for Anna. She becomes aware, from her subtle and penetrating intuitions, that there *is* something between her lover and the girl, after all his denials. She says to herself, 'If there's nothing between them they'll look at each other; if there *is* something they won't'—and they don't.

From this moment she becomes aware of Darrow's treacherous duplicity: 'She had been suddenly endowed with the fatal gift of reading the secret sense of every seemingly spontaneous movement. . .' (*R*, p. 251). And as we shall see, this perception eventually becomes one which makes her feel she can never again believe anything he says, and makes her feel there is a male world in which this kind of duplicity is endemic—makes her wonder, even, whether her late husband did not have other women in Paris, whether men in general all have illicit passions about which they remain silent.

This dread makes her perceive that not only does Darrow's duplicity threaten her own emotional life but also that of her stepson, the youth she loves so dearly; she tries to protect Owen against any thought that Darrow menaces his own love: 'Owen . . . is romantic and extravagant and he worships Sophy . . . Owen is like my son . . . I can't let him think you had anything to do with it. . .' (*R*, p. 254). But in Darrow's eyes she reads 'the forbearance of a man resigned to the discussion of non-existent problems'.

The subtle tragi-comedy of *The Reef* lies in scenes like this, in which Darrow is portrayed as a master of managing difficult situations, acting a duplicity and putting on a mask—while Anna's woman's instincts search him, until she sees the real truth in his eyes. Here she presses her inquiry as to why Darrow has been having long secret *tête-à-têtes* with Sophy. 'She felt a warning tremor as she spoke, as though some instinct deeper than reason surged up in defense of its treasure' (*R*, p. 255). Darrow's face is unstirred except for the 'flit of his half-amused smile' and he declares he has been trying to get to know Sophy so he could judge her.

> She listened with a growing sense of reassurance, struggling to separate the abstract sense of his words from the persuasion in which his eyes and voice enveloped them.
>
> 'I see—I do see,' she murmured. (*R*, p. 255)

Like Oedipus, Anna must go on inquiring and questioning, from the depths of her female authenticity, even though it threatens her with doom to do so.

Any estrangement between Owen and Darrow, Anna declares, would lull her; here, there is a fatal sense that the blood-is-thicker-than-water quality of her relationship with her stepson (though he is *not* of her blood) counts as primary for her, because she is a woman, because it is like a mother's concern for her son. The love relationship with a man (a woman knows) is never in that primary dimension.

But Darrow goes through physical anguish, too, and his experience becomes a 'moral teething'. Waiting to have another exchange with Sophy, he feels 'a relentless hand' tearing away 'all the tender fibres of association that bound him to the peaceful room'. Here he has drunk his deepest draughts of happiness, 'had had his lips at the fountain-head of its overflowing rivers; but now that source was poisoned and he would taste no more of an untainted cup' (*R*, p. 258). He feels 'an actual physical anguish'. He has been insincere again—letting Anna think he had consented to speak to Sophy because she asked it.

> In reality he had been feverishly casting about for the pretext she had given him; and for some reason this trivial hypocrisy weighed on him more than all *his heavy burden of deceit*. (*R*, p. 158; my italics)

The book ends in ambivalence, as we shall see, because the relationship between Darrow and Anna has been spoiled for ever by the deceit he has had to practice, and the hypocrisy he has had to enter into even in trivial questions like this, in every sphere of their encounter; she can never trust him, while every 'explanation' he gives seems to have a radical untruth behind it.

Darrow has betrayed both women. Now, when Sophy comes to him, tormented by impossible love for him, she is a wreck:

> He was profoundly moved by the change in the girl's appearance. At sight of him she had fixed a smile: *but it lit up her wretchedness like a candle-flame held to a dead face* (*R*, p. 259; my italics)

She lifts a hand to brush aside a lock of hair with a gesture 'that was burnt into his memory'—for, in seducing Sophy, he has entered into a sexual experience that has worked itself into his 'psychic tissue'; he has done fatal damage to Sophy, Anna and himself.

Darrow has warned Sophy that she should not marry a man she does not love; it is this advice (which comes ironically from him) that has revealed to her that she loves Darrow himself. In contemplating this fact Darrow has a glimpse of his own male inadequacy:

> He stopped before the writing table, where his photograph, well-dressed, handsome, self-sufficient—the portrait of a man of the world, confident in his ability to deal adequately with the most delicate situations—*offered its huge fatuity to his gaze.* (*R*, p. 260; my italics)

Darrow breaks out, 'It's I who ought to go.' But Sophy, with that *terre à terre* capacity of woman, declares 'what good would that do any of us—now?'

There seems nothing he can say that was not foolish or cruel or contemptible. Astonishingly, he tries to persuade Sophy to try to forget: 'Time modifies . . . rubs out . . . more quickly than you think.' But Sophy declares, 'For me . . . you'll always be here.' She does not want to forget: 'I want to keep you all to myself.' She has that sterling quality of true shamelessness about the affair:

> 'I wonder what your feeling for me was? It seems queer that I've never really known—I suppose we *don't* know much about that kind of feeling. Is it like taking a drink when you're thirsty? . . . I used to feel as if all of me was in the palm of your hand. . . . Don't for a minute think I'm sorry. It was worth every penny it cost. My mistake was in being ashamed, just at first, of its having cost such a lot. I tried to carry it off as a joke—to talk of it myself as an "adventure" . . . I've made my choice—that's all: I've had you and I mean to keep you.' Her face was shining like her eyes. 'To keep you hidden away here,' she ended, and put her hand upon her breast. (*R*, p. 263)

While Sophy betrays a female incomprehension of male modes, Darrow in the subsequent pages contemplates them in himself. She has declared that she has 'risked more, but that I'd won more, too—such worlds!' The sexual encounter has come to mean a great deal to her: he was good to her, she declares later.

Darrow reflects that, in the conventional male way (as with women who were 'not ladies'), he tried to separate sex from love.

> He remembered distinctly enough that he had not meant the perilous passion—even in its most transient form—to play a part in their relation. *In that respect his attitude had been above reproach.* (*R*, p. 264; my italics)

The latter is perhaps the strangest sentence in the book, and one is puzzled to think what Edith Wharton meant by it. He engaged with Sophy as 'the frank and easy comrade he had expected to find her': 'Her enjoyment had been unclouded and his pleasure in it undisturbed.' He recalls the way in which they had felt a sense of well-being, her charming gestures and atmosphere had taken the place of talk ('when her light chatter about people had failed') and a kiss had seemed a natural substitute for speech. The kiss had saved their venture from disaster.

The disaster seems to be that 'his wounded vanity . . . seeking balm for its hurt [had] yearned to dip deeper into the healing pool of her compassion.' She had 'committed the fatal error of saying that she could see he was unhappy' and entreated him to tell her why. His (first) kiss had snatched them out of this threat of a too-serious encounter with reality;

he did not have to listen to her any longer, and this added immensely to her charm.

He saw, in their idyll in the Paris woods, the mare's tails of an advancing depression, and later the rain came. The rain drove them back to the hotel; they were both rather irritable 'and vaguely disposed to resist one another's suggestions': it was this drift of circumstances that led them to go to bed together.

These reminiscences put a slightly different light on the encounter: 'the whole episode was still obscure to him.' He had wanted to give Sophy 'a few days of harmless pleasuring'. But he does dimly perceive that he did want 'the balm of her compassion': 'In his confused memory of the situation he seemed not to have been guiltless of such yearnings.' He tried to resist this, but 'a shade of lassitude had come over their intercourse.'

The kiss turns the relationship into a fairy tale:

> her presence as a part of the charmed stillness of the summer woods, as the element of vague well-being that *suffused his senses and lulled to sleep the ache of wounded pride.* (*R*, p. 266; my italics)

So, he dimly perceives the way in which he has been using Sophy to heal his sense of humiliation at Anna's telegram. He tried to keep the relationship in the realm of fantasy-encounter, even when Sophy offered 'compassion' and seriousness. But the lapse into sexual meeting came almost from dolefulness, tedium and irritation: the fall was caused by the rain. Darrow seems here, too, to have forgotten how he looked out at the rain in self-contempt, loathing and disgust.

This passage in Chapter XXVI does not much further illuminate what we know from the beginning, and does not quite get right the male attitude to such an adventure. We are not sure how to take his sense of how he feels himself to be 'above reproach' in not allowing love to enter into the matter, nor how to take 'was it he, then, who, in the sequel, had grown impatient of the bonds he had set himself?' If Darrow is going through a process of moral development, there are not enough signs of this in this meditation. He continues to reflect within his own egoism and shows no further insights into the nature of woman's reality or Sophy's experience of the encounter—whose truth now begins to manifest itself in her wrecked face.

After this musing reflection we have one of those false upward movements in the spirit of our response: Anna has persuaded herself she has been thick-skinned and obtuse; Sophy has explained everything. She almost apologizes to Darrow for Owen's suspicions: 'because I understand better how one can torture oneself over unrealities.' To Darrow this is amazing: 'Her gaze, so grave and yet so sweet, was like a deep pool into which he could plunge and hide himself from the hard glare of his misery' (*R*, p. 270). *'Because'*, Anna goes on, *'I'd dreamed the horror too!'* And she fixes on Sophy's pink cloak which the girl has worn after dinner. She recalls Owen's account of Darrow with a woman in a similar cloak at the theatre, and again, Oedipus-like, she presses towards the truth, following, however, her woman's insights.

She is 'happier now to have been so foolish!' But her new confidence in him, in 'one of her rare gestures of surrender, is fatal: this is the most fatal moment in the pool.'

> Her lips were parted in a noiseless laugh and the tremor of her lashes made their shadow move on her cheek. He looked at her through a mist of pain and saw all her offered beauty held up like a cup to his lips; but as he stooped to it a darkness seemed to fall between them, her arms slipped from his shoulders and she drew away from him abruptly.
>
> 'But she *was* with you, then?' she exclaimed: and then, as he stared at her: 'Oh, don't say no! Only go and look at your eyes!' (*R*, p. 272)

Darrow cannot mask and act any more: 'He knew he could no more hide from her what was written there than he could efface from his soul the fiery record of what he had just lived through.'

> There before him, staring him in the eyes, and reflecting itself in all his lineaments, was the overwhelming fact of Sophy Viner's passion and of the act by which she had attested it. (*R*, p. 272)

Darrow tries still to be plausible, but he hears 'himself speak as though the words had proceeded from other lips', and makes a slip, about the Farlows not knowing. Anna is in doubt and misery, and declares she will get the truth from Sophy. She tries to invent reasons why Sophy wanted her visit to Paris to be kept secret, but continues to pursue the truth; at last she perceives that Sophy is leaving because she loves Darrow. Has she given him up? He declares she has.

A moment before she 'had lifted her arms to his neck' and 'she had been wrapped in a sense of complete security': 'All the spirits of doubt had been exorcised, and her love was once more the clear habitation in which every thought and feeling could move in blissful freedom' (*R*, p. 277). But now, after looking in Darrow's eyes, 'she had seemed to look into the very ruins of his soul'. What seemed all light and life was now 'a place of graves'.

A motto for the novel could be

> There is no art
> To find the mind's construction in the face . . .

—the discovery of what lies behind the eyes is a perception of death, for the discovery if found in the face is itself the death of the soul, between two people. And we have that same undercurrent of death between lovers, as we have at the end of *The House of Mirth*.

Anna now fully understands the secret: Darrow has met the girl in Paris and has been 'overmastered by her passion'. She goes on declaring, 'I must believe him', and tries to believe that Darrow's main and generous concern has been to protect Sophy's piteous secret. Too late, Owen comes to her, to declare, after a talk with Sophy, that everything is all right—and Anna feels she must keep the truth from him. She must talk to Sophy, and as she waits she reflects upon 'her inability to deal with the oblique and the tortuous'.

> She had lacked the hard teachings of experience, and an instinctive disdain for whatever was less clear and open than her own conscience had kept her from learning anything of the intricacies and contradictions of other hearts. She said to herself, 'I must find out—'yet everything in her recoiled from the means by which she felt it must be done. (*R*, p. 282)

Anna now sees Sophy 'as that unknown peril lurking in the background of every woman's thoughts about her lover'. She notes in the girl 'graces and snares never before perceived', and this is enough to 'make her ashamed of the darkness it lit up in her heart'. At first their encounter is one of defiance and distrust; but then she comes out with it: 'Is there any reason why you shouldn't marry Owen. . . . Do you love someone else?' (*R*, p. 284). Sophy gives her a glance of indescribable reproach: 'Ah, you might have waited!'

'. . . Of course I can't marry him', she declares: Anna is trembling with a confused compassion. She tries to say she has divined the truth: Darrow has not told. But all Sophy can say is '. . . in your place I should have guessed it sooner.' These words go through Anna 'like a sword'. Anna regards Sophy, however, as young, exposed and desolate ('What thoughts must she be hiding in her heart'). Anna is perplexed, however, by the precocity of Sophy, who seems numb to her grasp. ' "I suppose I'm not more than half a woman," she mused, "for I don't want my happiness to hurt her" ' (*R*, p. 286). Sophy lays her lips on Anna's hand in a stream of weeping, as though 'Anna's touch had released the waters of some deep spring of pain.' The girl flings back from the door, 'He was good to me—no one was ever so good.' It is an extraordinary scene, which could only have been written by a woman (and may, in its intensity, remind us of the classical scene between Dorothea and Rosamund Lydgate in *Middlemarch*).

Anna seeks some 'channel of escape to the flood of her pent-up anguish'. The situation evokes many 'hungry ghosts': 'her youthful disappointment, *the failure of her marriage*' (my italics). We have not really so far understood that her marriage was a failure, and again I believe this phrase slips out from Edith Wharton's own identification with her subtle heroine. These, however, were 'negative sorrows'; now she was suffering 'as a hurt animal must, blindly, furiously, with the single fierce animal longing that the awful pain should stop.' She meets Darrow with the cry, 'Don't! It's useless. I know everything. . . .'

Darrow, surely not with duplicitousness but effrontery, says it is not like her to be afraid; as soon as Sophy is mentioned it strikes her 'how the girl must have loved him to be so generous—*what memories there must be between them!'* (*R*, p. 289; my italics).

The book now moves through complexities in which Anna is torn between wanting to keep Darrow and letting 'his nearness . . . and all the unseen influences that flowed from him . . . dissolve her soul to weakness' (*R*, p. 291), and summoning her strength either to let him go or detach herself. From time to time she is overcome by sobs. Darrow is no longer duplicitous, but almost sickly in his appeals to moral considerations he has long ago forfeited the right to invoke: 'It's not worthy of either of us to be afraid . . . in the name of common charity. . . .' Anna just does not want to hear the girl's name again, but he persists with even a kind of sermon:

> You've always said you wanted, above all, to look at life, at the human problem, as it is, without fear and without hypocrisy; and it's not always a pleasant thing to look at . . . all I ask you is to be generous to Miss Viner. (*R*, p. 292)

She tells him he can marry Sophy; he declares this is the worst fate she could wish her. '. . . what *is* she? What are you? It's too horrible! On your way here . . . to *me*. . . .' In this scene Darrow is quite sickeningly seeking to be plausible:

> I was on my way to you—after repeated delays and postponements of your own making. At the very last you turned me back with a mere word—and without explanation. I waited for a letter; and none came. I'm not saying this to justify myself. I'm simply trying to make you understand. I felt hurt and bitter and bewildered. I thought you meant to give me up. And suddenly, in my way, I found some one to be sorry for, to be of use to. . . . The rest was a moment's folly . . . a flash of madness. . . . (*R*, p. 293)

Here, I believe, we may plumb not only Edith Wharton's delineation of the unsatisfactory man, but also the weakness of her concept of man, such as we shall examine later in *The Gods Arrive*. The man is so often a child—a child who finds the slightest rejection so intolerable that he can only make emotional demands that are appropriate as from an infant to mother. It is as if trying to play on that maternal capacity to pardon infant behaviour that Darrow is gambling here. The answer is to invoke the phrase *sub specie aeternitatis*: does he, did he, love Anna thus, for if so, he would not surely have used such lame excuses for an infidelity, as the frustration of a hope for a letter from her?

Darrow goes on to accuse Anna of judging Sophy 'by conventional standards'—provoking in her an 'almost physical repugnance': 'I always thought her an adventuress', which Sophy is, of course. 'She had the excuse of her loneliness, her unhappiness—of miseries and humiliations that a woman like you can't even guess' (*R*, p. 293). But this is still specious when, as we have just learnt from his reminiscence, he had stopped listening to Sophy's tales of Mrs. Murrett. Every word he says throws 'a disintegrating light on their own past', and she is appalled to think that 'his security was the security of falsehood'; he has come to her from the liaison for which he gives such excuses—and if he meant he had forgotten, that was worse.

But, strangely, Anna wants to know more: she is continually aware of her lack of knowledge of 'life' and seems to feel inadequate because of this.

> How did people enter on such adventures, how pass out of them *without more visible traces of their havoc*? Her imagination recoiled from the vision of a sudden debasing familiarity: *it seemed to her that her thoughts would never again be pure.* (*R*, p. 244; my italics)

The phrases I have italicized come, I believe, from puzzlements of Edith Wharton; Henry James would, I believe, have been more strongly moral about the inauthenticity of Darrow's lapse, but then he did not know the snares of sexual passion (and the *allowances* men and women make for their own lapses) as Edith Wharton did.

Darrow can even say, 'I swear to you . . . It was simply that and nothing more', which makes Anna wonder at his composure. Like enemies, they face each other, he with charges of her uncomprehension, and she with protests that she does not want to understand such things.

They feel they are 'beings of different language'. Book IV ends with her horror of his departure, which leaves an empty space, and with her vision of herself throwing herself into his arms, whereupon she thinks agonizingly, 'I shall never know what that girl has known.'

Edith Wharton, however, is too subtle to leave it at that.

Anna *is* to know what Sophy has known, but is to suffer, on each occasion when she shares an experience with Darrow, the horrible pangs of imagining what it was like for Sophy when she had the same experience: a permanent poisoning of consciousness.

In Book V she goes to Paris, to try to find out if Owen has gone to Sophy; we find her in Chapter XXX in Adelaide Panter's flat. Adelaide brings her Sophy, who wants to tell Owen the truth. She is appalled to hear Anna is giving Darrow up: she went away so he should not have to lose Anna. She declares to Anna that 'He's never loved anyone else . . . he never cared for me.' Sophy urges that she's not ashamed of having loved him: 'he never said a word to mislead me' (which, as we have seen, is not strictly true). Anna is only conscious of being in the presence of an intenser passion than she had ever felt. Sophy urges her to go back to Givré, to hide her attempt to find Owen from him. 'Can't I move you? Some day you'll know'—words which are to reverberate in Anna, once she does learn.

Left to herself for an evening, Anna has a dream of Darrow putting his arms around her and admiring her hair; she awakes smiling, only to break down into sobs. At that moment Darrow arrives back from London, and he comes towards her and takes her in his arms, as though he had found her after a long search. She draws his face down to kiss him.

She hesitates to encourage Darrow to return to Givré', as Sophy has suggested, in order to allay Owen's fears and prevent his pain: that seems to her an unacceptable fraud. Obliged to admit his episode with Sophy was a 'case of not feeling', Darrow comes out with more specious pleading (he has a capacity to talk like a B.B.C. 'Prayer for the Day'):

> When you've lived a little longer you'll see what complex blunderers we all are: how we're struck blind sometimes and made sometimes—and then . . . we have to work . . . [to] build up the precious things . . . life's just a perpetual piecing together of broken bits. (*R*, p. 315)

And then (urged to marry Sophy) he describes the Reef itself:

> It seemed such a slight thing—all on the surface—and I've gone aground on it because it *was* on the surface. I see the horror of it just as you did. But I see, a little more clearly, the extent, and the limits, of my wrong. It's not as black as you imagine. (*R*, p. 316)

The shame is that Sophy loves him: 'Is it anything to be proud of, to know so little of the strings that pull us', he confesses. She says, however, that she does not condemn him, but she is not as repelled as she should be by his persistent plausibility, which is, actually, very American.

Anna's body and soul are divided against themselves: she is actually discovering 'instincts and desires, which, muted and unmarked, had gone to and fro in the dim passages of her mind'. Her growing acquaintance with Darrow's weaknesses is actually awakening in her her recognition of her own passion.

Owen walks in, and she declares (to his astonishment) that Darrow is going back to Givré with her; the 'fraud' she earlier dismissed is perpetrated by herself. Left alone she falls into Darrow's arms again: 'all her fears seemed to fall from her as he held her.' She feels 'secret shames and rancours'—'yet richer, deeper, more enslaving': *'She knew now that she could never give him up'* (my italics). 'She and Darrow belonged to each other, and . . . he was right in saying no past folly could ever put them asunder' (*R*, p. 319).

She is now aware of another turmoil in her, between 'what thought in her and what blindly wanted'. She has, strangely, an 'absolute trust in Sophy Viner', even though she cannot make her out; for she had concealed from Owen the fact that she had given herself to Darrow 'with no more apparent sense of debasement than the vulgarest of adventurers', yet had 'instantly obeyed the voice of her heart when it bade her part from the one and serve the other'. She finds veils between herself and understanding of Sophy's background. She wonders if her own husband ever had women in Paris; then she realizes she is fantasizing this to shield Darrow, trying to persuade herself that 'all men are like that.' She upbraids herself for persisting in her pursuit of truth: if she had held her tongue nothing need have come out. Yet, as a woman, one must be aware of levels of being, and questions of the deepest authenticity of being, that she cannot ignore.

Arriving at Givré, she is aware that Darrow always knows what to do, but sensing that his tact is a kind of professional expertness, she is filled with repugnance. The currents flow between them, but she has doubts about giving Effie a father like Darrow: 'there was every reason for not marrying a man in whom her faith was not complete'; '*she would never again know if he were speaking the truth or not*' (*R*, p. 325; my italics).

So, she continues to vacillate, deciding at one moment to marry Darrow (*R*, p. 328), being filled with quiet joy (*R*, p. 329); when she is away from him she frets—and when she is with him she is benumbed. She is tormented by visions of his past: 'Had such things happened to him before? . . . Was it a link in a chain of similar experiments . . . the thought of it dishonoured her whole past' (*R*, p. 330). If she watches him, she reflects that other women have done so. And, like Anna Karenina, she wonders whether she has the art to keep him. Is he capable of loyalty? They speak of Sophy Viner, and she wants to know more about their *affaire*—but he (rightly) refuses.

In the next chapter (XXXV) she decides she must let him know she cannot be his wife. She is appalled by the spectre of herself as Effie's mother, the girl growing up under the influence of the woman she feels herself becoming. She believes Sophy Viner, in renunciation, has chosen the better path.

Darrow's summons comes from the Ambassador, whom he must meet in Paris. She summons her powers and is determined to tell him, appalled by the spectacle of life without him—of being left 'alone among her shrunken thoughts'.

In Chapter XXXVI, however, they drift into bed. He demands his answer. But she persists in quizzing him: 'Do such things happen to men often?' Such a thing never happened to him, he declares. Had it begun before he went to Paris? No. Did he know she was easy? They move towards an uneasy good night, but her grief breaks and she leans against him and presses her head against his arm.

She finds herself in his room, and thinks bitterly 'this is what Sophy Viner knew', ashamed by this detested vision. He is waiting for her to depart and it is clear *no other possibility has crossed his mind.* Something whispers in her, 'Why not . . . why not?' as if his tact were a slight on her potentialities for desire. She longs to be for him *all that Sophy Viner had been,* and even reflects, 'Don't I feel things as other women do?' She sees a note-case she had given him, and touches it: the contact makes her tremble, and her heart rocks like a boat on memories of her girlish past with him. Suddenly Darrow takes her in his arms, and she opens her eyes 'to the flood of light in his'.

'She was his now': but she is troubled by the thought that 'will it become a matter of course to him so soon'; she finds it hard to bear his public demeanour in the train next day to Paris. But now she even fears he will grow indifferent to her, as he is to Sophy Viner, so she feels she is reliving Sophy's experience. But Anna also feels the possessive pride of the woman in love, about their 'happy secret'.

They meet Owen, and she senses with a pang that 'he knows'. She meets Darrow and intends to tell him that. He is free and takes her to a restaurant (she notes a shadow on his face as he changes an impulse which would have taken them to the café to which he took Sophy). He suggests the theatre, but she wonders if it is the one where he took Sophy. She even begins to quiz him on this: 'I can't go on in the darkness any longer!' she cries. I want to know everything, she declares, but again, he rightly refuses. Darrow is appalled: ' "No, but things can't go on like this." He paused, as if to measure his words. "I fill you with aversion," he exclaimed' (*R*, p. 358). He is appalled by the price she is paying, by giving him 'all the chances a woman could'. He is leaving her, again for ever, but she breaks again. 'Why, he's mine—he's mine! He's no one else's!' she cries: '. . . the look in his eyes swept away all her terrors.'

And is her conclusion to this chapter conclusive? 'She no longer understood what had prompted her senseless outcry: and the mortal sweetness of loving him became again the one real fact in the world' (*R*, p. 360).

But there is another chapter, XXXIX, and in this she wakes 'to a humiliated memory of the previous evening'; she had learned that it was beyond her power to avoid making scenes like that, when she recoiled from him as he held her cloak. She saw 'he and she were profoundly and inextricably bound together as two trees with interwoven roots.' She can only escape from her plight, she considers, by some external chance.

The only hope for such a chance seems to lie with Sophy Viner. She will go to her and tell her she has given Darrow up. But Sophy has left her address and is staying with her sister. The scene at the sister's is Dickensian: hers is the vulgar world of the shabby entertainer, in all its seediness. Sophy has gone to India with Mrs. Murrett. Sophy has sunk back into a coarse and humiliating world, but nobly, in renunciation. Anna 'sits motionless, 'gazing at the disordered room, the pink bed, the trivial face among the pillows'. This is the world from which the strange little adventuress emerged, to threaten her life.

But now there can be no chance through Sophy's presence to enable her to leave Darrow. So, presumably, she will have to continue, between falling into his arms in desperation, and being tormented on the cross of suspicion, aware that she is but sharing the intimacies he gave initially to that frank and honest but light-headed adventuress. Her chance of the happiness she once contemplated is forever spoiled by the unsatisfactory man. To find Sophy Viner the heroine in such a triangle is absurd. The destruction of three emotional lives is the consequence of the foundering on the reef of inauthenticity and, essentially, on the failure of the man to understand and respect woman.

# 3

# *The Custom of the Country*

*The Custom of the Country* is the one novel which only Edith Wharton could have written. It is a *tour de force*, embracing a number of worlds: Apex America, the Washington Square *milieu* of those who have made it, the world of Anglicized traditional New York families, fashionable Paris life, and the life of the French aristocracy. All are done from first hand knowledge, with superb and penetrating irony. (The names strike one from the beginning as being hilariously right, for their background: Spragg (and 'Undine' itself, from *ondoyant*, the name given to Mr. Spragg's hair crimper), Mrs. Spoof, Indiana Trusk, Mabel Blitch.)

But besides this sociological irony there is an undercurrent of wisdom about sexuality. Undine Spragg is a complex protagonist, and the female view of her sexuality is superbly done. Her main impulse is that of voraciousness: she is sublimely beautiful and spoiled, and her central impulse is to employ her beauty to gain everything she wants. There is a woman of this kind in the two later works, *Hudson River Bracketted* and *The Gods Arrive*, Floss Delaney, who is a ruthless manipulator, but Floss is a simple gold-digger beside Undine. Undine is absolutely ruthless, in her pursuit of her goals—and her greed is integral with her idea of herself. She is, for instance, continually aware of herself in mirrors, and when she is alone in Italy with Ralph on honeymoon, what bores her is not so much the absence of shops and balls, for excitement, but the absence of the *world*, to reflect her. She is throughout preoccupied with how people regard her, and it is when she is not *reflected* in this way that she suffers distress.

A ray of the same light fell on her where she stood in the unlit

> sitting room, and her reflection bloomed out like a flower from the mirror that faced her. . . . (CC, p. 300)

> She had dropped her cloak and stood before the wardrobe mirror studying her reflection when he came up behind her and she saw he was looking at it too. (CC, p. 375)

Her sexual life is only a subsidiary element in this *need to be seen*. The normal male reader might expect the sexual theme to be related to this voracious need, and no doubt it is. But there is a sense in which sexual love is something to which in itself Undine is *indifferent*. One of the French women says, 'Ah, you funny Americans. Why do you all behave as if love were a secret infirmity?' (CC, p. 338). Undine's attitude to sex is totally subservient to her husband's or lover's rôle in 'society'.

This is a woman's view. To a male writer one might expect that authenticity would have its focus in sexual experience. Edith Wharton knows better. This novel, although of course it is about divorce (divorce being 'the custom'), does not have sexuality at its centre at all; sensuality is not Undine Spragg's primary preoccupation. Her liaisons are subservient to an overall concern with how-I-am-seen-in-the-world, in terms of manic success.

At the same time it must be said that Undine Spragg is a fully realized woman—as complicated as Cleopatra. She suffers so much, over her second husband's death, for instance, that the reader even finds relief in the last episode, in which she takes refuge in the arms of Elmer Moffat—with whom she encounters the good, solid old American attitudes. Perhaps the great virtues of the novel can best be brought out by examining this episode first.

When Undine goes to Moffat's apartment, 'She knew now what she had come for—to keep him from every one else, to keep him for herself alone' (CC, p. 567).* Her view of Moffat is significantly different from that of Ralph, at the moment when Moffat reveals to him that he has been Undine's husband:

> His redness, his glossiness, his baldness, and the carefully brushed ring of hair encircling it; the square line of his

* References are to the Macmillan edition of 1913.

> shoulders, the too careful fit of his clothes, the prominent lustre of his scarf-pin, the growth of short black hair on his manicured hands, even the tiny cracks and crows'-feet beginning to show in the close surface of his complexion: all these solid witnesses to his reality and his proximity pressed on Ralph with the mounting pang of physical nausea. (CC, p. 468)

In the final episodes, Moffat's possessions speak of his 'success' and Undine takes her place among them; here, one of the possessions symbolizes Undine: 'Ralph's eyes roamed towards the crystal toy that stood on the desk beside Moffat's hand. Faugh! That a hand should have touched it!' (CC, p. 468). Ralph's shock is to find he has had Undine only second to Moffat: 'it' is Undine's body.

Ralph's set of values is not only utterly foreign to Moffat; Moffat would not even understand them. He feels

> the uselessness, the irrelevance of all the old attitudes of appropriation and defiance. He seemed to be stumbling about in his inherited prejudices like a modern man in mediaeval armour. . . . 'He doesn't even know what I'm feeling,' flashed through Ralph; and the whole archaic structure of his rites and sanctions tumbled down about him. (CC, p. 469)

But what Undine sees is 'Europe' bought by Moffat:

> She advanced into the room and slowly looked about her. The big vulgar writing-table wreathed in bronze was heaped with letters and papers. Among them stood a lapis bowl in a Renaissance mounting of enamel and a vase of Phoenician glass that was like a bit of rainbow caught in cobwebs. On a table against the window a little Greek marble lifted its pure lines. On every side some rare and sensitive object seemed to be shrinking back from the false colours and crude contours of the hotel furniture. (CC, p. 567)

The precious object becomes a symbol of Undine as Ralph has idolized her.

This echoes the description of the Spragg apartment at the beginning of the book:

> The Spragg rooms were known as one of the Looey suites, and the drawing-room walls, above their wains-cotting of highly-varnished mahogany, were hung with salmon-pink

> damask and adorned with oval portraits of Marie Antoinette and the Princess de Lamballe. In the centre of the florid carpet a gilt table with a top of Mexican onyx sustained a palm in a gilt basket tied with a pink bow. . . . (CC, p. 4)

This accounts for the sense of relief we experience in the final episodes: in going back to Moffat, Undine is *going home*. She has been bored on honeymoon with Ralph; she has made a serious mistake giving herself to Peter Van Degen for two months:

> She had gone away with Peter because, after the decisive scene in which she had put her power to the test, to yield to him seemed the surest means of victory. . . . She too had wandered from place to place, spending a great deal of money, always more and more money . . . but presently she began to perceive that her companion's view of their relation was not the same as hers. She saw that he had always meant to be an unavowed tie . . . since Undine had insisted on being carried off like a sentimental school-girl he meant to shroud the affair in mystery, and was as zealous in concealing their relation as she was bent on proclaiming it. (CC, p. 365)

—and she ends her marriage to Raymond de Chelles more or less as a prisoner, suffering a deliberate snub to her sexuality, between the family's wish for her to produce a child and his cool rejection ('You never looked better; your dress is extremely becoming. Goodnight, my dear', he said, kissing her hand as he turned away (CC, p. 520)).

> The dullness of her life seemed to have passed into her blood: her complexion was less animated, her hair less shining. The change in her looks alarmed her, and she scanned the fashion-papers for new scents and powders, and experimented in facial bandaging, electric massage and other processes of renovation. . . . Her constitutional restlessness lapsed into an apathy like Mrs. Spragg's. (CC, p. 522)

Edith Wharton often depicts couples whose sexual life is suspended. After a strange passage in New York, after her son's birth, it is made plain to us that Undine is not Peter Van Degen's mistress: 'was it possible he might become a ''bother'' . . . Undine was not greatly alarmed—she still had full faith in her powers of self-defence. . .' (CC, p. 228);

> Undine . . . had never been more sure of her power to keep her friend in the desired state of adoring submission. But Peter, as he grew more adoring, became less submissive; and there came a moment when she needed all her wits to save the situation. . . . (CC, p. 230)

But by a series of manipulations, she gets away by herself to Paris, where Van Degen resumes his assault:

> Undine's heart was beating fast, but she felt within her a stronger lucid force of resistance. Because of that sense of security she left her hands in Van Degen's. So Mr. Spragg might have felt at the tensest hour of the Pure Water move. She leaned forward, holding off her suitor by the pressure of her bent-back palms.
>
> 'Kiss me goodbye, Peter; I sail on Wednesday,' she said.
>
> It was the first time she had permitted him a kiss, and as his face darkened down on her she felt a moment's recoil. *But her physical reactions were never very acute; she always vaguely wondered why people made 'such a fuss', were so violently for or against such demonstrations. A cool spirit within her seemed to watch over and regulate her sensations, and leave her capable of measuring the intensity of those she provoked.* (CC, p. 294; my italics)

The kiss establishes a new situation between them, however, and, after an incident over a cablegram from America, she gives herself at last to Van Degen:

> She turned her eyes from the mirror and let them rest on his face, which looked as small and withered as an old man's, with a lower lip that trembled queerly. (CC, p. 301)

The cablegram, however, was one which had demanded her presence by the side of her sick husband, and this had been followed by another to Van Degen himself from her husband's sister asking Van Degen to find out where she was and to tell her to come straight back (CC, p. 359). From this he perceives that she has ignored her sick husband's plea. When Indiana tells her, Undine declares: '. . . it made no earthly difference to him at the time. . . .' But:

> 'It came over him gradually, he said. One day when he wasn't feeling very well, he thought to himself: "Would she act like that to *me* if I was dying?" And after that he never felt the same to you'. . . . 'Men have their feelings too—even

when they're carried away by passion.' . . . 'I don't know as I can blame him Undine. You see, you were his ideal.' (*CC*, p. 360)

But to return to the final episodes. 'You're so strong', Undine says to Moffat—'She had never spoken more sincerely', and she feels again 'the instinctive yearning of her nature to be one with his'.

Undine, in this final encounter, is not only sincere: she does not use 'any of the arts of cajolery'. She tells Moffat, 'It's the only time I really cared—all through!' She offers to be his mistress: 'I've always felt, all through everything, that I *belonged* to you' (my italics).

To her astonishment, Elmer is appalled at the behaviour of the French, and refuses to accept her as his mistress:

> Look here, Undine, if I'm to have you again I don't want to have you in that way. That time out in Apex, when everybody in the place was against me, and I was down and out, you stood up to them and stuck by me. . . . There are things a man doesn't do. . . . (*CC, p. 573)*

He offers her a proper Apex divorce ('You're an American, ain't ya? What you want is the home-made article.')

> No, no, don't cry—it ain't that kind of story . . . but I'll have a deck suite for you on the *Semantic* if you'll sail with me the day after tomorrow. (CC, p. 576)

Surprisingly, without forfeiting any of the reader's sympathy, Edith Wharton makes it a triumph—of American Apex good sense. But she retains her insights into the moral consequences of Undine's behaviour. She sets the last chapter of all through the eyes of Paul, and we have to try to remember whose child he is. He is now 9. Mr. and Mrs. Moffat have been married for two years, and he feels lonely. The father he liked best has abruptly disappeared from his life:

> . . . his room, in which there was not a toy or a book, or one of his dear battered relics (none of the new servants—they were always new—could find his things, or think where they had been put), seemed the loneliest spot in the whole house. (CC, p. 577)

He wanders through the rooms: in the library the bookcases

cannot be opened because the books are too valuable to take out. 'Not a single volume had slipped its golden prison.'

He finds the ubiquitous Mrs. Heeney whom his mother has brought from New York—the masseuse we met at the Spragg's, and this woman goes over her 'clippings' for him. It is, of course, profoundly symbolic that here we have a servant-admirer of the family talking to the child of the second marriage, who sees Undine as she is best seen—in the newspaper gossip columns. Paul makes a betraying confusion: when Mrs. Heeney refers to his Papa at Grandma Spraggs, he declares that his Papa never went to America: 'The boy blushed also, conscious that it must have been wrong to forget, and yet not seeing how he was to blame' (*CC*, p. 582). The clippings reveal that 'the necklace, which was formerly the property of an Austrian Archduchess, is composed of five hundred perfectly matched pearls. . . .' But the child asks, 'why is mother married to Mr. Moffat now?'

The account of the divorce is hilarious:

> The hearing began at seven ten p.m. and at eight o'clock the bridal couple were steaming out of the station. . . . Judge Toomey, who is a personal friend of Mr. Moffat, held a night session and rushed it through. . . . (*CC*, p. 585)

Then Judge Toomey doubles as best man! But: 'At the trial Mrs. Spragg de Chelles, who wore copper velvet and sables, gave evidence as to the brutality of her French husband. . .' (*CC*, p. 585). 'Now you see how it all happened,' says Mrs. Heeney.

> Paul was not sure he did; but he made no answer . . . she had said things that weren't true of his French father. Something he had half-guessed in her, and averted his frightened thoughts from, took his little heart in an iron grasp. She said things that weren't true. . . . That was what he had always feared to find out. . . . She had said before a lot of people things that were awfully false about his dear French father. (*CC*, p. 586)

Asked about the tapestries which Moffat has purchased from de Chelles, Paul hopes that perhaps 'his French father might be coming too'. (Undine has rushed off to dress, Moffat protesting, 'Can't you ever give him a minute's time?') When Mr. Moffat declares, 'it was like drawing teeth for him to let them go', Paul bursts into tears, and yet cannot say why; 'he could only sob and sob as the great surges of loneliness broke over him.'

Undine is holding a dinner party: 'It was only necessary to give people the time to pretend they had forgotten: and already they were pretending beautifully' (*CC*, p. 590). She had at first been dazzled by Moffat, but now she sees his defects and was irritated by them.

> When his loudness and redness, his misplaced joviality, his familiarity with the servants, his alternating swagger and ceremony with her friends, jarred on perceptions that had developed in her unawares. . . . (*CC*, p. 591)

Now and then she caught herself thinking that his two predecessors ('—who were gradually becoming merged in her memory—') would have behaved differently. 'And the comparison was almost always to Moffat's disadvantage.'

This evening, however, she is well disposed towards her husband 'and deepened the sense of well-being with which—according to her invariable habit—she walked up to the mirror above the mantelpiece and studied the image it reflected' (*CC*, p. 592). But she has to be told that she will never be an ambassador's wife. So, though 'She turned to give herself a last look in the glass, saw the blaze of her rubies, the glitter of her hair, and remembered the brilliant names on her list' (*CC*, p. 594)—including, to her amusement, that of Peter Van Degen—'a tiny cloud remained. . .'.

All the same, Undine is clearly an American, and the American hypocrisy *nearly* includes her, although there remains 'something that neither beauty nor influence nor millions could ever buy for her.'

*The Custom of the Country* is however by no means a superficial caricature of American greed, because Edith Wharton follows Undine's progress with a deep awareness of female experience. Undine grows, she changes, she suffers; she makes blunders, she is frustrated and sinks into apathy. She is observed—as she is created—by someone close to her, and once again the quality of male experience fails her again and again: Ralph is too 'traditional', and belongs too absolutely to the old-fashioned mode of civilized America; de Chelles is too much the aristocrat, and expects his wife to put up with his own infidelities and the denial or her right to be a mother (not that Undine wants to be a mother—but she would like to provide an heir). Only Moffat satisfies her, in the end, despite her dissatisfactions with him, because of his immense purchasing power.

For a moment, just after she is married to Ralph, she seems to fit into the Anglo-Saxon picture of married love—and the mood of the book changes:

> Ralph loved the heavy Italian summer, as he had loved the spring days leading up to it: the long line of dancing days that had drawn them on and on ever since they had left their ship at Naples four months earlier. Four months of beauty, changeful, inexhaustible, weaving itself about him in shapes of softness and strength; and beside him, hand in hand with him, embodying that spirit of shifting magic, the radiant creature through whose eyes he saw it. (CC, p. 139)

But it dawns on him that she is bred by the Italian summer: 'it came to him, with the sharpness of a knife-thrust, that a crowd was what she wanted—that she was sick to death of being alone with him' (CC, p. 147). In this realization, he discovers that his wife has no inner resources:

> Her mind was as destitute of beauty and mystery as the prairie school-house in which she had been educated; and her ideals seemed to Ralph as pathetic as the ornaments made of corks and cigar-bands with which her infant hands had been taught to adorn it. (CC, p. 147)

'Her pliancy and variety were imitative rather than spontaneous': Ralph is trying hard to understand her, and yet he cannot admit this to himself.

Beneath Undine's selfishness, her cruel coldness, her greed and ambition, Edith Wharton detects a profound insecurity. 'She had taken but a lukewarm interest in the diversions of her playmates': 'Already Undine's chief delight was to "dress up" in her mother's Sunday skirt and "play lady" before the wardrobe mirror' (CC, p. 22). Throughout the novel, Undine is seen from time to time seeking reflection in mirrors.

> The taste had outlasted childhood, and she still practised the same secret pantomime, gliding in, settling her skirts, swaying her fan, moving her lips in soundless talk and laughter. . . .
> For a while she carried on her chat with an imaginary circle of admirers, twisting this way and that, fanning, fidgeting, twitching at her draperies, as she did in real life when people were noticing her. (*CC*, p. 22)

In the end, it is Moffat who gives her the ultimate reflection she seeks:

> '. . . when the swells are hard-up nowadays they generally chip off an heirloom'. . . .
> She tried to check herself, to summon up a glittering evocation; but his face, his voice, the very words he used, were like so many hammer-strokes demolishing the unrealities that imprisoned her. Here was someone who spoke her language, who knew her meanings, who understood instinctively all the deep-seated wants for which her vocabulary had no terms; and as she talked she once more seemed to herself intelligent, eloquent and interesting. (*CC*, p. 536)

Another view of the disposal of heirlooms is put by her husband Raymond de Celles:

> . . . You come among us from a country we don't know, and can't imagine, a country you care for so little that before you've been a day in ours you've forgotten the very house you were born in—if it wasn't torn down before you knew it. You come among us speaking our language and not knowing what we mean; wanting the things we want, and not knowing why we want them; aping our weaknesses, exaggerating our follies, ignoring or ridiculing all we care about—you come from hotels as big as towns, and from towns as flimsy as paper, where the streets haven't had time to be named, and the buildings are demolished before they're dry, and the people are as proud of changing as we are of holding to what we have—and we're fools enough to imagine that because you copy our ways and pick up our slang you understand anything about the things that make life decent and honourable for us! (*CC*, p. 545)

The book ends in a tussle between the American idea and the European one—a very Jamesian theme, of course—and one suspects in Edith Wharton a satisfaction (to put it no higher) with the American way. At last, Undine finds a man who is not primarily interested in sexuality, but in exerting his will and power (as, indeed, he always has).

Undine has had a deep satisfaction in her third husband.

> The three months since her marriage had been more nearly like what she had dreamed of than any of her previous experiments in happiness. At last she had what she wanted, and for the first time the glow of triumph was warmed by a deeper feeling. Her husband was really charming (it was odd how he reminded her of Ralph), and after her bitter two years of loneliness and humiliation it was delicious to find herself once more adored and protected. (*CC*, p. 480)

But Raymond is possessive: he is less reluctant to show that he is jealous of her, and is 'eager for reciprocal assurances of constancy'. Her domination over him involves, however, a corresponding loss of independence. She has to give her husband a circumstantial report on every hour she spends away from him.

Then, suddenly, the 'lights went out', as Raymond said. '. . . The world's had you long enough, and it's my turn. What do you say to going down to Saint Désert?' (*CC*, p. 489). There follows a marvellous picture of the family problems, including Raymond's responsibility for setting up his brother Hubert in apartments in Paris. Quarrels over this incident put a strain on their relationship; Raymond declares, 'I must look out for the future of our son' (*CC*, p. 502).

> Undine flushed to the forehead. She had grown accustomed to such allusions and the thought of having a child no longer filled her with the resentful terror she had felt before Paul's birth. But all these lightly-noted sentiments went down in the rush of her resentment. . . . (*CC*, p. 503)

Undine, however, has to accept the expenditure on Hubert, and yet the incident reveals how far apart they are.

> The very absence of external pressure, of any tactless assertion of authority on her husband's part, intensified the sense of her helplessness. He simply left it to her to infer that, important

> as she might be to him in certain ways, there were others in which she did not weigh a feather. (CC, p. 505)

Their outward relations have not changed, while Raymond meets her advances with a good grace. Raymond is as 'lovely' to her as ever, but

> She had a startled sense of not giving him all he expected of her. She had admired him, before their marriage . . . during the honeymoon he had been the most ardent of lovers. . . . But Raymond, to her surprise, had again developed a disturbing resemblance to his predecessors. . . . (CC, p. 506)

'Little by little their talk died down to monosyllables.' Madame de Trézac hints that it is her childlessness that is making her husband less interested in her.

So, she tackles him; she determines to speak, even though 'the barrier of his indifference hung between them.'

> She had not yet found the word, and already his tone told her she was too late. A year ago, if she had slipped her hand in his, she would not have had that answer.
>
> 'Your mother blames me for not having our child. Everybody thinks it's my fault.'
>
> . . .
>
> 'My mother's ideas are old-fashioned; and I don't know that it is anybody's business but yours and mine.'
>
> 'Yes, but—'
>
> . . .
>
> In the ante chamber Raymond paused to take her cloak from her shoulders, and his eyes rested upon her with a faint smile of approval.
>
> 'You never looked better; your dress is extremely becoming. Good night, my dear,' he said, kissing her hand as he turned away. (CC, p. 510)

Undine feels 'wounded pride', and feels confident that Raymond will 'come back', as Ralph 'always had, to the last'. But her attitudes, to Hubert and the family, have had a dire effect; her husband is not going to make love to her, and she is condemned to a permanent state of impotence. Of the conditions of her new life, 'as the days passed she began to understand that they would continue to succeed each other till the end' (CC, p. 511). The family even attributes the collapse of the marriage to extraordinary experiences on their honeymoon! Without sex, Undine goes drab: 'her complexion was less animated, her hair less shining'. Her husband is now well on the way to denying her existence: 'He looked at her as though the place where she stood were empty.' And on her part she suffers a profound humiliation, for 'she could not conceive that anyone could tire of her of whom she had not at first tired. . . (CC, p. 524). She is 'humiliated by his indifference', and the appalling contradiction, between her husband's insistence on her outward compliance in his affairs and those of the 'family', and his personal coldness—while (as others tell her) he is desporting himself with other women. Escape seems impossible:

> Even when, at the close of their talk, she had burst out: 'If you grudge me everything I care about we'd better separate,' he had merely answered with a shrug, 'It's one of the things we don't do—' and the answer had been like the slamming of an iron door in her face. (CC, p. 528)

The degree to which this French Catholic world has impinged upon Undine becomes clear when she resists Elmer Moffatt, in the end, and he refuses to enter into an illicit liaison with her. She cries out:

> 'How can I? Such things are not done out here. Why, I'm a Catholic, and the Catholic Church—' she broke off, reading the end in his face. 'But later, perhaps . . . things might change. Oh, Elmer, if only you'd stay over here and let me see you sometimes!'
>
> 'Yes—the way your friends see each other. We're differently made out in Apex. When I want that sort of thing I go down to North Fifth Street for it.' (CC, p. 573)

'North Fifth Street' is the notorious 'saloon' street, from which came the woman with whom Elmer walked up Eubow Avenue after his disgrace at the temperance supper, when he 'lost the support of the feminine community' (CC, p. 553), except Undine.

His view of marriage and sex is quite different from that of his European contemporaries:

> She paled under the retort, but her heart beat high with it. What he asked was impossible—and she gloried in his asking it. Feeling her power, she tried to temporize. 'At least if you stayed we could be friends—I shouldn't feel so terribly alone.'

> He laughed, impatiently. 'Don't talk magazine stuff to me, Undine Spragg. I guess we want each other the same way. Only our ideas are different. You've got all muddled, living out here among a lot of loafers who call it a career to run around after every petticoat. I've got my job out at home, and I belong where my job is.' (CC, p. 573)

Belonging to Apex and to the 'job' means he has to have a wife and stay out of compromising sexual liaisons (except on North Fifth Street). His down-to-earth manner annihiliates her: 'She wished he would come nearer, or look at her differently: *she felt, under his cool eye, no more compelling than a woman of wax in a showcase*' (CC, p. 574; my italics) Yet she keeps up her resistance:

> 'How could I get a divorce? With my religion—'
>
> 'Why, you were born a Baptist, weren't you? That's where you used to attend church when I waited round the corner. . . . If you'll come along home with me I'll see you get your divorce all right. Who cares what they do over here? You're an American aren't you? What you want is the home-made article.'

But there is still a resistance in her, and we are perplexed, surely, to wonder what it is?

> Her defense was drawn from reasons he did not understand, or based on difficulties that did not exist for him. . . .
>
> 'You don't know—you don't understand—' She kept repeating; but she knew that his ignorance was part of his terrible power, and that it was hopeless to try to make him feel *the value of what he was asking her to give up.* (CC, p. 575; my italics)

'I mean to have the best'—that is Moffatt's motto (CC, p. 538). His final plea is blunt:

> 'See here, Undine,' he said slowly, as if he measured her resistance though he couldn't fathom it, 'I guess it had better be yes or no right here. . . . No, no, don't cry—it ain't that kind of a story. . . .' (CC, pp. 575–76)

He is absolutely what she deserves, and yet there is an appeal in his directness, just as there was in their original involvement with one another, on which she reflects just before this episode. Undine is seriously limited; 'her entrances were always triumphs: *but they had no sequel.* As soon as people began to talk *they ceased to see her*'(CC, p. 541; my italics) She cannot sustain interest in people, not by her beauty alone—especially in situations where 'people down here don't go on looking at each other forever' (Madame de Trézac (CC, p. 542) ).

Moffatt has always been a perfect fit for Undine, since those first Apex days on which she reflects, in Chapter XLIII: 'She had been drawn to Elmer Moffatt from the first':

> he had taken instant possession of Undine, sitting in the big 'stage' beside her on the 'ride' to the grove, supplanting Millard Birch (to whom she was still, though intermittently and incompletely engaged), swinging her between the trees, rowing her on the lake, catching and kissing her in 'forfeits', awarding her the first prize in a Beauty Show he hilariously organized and gallantly carried out, and finally (no one knew how) contriving to borrow a buggy and a fast colt from old Milvey, and driving her off with her at a two-forty gait while Millard and the others took their dust in the crawling stage. (CC, p. 548)

There is a relish for this simple Apex life, in the very language itself, and its idiom: 'fast colt', 'two-forty gait', 'took their dust'. Moffatt is 'of' small town America: 'he simply appeared one day behind the counter in Luckaback's Dollar Shoe-Store.' He boarded on the edge of the 'red-light slum' and never showed any desire to improve or refine himself. In driving away with him Undine 'tasted the public triumph which was necessary to her personal enjoyment'. The Sons of Jonadab invited him to give their Fourth of July oration, and Undine sits beneath the platform 'all in white, with a red rose in her breast'. He gets drunk and provides a catastrophe and scandal. His later conduct confirms the impression of him as an irresponsible loafer and hopeless failure, as he walks up Eubow Avenue with a prostitute.

> Undine's estimate of people had always been based on their apparent power of getting what they wanted—providing it came under the category of things she understood wanting success was beauty and romance to her; yet it was at the moment when Elmer Moffatt's failure was most complete and flagrant that she suddenly felt the extent of his power. (CC, p. 554)

Elmer was dismissed from his surveyor's office and on the day of his dismissal he cheerfully asked Undine to take a walk with him. She sees Millard Birch's mother looking disapprovingly at her—and agrees.

> She was in a mood of aimless discontent and unrest, tired of her engagement to Millard Birch, disappointed with Moffatt, half-ashamed of being seen with him, and *yet not sorry to have it known that she was independent enough to choose her companions without regard to the Apex verdict.* (CC, p. 554; my italics)

His disdain for Apex, and 'the affirmation of a soaring self-confidence . . . seemed to lift her on wings.'

> It was strange that Elmer Moffatt, a shiftless outcast from even the small world she despised, should give her, in the very moment of his downfall, the sense of being able to succeed where she had failed. (CC, p. 535)

She gives herself to Elmer, and they go away on the 'Limited' Express—only, later, for Elmer to be bought off by Mr. Spragg.

In the end, as we have seen, Elmer is not everything Undine would wish for. He has cheated Raymond de Celles of his tapestries, she reflects, and the satisfaction this yields goes with a last glimpse of her seeking reflection in her mirror:

> These facts disposed her favourably towards her husband, and deepened the sense of well-being with which—according to her invariable habit—she walked up to the mirror above the mantelpiece and studied the image it reflected. (CC, p. 592)

Her husband comes in, his shirt front as glossy as his baldness: 'and in his buttonhole he wore the red ribbon bestowed on him for waiving his claim to a Velasquez that was wanted for the *Louvre*. . .' (CC, p. 592).

The presentation of Undine is ironic to the last—and made bitterly critical in the rendering of the isolation and deprivation of her only son. But she has come 'home', and she has achieved her kind of triumph. Even Van Degen is coming as a guest to her dinner.

The 'new' America is triumphant, too. Ralph Marvell was unsatisfactory, because he assumed that Undine's beauty was the face of intelligence and sensitivity, whereas it was but the mask of a voracious compensation for a sort of emptiness.

He fell short of her success because he let her go to Europe without him—and failed to sustain his rôle as her lover, failing totally to understand her. Her French husband involves her in the toils of his aristocratic family, and then cuts off sexual relations with her, because of her attitude to his duty to Hubert; he also deceives her by his amorous adventures, assuming that she will have to put up with them. In the end, she re-marries Moffatt, thus reverting to the world of Apex. Moffatt, now looking bald, stout and redder than ever, has shown himself throughout the novel, from time to time, as he makes his way up the social scale, by becoming rich; her French husband's tapestries are 'under her roof after all' and he 'and all his clan were by this time aware of it' (*CC*, p. 592). These facts deepen the sense of well-being with which 'she walked up to the mirror above the mantelpiece and studied the image it reflected' (*CC*, p. 592).

While the men in *The Custom of the Country* may be said to be unsatisfactory—in Ralph Marvell's case tragically so—the main truth with which the novel is concerned is that of *female unsatisfactoriness*. Undine has no inner resources, no culture, no persistence; once people begin to talk, she ceases to exist.

All the male preconceptions of what a woman is are challenged. She is not primarily interested in sexuality: Undine for the most part merely suffers passion and hardly gives it a thought (though when her French husband neglects her, she loses her tone and becomes hypochondriac). Pregnancy and childbirth are horrors to her, because she cannot enjoy her own femininity in that mode; her beauty is a brittle, external thing. Religion, family ties, culture mean little or nothing to her, and possessions are merely assets to be realized when there is need—need to keep the elegant run of shopping, visiting, dressing up and going 'out' into the reflecting circles of society. She likes 'attention', but is always making a calculation about what it adds up to—what it promises, towards more success, more réclame.

Interestingly enough, she is a kind of woman close to Edith Wharton herself: hers is the authoress's world, though she herself had no such beauty, but had immense personal resources, culture and feeling. But there is no doubt that she had something of Undine in herself, and a sympathy even for the 'new' America which is represented by Elmer Moffatt—who despises everyone, from Apex to New York City, and from French aristocracy to the English upper set. Elmer is 'strong' in a certain way that Edith Wharton admired, even as she comically 'places' him.

Where is the centre of the book? We are perplexed to find it—that is the great achievement. We are not 'with' any of the main groups, although we do sense good qualities in all of them—as with Mr. Spragg's compassion for Ralph. Apex is small town, the Spraggs are social climbers, Ralph is too cultivated and unrealistic (his book never gets written), de Celles is too much sunk in the family and the conservatism of a French past, Elmer is too ruthless and philistine—and Undine, well, she is insufferably and sufferingly egocentric. The only centre is the author's own sensitivity and intelligence.

# 4

# *Ethan Frome* and *Summer*

These two stories use Edith Wharton's experience of the primitive rural communities of New England that she explored by motor car from her house, The Mount, in Lenox. They are in the Hawthorne tradition, and she notes that

> insanity, incest and slow mental and moral starvation were hidden away behind the paintless wooden housefronts of the long village street, or in the isolated farm-houses on the neighbouring hills. (*A Backward Glance*, quoted by Glendenning, p. vi)

She used real-life events and places in both stories. There was a sledging accident near Lenox which left several people maimed for life, for example. But she also translated her own predicament into *Ethan Frome*, which was written after her experience of Morton Fullerton in 1908. As Victoria Glendenning declares in her introduction, Edith felt 'trapped and stifled' in her sexless marriage with Teddy, who was unfaithful and also suffering from melancholia and mental instability. Like Ethan, she had briefly glimpsed happiness with someone else. Lewis reports that passages from the Diary she kept in 1908 describing her excitement over Morton Fullerton were transcribed into the scenes between Ethan and Mattie, while the quarrels between Ethan and sickly Zeena echoed those between Edith and Teddy. Both Edith and Teddy used, like Zeena, illness as an emotional weapon against one another. The sharp contrasts in the writing, between the household dominated by Zeena, and the same scene enlivened by the presence of Mattie, derives directly from Edith's own experience: on the one hand, death: 'The light . . . deepened fantastically the hollows and prominences of her high-boned face' (*EF*, p. 29)*; on the other, life:

> She held the light . . . and it drew out with the same distinctness her slim young throat and the brown wrist no bigger than a child's. Then striking upwards, it threw a lustrous fleck on her lips, edged her eyes with velvet shade, and laid a milky whiteness above the black curve of her brows. (*EF*, p. 43)

Involved in his fantasies of joyful abandonment, and unable to escape from the prison of his marriage when Zeena orders Mattie away, Ethan takes Mattie for a sleigh-ride, and makes a ridiculous suicide attempt with her. This last sleigh-ride seems symbolic of a sexual act, and it culminates in the crippling of both Ethan and Mattie. Zeena, after the catastrophe, becomes dominant and mysteriously cured, as Victoria Glendenning points out. But we could also interpret this novel as one that yet again emerges from a deep unconscious fear of sexual intercourse. Mattie is noticeably a 'child' as in the quotation above, and the father's desperate venture is with a figure in his household who is in the position of a daughter. His sexual gesture towards her brings catastrophe and leads to perpetual misery, so that the daughter has to live, crippled for life, in the shadow of both destructive mother and desperate father. Perhaps we may find in this a deeper undercurrent than memories of Morton Fullerton, and detect in the leading characters a mother sick in her recoil from sex and emotion, and a father crippled by his guilty act, with their daughter suffering between them.

While *Ethan Frome* disturbed Edith Wharton's audience, she described *Summer* as her 'hot Ethan'. While Edith obviously had difficulties over the form of *Ethan Frome,* as when the narrator is forced to assume an authorial omniscience, the language and form of *Summer* seem to mark a consummate achievement. *Summer* is a marvellous *nouvelle,* which is even more clearly woven out of Edith Wharton's experience of her *affaire* with Morton Fullerton, and her subsequent discovery of his failure of commitment and his amazing capacity for multiple relationships. It is written passionately out of her predicament as a sexual being—not a direct transmuting

* References are to the Oxford Classics Edition of 1982.

of the material, but a myth inspired by her own life. The passional experiences of her *affaire* gave her the insights to explore the predicament of the simple young woman heroine, Charity Royall. The book brings to life vividly the scenes in the village, the vitality of Charity, and the nature of her passion. Inevitably, because of the frankness of its subject-matter, *Summer* was not well received, but Joseph Conrad and Howard Sturgis thought very highly of it. Conrad wrote, 'I've always loved your rhythms, so very fine, distinct and subtle. On opening the book I let myself be carried on by them. . . . Truly it was a great delight' (R. W. B. Lewis, p. 398).

The tale reads as if inspired, and, indeed, it contains all the elements that are close to Edith Wharton's heart. Lawyer Royall dominates the book: Edith Wharton herself said, 'he *is* the book'—and he is clearly a father figure, so the relationship with Charity is incestuous. Cynthia Wolff declares that 'Incest, as Edith Wharton renders it, is irresistably attractive', and once again we have a theme in which a young woman finds peace and security in a marriage with a father-figure.

Symbolic here, too, is the episode in which Edith Wharton 'gets rid of Mother'—an appalling scene in which the primitive nature of the Mountain community is revealed, as Charity goes back to the place of her birth. This is one of the most moving and terrible scenes in Edith Wharton, in which the simple ritual of the Burial Service is woven in counterpoint with the terror of death with the brutal bickering of the mountain people in the background. But we should note that the mother who is being buried has rejected Charity and is a stranger to her—the symbolic significance of which will be evident.

Charity, of course, is very different from Edith Wharton, but she is yet another alter ego; we see the world of the remote village through her eyes, and we experience through her the yearnings to fulfil herself sexually, from adolescence to motherhood. She dreams erotic fantasies of being wooed and married by the young stranger who turns up at her library, and by degrees she comes to be seduced by him—going to live with him in an empty house in the woods. But Lucius Harney has another woman whom he is going to marry. Their union is a joy, but Charity, like Edith Wharton with Morton Fullerton, gradually becomes aware that this man has relationships with other women; like Sophy Viner, she has no guilt about giving herself to Lucius: she even writes to him to urge him to marry Annabel Balch. But now the reality of sexual experience forces itself upon her, for she is to have a child—and so she needs shelter and sustenance. Lawyer Royall marries her, and displays his consideration by sitting all night in a chair on their wedding night, so she shall not be frightened. In the end, there is something like love between them:

> '. . . You're a good girl, Charity.' Their eyes met, and something rose in his that she had never seen there: a look that made her feel ashamed and yet secure.
>
> 'I guess you're good, too,' she said, shyly and quickly. He smiled without answering, and they went out of the room together and dropped down to the hall in the glittering lift.
>
> Late that evening, in the cold autumn moonlight, they drove up to the door of the red house. (*S*, p. 248)

What is the 'upshot' of the tale? It is not that Charity has conformed to the standards of society, and so is faced with a life of misery and deadness—for Lawyer Royall genuinely loves her. It is not a romance in which a woman achieves a momentary satisfaction of her passion at the cost of everything. (She writes in the end to Lucius Harney, 'I'm married to Mr. Royall. I'll always remember you. CHARITY'.) It is not a championship of femininity in a harsh world dominated by males and their moral codes. But it does have behind it the Wharton unconscious mythology, of getting rid of Mother and marrying Father. And as a study of sexuality it has the vitality and power of that perplexing tale, Shakespeare's *Antony and Cleopatra*, which leaves one unable to reach in the 'upshot' any firm conclusion, any 'message' or 'moral': each time one reads the story, one feels a different complex of responses. One is, on the one hand, grateful for the richness of experience the girl has had, in her studied recklessness; on the other, one is appalled by her suffering. One is glad of the sensitivity of her response to the world and to 'life', even to the young man who carelessly seduces her. Yet even he is not to be condemned, because he has shown a profound interest in her being—even though he is committed elsewhere, in the real world to which he belongs. He does not simply exploit her with contempt, but cherishes her as a rare creature—until, that is, she becomes an embarrassment, as she begins to be part of his reality.

The novel, we may say, celebrates 'life' and 'being'—that vitality of being that can transcend the characters' sordid origins, their unpropitious conditions, their deceptive fantasies, and even their betrayal of one another. This is its fundamental positive. Q. D. Leavis merely said, of Edith Wharton that the only positive in her work was 'the simple goodness of the decent poor. . .'. 'But beyond that Mrs. Wharton has only negatives, her values emerging I suppose as something other than what she exposes as worthless. . .'. This is not very nourishing. . .' (*Scrutiny*, Vol. VII, p. 275). This is not even true of *The Custom of the Country*; it is patently untrue of *Summer*. The positives that emerge from the latter are those of being alive—of fulfilment of being—even though circumstances and the *unsatisfactoriness of a man* bring about devastating pain and loss. (We need to note, however, that the most terrible, life-destroying, cheating and menacing character in *Summer* is the woman abortionist.)

It might seem a strange claim for a novel that explores the darkest horrors of human nature, yet Charity is singularly unscathed even at the end. Like Marina in Shakespeare's *Pericles*, she displays an intuitive moral courage, which is symbolized by her rejection of Lawyer Royall at the threshold of her room. (We may recall that the *threshold* was the place at which Edith Wharton, as a child, was seized by a profound phobia, a dreadful fear of being pursued by some nameless horror.)

The progress of Charity Royall's sexual awakening is delicately traced, and Edith Wharton embodies in it her own discovery of passion—that sense of a secret between two people that can defy all their social obligations: 'It was a joy to Charity to sing: it seemed as though, for the first time, her secret rapture might burst from her and flash its defiance at the world' (*S*, p. 191). Lucius Harney appears at the library where she works, looking for books on local architecture. He belongs to a world of culture and sophistication that is quite alien to her, but she sees him just as a woman would:

> She had liked the young man's looks, and his short-sighted eyes, and his odd way of speaking, that was abrupt yet soft, just as his hands were sunburnt and sinewy, yet with smooth nails like a woman's. (*S*, p. 107)

> Strangely, while she knows she 'rules' in Lawyer Royall's house: confusedly, the young man in the library had made her feel for the first time what might be the sweetness of dependence. (*S*, p. 107)

Lawyer Royall brought her down from the mountain; he was her guardian, although he had not legally adopted her. He kept her at home because he was lonesome. One night, when she was 17:

> She was awakened by a rattling at her door and jumped out of bed. She heard Mr. Royall's voice, low and peremptory, and opened the door . . . when she saw him in the doorway, a ray from the autumn moon falling on his discomposed face, she understood.
>
> For a moment they looked at each other in silence; then, as he put his foot across the threshold, she stretched out her arm and stopped him.
>
> 'You go right back from here,' she said, in a shrill voice that startled her; 'you ain't going to have that key tonight.'
>
> 'Charity, let me in. I don't want the key. I'm a lonesome man,' he began, in the deep voice that sometimes moved her.
>
> Her heart gave a startled plunge, but she continued to hold him back contemptuously. 'Well, I guess you made a mistake, then. This ain't your wife's room any longer.' (*S*, p. 111)

'She was not frightened, she simply felt a deep disgust'—and seeing this disgust in her face, he withdraws. '. . . a belated sense of fear came to her with the consciousness of victory.'

Later, she entrenches her position, when Lawyer Royall asks her to marry him:

> 'Marry you? Me!' she burst out with a scornful laugh. 'Was that what you came to ask me the other night. . . . How long is it since you looked in the glass?' She straightened herself, insolently conscious of her youth and strength. . . . (*S*, p. 114)

He responds 'as though the blaze of her scorn had blinded him'.

The result is that she triumphs in his house: 'She needed no one to defend her: his humbled pride was her surest protection.' When she rebuffs him, he declares that 'People ain't been fair to me'; so, Royall is shown to have scruples, to be susceptible to decent feelings and respect: he is not a villain, but a sad and lonely man.

The developing relationship between Charity and Lucius is of the essence of summer: 'There had never been such a June in Eagle County.' Charity's adolescent fantasies are related to her participation in the natural life of summer, as expressed in Lawrentian terms:

> Directly in her line of vision a blackberry branch laid its frail white flowers and blue-green leaves against the sky. Just beyond, a tuft of sweet-fern uncurled between the beaded shoots of the grass, and a small yellow butterfly vibrated over them like a fleck of sunshine. This was all she saw; but she felt, above her and about her, the strong growth of the beeches clothing the ridge, the rounding of pale green cones on countless spruce-branches, the push of myriads of sweet-fern fronds in the cracks of the stony slope below the wood, and the crowding shoots of meadowsweet and yellow flags in the pasture beyond. All this bubbling of sap and slipping of sheaths and bursting of calyxes was carried to her on mingled currents of fragrance. . . . (*S*, p. 124)

All 'were merged in a moist earth-smell that was like the breath of some huge sun-warmed animal'.

She ponders visiting the Mountain, and discusses this with Lucius, who would like to go there.

> 'It's queer, you know,' he continued, 'that, just over there, on top of that hill, there should be a handful of people who don't give a damn for anybody.'
>
> The words thrilled her. They seemed the clue to her own revolts and defiances. . . . (*S*, p. 130)

She tells him she comes from the Mountain, and 'He picked up her hand and laid a kiss on the sunburnt knuckles.' Later, of course, we are to know what things are like in this community who 'don't give a damn for anybody', but we suspect that her words give Lucius Harney a different interest in Charity as a rebel.

A different view of the people of the Mountain is given by Lawyer Royall; he refers to fetching a little girl whom her father wanted 'reared like a Christian':

> 'Oh, yes; there was a mother. But she was glad enough to have her go. She'd have given her to anybody. . . .'
>
> . . .
>
> 'My God, how ghastly,' Harney murmured; and Charity, choking with humiliation, sprang to her feet and ran upstairs. . . . (*S*, p. 134)

While the narration sticks close to Charity's experience, her vision of the world, we are brought to perceive enough of Harney's real world to realize that he is taking an interest in Charity in a quite different dimension; she is puzzled by the references of the clergyman Mr. Miles to one 'Miss Balch':

> Charity thought she detected a look of constraint in Harney's eyes. She fancied he did not wish to be alone with her; and with a sudden pang she wondered if he repented the tender things he had said to her the night before. (*S*, p. 146)

But when she goes to look in at his window, after sensing a crisis (Lawyer Royall has told Harney he must leave), she develops new feelings for the young man. She watches without making any sign:

> It was not the fear of any sanction, human or heavenly; she had never in her life been afraid. It was simply that she had suddenly understood what would happen if she went in. . . . Since the day before, she had known exactly what she would feel if Harney should take her in his arms: the melting of palm into palm and mouth on mouth, and the long flame burning her from head to foot. (*S*, p. 154)

(*Cf.* Palm to palm, heart to breast in the gloom . . .
  And the shadow-mouths melted on one . . .
    The faint red lamp . . .
  . . . kindled a mystic flame . . . ('Terminus') )

But Charity does not want to be taken like the other village girls; she has a 'wondering pride in his liking for her', she cannot cheapen herself to Harney; she must not do anything to debase the image of herself he would carry away: *'If he wanted her he must seek her.'*

Yet, surely, we must see her as being to some extent deceived, albeit by a youth who is confused and perplexed? Edith Wharton, however, maintains a position from which such confusion is not to be condemned. She certainly does not share Royall's jealous condemnation. He is stirred by 'a deep and stern emotion'; when he accuses Charity of staying the night with Lucius, she exclaims, 'Oh, how I've always hated you!' She is appalled by his 'fingering of her dreams', and by the 'outrage of his interference'. She tells Royall how she watched Harney but 'I dursn't go in for fear he'd think I'd come after him'—and cries out, 'As long as I live I'll never forgive you!' The revelation makes Royall seem very old: 'Age seemed to have come down on him as winter comes on the hills after a storm'; for it is the essential goodness of adolescent feelings, their hesitancies and the growing affection she has for Harney that are remote from him, jealous as he is. He declares, 'if he'd wanted you the right way he'd have said so.'

Royall proposes to her again: 'you've always known I loved you the way a man loves a decent woman.' 'Nothing in his appeal reaches her heart, and she thought only of words to wound and wither.' She sees the old life closing in on her. Royall goes on to offer to marry her to Harney, but she remembers a muddy boot coming down on the white-bramble flowers: 'something transient and exquisite had flowered in her, and she had stood by and seen it trampled to earth. . .' (*S*, p. 158). Harney sends her a torn page with a message to meet him. He is by no means ardent in his attentions:

> It seemed to be enough for him to breathe her nearness like a flower's: and since his pleasure at being with her, and his sense of her youth and her grace, perpetually shone in his eyes and softened the inflection of his voice, his reserve did not suggest coldness, but the deference due to a girl of his own class. (*S*, p. 164)

So, Harney seems here to be truly enthralled by Charity, and their love grows in the summer atmosphere:

> . . . to Charity the heat was a stimulant: it enveloped the whole world in the same glow that burned at her heart. Now and then a lurch of the train flung her against Harney, and through her thin muslin she felt the touch of his sleeve. She steadied herself, their eyes met, and the flaming breath of the day seemed to enclose them. (*S*, p. 164)

He buys her a blue pin, takes her to a French restaurant, and then out to the lake. Just before they secure a boat,

Charity sees the house of Dr. Merkle: why is it introduced here?

> . . . suddenly she remembered Ally Hawes' words: 'the house was at the corner of King Street and Lake Avenue. . . . There's a big black sign across the front. . . .' Through all the heat and the rapture a shiver of cold ran over her. (*S*, p. 170)

It must be because Edith Wharton wished to remind us of the dangers of that rapture?

Charity is made aware of her distance from Harney. It is important to emphasize this element in the story to counter critical misrepresentation like that of Cynthia Wolff, who declares: 'Charity and Lucius share their youth, and they call to each other (very gently and softly now at first) in a sweet unspoken language of eyes and laughter.' There is an ominous indication all through that Harney is being duplicitous. At one point he lies in the bottom of the boat without speaking:

> Ever since their meeting at the Creston pool he had been subject to these brooding silences, which were as different as possible from the pauses when they ceased to speak because words were needless. . . . (*S*, p. 170)

She thinks of the ten dollars he had given to the driver: 'with ten dollars he might have bought her an engagement ring.'

> Harney would never buy her an engagement ring: they were friends and comrades, but no more. He had been perfectly fair to her: he had never said a word to mislead her. She wondered what the girl was like whose hand was waiting for his ring. (*S*, p. 171)

At the end of the firework set pieces, Charity 'seemed to have been caught up into the stars'. Harney suddenly kisses her.

> In the obscurity she felt her head clasped by two hands: her face was drawn backward, and Harney's lips were pressed on hers. With sudden vehemence he wound his arms about her, holding her head against his breast while she gave him back his kisses. An unknown Harney had revealed himself, a Harney who dominated her and yet over whom she felt

> herself possessed of a new mysterious power. (*S*, p. 174)

Stumbling about in the melée they encounter Royall: 'his face, a livid brown, with red blotches of anger and lips sunken in like an old man's, was a lamentable ruin in the searching glare.' Like the ghost of a father-phantom he calls out to Charity: 'You whore—you damn—bare-headed whore, you!' Charity is ashamed to be seen hatless, with Harney, confronting this drunken crew, 'headed by her guardian's pitiable figure'. Royall's acquaintance with disreputable girls is new and dreadful to her. She calls to Royall, 'you come right home with me', but finds herself sobbing desperately, clinging to Harney's arm.

It is like one of those occasions in the work of D. H. Lawrence in which a young couple's love-making is interrupted by the appearance of the moon—representing the mother's face—only here it is the Father. Phenomenologically, it has that kind of significance.

Charity sets off next day to the Mountain, but she encounters Harney. He is looking at her with

> the passionate absorbed expression she had seen in his eyes after they had kissed on the stand at Nettleton. He was the new Harney again, the Harney abruptly revealed in that embrace, who seemed so penetrated with joy of her presence that he was utterly careless of what she was thinking or feeling. (*S*, p. 182)

—that is, we may remind ourselves, he is very like Morton Fullerton, whose letters reveal him 'utterly enraptured by passion'. They go to a desolate abandoned house; she tells him of Royall's desire for her, and her determination never to go back.

> But once more, as she spoke, she became aware that he was no longer listening. He came close and caught her to him as if he were snatching her from some imminent peril: his impetuous eyes were in hers, and she could feel the hard beat of his heart as he held her against it.
>
> 'Kiss me again—like last night,' he said, pushing her hair back as if to draw her whole face up into his kiss. (*S*, p. 184)

She and Harney are now living in the deserted house.

> Everything unrelated to the hours spent in that tranquil place was as faint as the remembrance of a dream. *The only reality was the wondrous unfolding of her new self, the reaching out to the light of all her contracted tendrils. She had lived all her life among people whose sensibilities seemed to have withered for lack of use . . . she had always thought of love as something confused and furtive, and he made it as bright and open as the summer air*. . . . (*S*, p. 190; my italics)

This is surely autobiographical, and thus we can see that the title *Summer* is linked with Edith Wharton's feelings about being renewed in the summer of life (the phrases italicized above do not fit so well the unawakened life of an adolescent girl in Charity's situation, after all).

Harney has camped in the house, swum in a brown pool he knows of, and wandered about the countryside. 'And in the afternoon Charity came to him.' Reflecting on the experience,

> her short hours with him flamed out like forest fires. Nothing else mattered, neither the good nor the bad, or what might have seemed so before she knew him. He had caught her up and carried her away into a new world, from which, at stated hours, the ghost of her came back to perform customary acts, but all so thinly and unsubstantially that she sometimes wondered that the people she went among could see her. (*S*, p. 191)

—another autobiographical paragraph. Yet, as the evening falls, 'Charity's heart contracted. The first fall of night after a day of radiance often gave her a sense of hidden menace. . .' (*S*, p. 192).

His 'technique' obliterates the reality of other modes and relationships, as did Morton Fullerton's:

> He had his arms about her, and his kisses were in her hair and on her lips. Under his touch things deep down in her struggled to the light and sprang up like flowers in sunshine. . . . She hardly heard his excuses for being late: in his absence a thousand doubts tormented her, but as soon as he appeared she ceased to wonder where he had come from, what had delayed him, who had kept him from her. . . . (*S*, p. 192)

He chaffs her, about dancing with any other girl at the dance in the Town Hall: 'Any other girl? Were there any others?

She had forgotten even that peril, so enclosed did he and she seem in their secret world. . .' (*S*, p. 193). At the dance, Lawyer Royall gives a speech about being good, 'in the place we live in'. Charity sees Harney with Annabel Balch, her face reflecting something he has said to her.

> In a flash, they had shown her the reality of her situation. Behind the frail screen of her lover's caresses was the whole inscrutable mystery of his life: his relationships with other people—with other women . . . the net of influences and interests and ambitions in which every man's life is entangled. . . . (*S*, p. 198–99)

Yet she feels no jealousy:

> In the foreground, hiding all else, there was the glow of his presence, the light and shadow of his face, the way his short-sighted eyes, at her approach, widened and deepened as if to draw her down into them; and, above all, the flash of youth and tenderness in which his words enclosed her. (*S*, p. 199)

But she does feel 'a terror of the unknown, of all the mysterious attractions that must even now be dragging him away from her, and of her own powerlessness to contend with them'.

> She had given him all she had—but what was it compared to the other gifts life held for him. She understood now the case of girls like herself to whom this kind of thing happened. They gave all they had, but their all was not enough: it could buy no more than a few moments. . . . (*S*, p. 199)

This, again, is autobiographical, and, if examined, reveals the limitations of Edith Wharton's view of love. There is a confusion in this story, between the apparent equal flowering of a love relationship and the perception that, by any realistic account, Harney is a cruel trifler. Yet Edith Wharton, so grateful for her awakening, cannot depict him as such: he is the unsatisfactory man, but the woman must find this as her own fault: she gave all she had, but this was not enough. There can be no equality and harmony between men and women on this principle, yet (as we have already declared)

Edith Wharton's predicament was that *this* uncommitted, hypnotized, rapturously passionate, but amoral and *dissociated* experience—dissociated from whole being—was what she wanted.

The Reverend Miles is uttering platitudes about 'A rich harvest of hallowed memories' as Charity faints face downwards at Lawyer Royall's feet.

Charity is waiting for Harney in the isolated house, when Royall comes in. He proclaims his 'right' to care for her: 'the right to try to keep you out of trouble'. 'Better wait till I'm in trouble', she replied—and the reader, of course, has already begun to suspect she is. Royall challenges Harney over whether he is going to marry Charity. He replies:

> 'Miss Royall is not a child. Isn't it rather absurd to talk of her as if she were? I believe she considers herself free to come and go as she pleases, without any questions from anyone. . . .' (*S*, p. 204)

Royall accuses Harney of not meaning to marry Charity: 'It's because you hadn't need to.' When he goes, Charity declares, 'I ain't ever been sorry—not a minute!'—like Sophy Viner. But the presence of Lawyer Royall has put a damper on the occasion; reality has intruded, and Harney is thrust back to reality:

> His voice seemed like a stranger's: nothing was left in it of the vibrations she knew. . . . They sat motionless, *in their attitude of confident endearment*, as if some strange death had surprised them. (*S*, p. 206; my italics)

Harney declares, 'we couldn't have come here much longer'—it is getting cold and damp:

> 'But it's been good, though, hasn't it Charity? . . . What's the matter—why do you stand there staring at me? Haven't the days been good?' He went up to her and caught her to his breast. 'And there'll be others—lots of others . . . jollier . . . even jollier . . . won't there, darling?'
>
> He turned her head back, feeling for the curve of her throat below the ear, and kissing her there, and on the hair and eyes and lips. She clung to him desperately, and as he drew her to his knees on the couch she felt as if they were being sucked down together into some bottomless abyss. . . . (*S*, p. 206)

Sexual intercourse has become death again. When they part, 'her doubts were deeper and less definable.' She felt that the gulf between them was too deep for marriage, and 'the bridge their passion had thrown across it was as insubstantial as a rainbow.'

Talking to Ally, Charity learns that Miss Balch is to marry Harney; Ally is sewing a lace blouse, and, in a fit of jealous rage, Charity tears it up. Astonishingly, she writes to Harney:

> I want you should marry Annabel Balch as you promised to. I think maybe you were afraid I'd feel too bad about it. I feel I'd rather you acted right.
>
> Your loving
> CHARITY
>
> (*S*, p. 211)

No doubt this is autobiographical, too; no doubt Edith Wharton is thinking of Fullerton's promises to Katherine—and her 'sense of decency', her recognition of the 'social component' of relationships. But on what grounds does Charity determine what is 'right'?

Her pregnancy obviously belongs to the 'social component'; yet Charity, as soon as she discovers she is pregnant, goes to the doctor who turns out to be an abortionist: a woman with a 'false, murderous smile'—'what was she offering but immunity from some unthinkable crime.' She is suddenly confronted by 'the grave surprise of motherhood'. Charity decides to leave, and since she has no money, has to deposit Harney's blue stone brooch as a pledge. In the train home she has a vision of her claim to become Harney's wife.

At home there is a letter from Harney in which she comes to recognize that 'every word and every reticence was an avowal of Annabel Balch's prior claim.' Yet she does not blame him:

> She did not even reproach him in her thoughts for having concealed from her that he was not free: she could not see anything more reprehensible in his conduct than her own. From the first she needed him more than he had wanted her, and the power that had swept them together had been as far beyond resistance as a great gale loosening the leaves of the forest. . . . (*S*, p. 216)

This surely is a record of Edith Wharton's feelings, about her *affaire* with Morton Fullerton, who was so able to charm his women into accepting his need for them. But how much does it belong to universal truth? Edith Wharton is also aware of the misery of this girl's predicament:

> A cold tremor ran over her, and the hard sobs struggled up into her throat and shook her from head to foot. For a while she was caught and tossed on great waves of anguish. . . . (*S*, p. 216)

She relives her short romance, and feels 'these things were hers': 'They had passed into her blood, and become part of her, they were building the child in her womb; *it was impossible to tear asunder strands of life so interwoven*. . .' (*S*, p. 217; my italics). But they are torn apart (Sophy Viner has a similar feeling that Darrow's memories have become part of her—a feeling no doubt Edith Wharton had consoled herself with).

Contemplating her situation, Charity eschews appealing to Harney; she has seen the results of the shotgun marriage. She decides to go back to the Mountain: 'She supposed it was something in her blood that made the Mountain the only answer . . . (*S*, p. 220)—though the real reason is surely unconscious: Edith Wharton feeling herself an unborn child must seek in the primitive unconscious for the mother, but yet, at the same time, must obliterate that mother, before marrying the father. Charity declares, 'This is where I was born . . . this is where I belong.' In a sense it is also a symbolic retreat to the unconscious primitive sources of passionate sexuality. The dead mother is seen so starkly; there is no coffin. Charity tries to 'compose her mother's body':

> She drew the stocking over the dreadful glistening leg, and pulled the skirt down to the battered upturned boots. As she did so, she looked at her mother's face, thin yet swollen, with lips parted in a frozen gasp above the broken teeth. There was no sign in it of anything human: she lay there like a dead dog in a ditch. (*S*, p. 227)

The resonance of the Burial Service, as against the mean interjections of the Mountain people, is superb, and tragic: 'Man that is born of woman hath but a short time to live and is full of misery' (*S*, p. 229). Charity decides to stay, but reflects on her mother's hopes, when she gave Charity herself to Lawyer Royall. The dreadful episode has an effect parallel to Fanny

Price's experience of her Portsmouth home: it brings home to her the advantages of Mansfield Park. 'Anything, anything was better than to add another life to the nest of misery on the Mountain.'

She tries to walk away, but she is weighed down by her child. The dreadful events up the Mountain seemed to have divided her for ever, from her 'short dream of bliss'. 'Even Harney's image had been blurred by that crushing experience.' Suddenly, she sees Lawyer Royall with his old buggy.

She feels a softening of her heart, as she thinks of the efforts he has made through the cold night. Royall announces his intention to marry her. She stands up, shaking and bewildered. ' "I know I ain't been fair to you always; but I want to be now . . . I want you to know . . . I want." Her voice failed her and she stopped' (*S*, p. 238). He replies, 'You want to be took home and took care of.' He takes a strong line, and she takes a sense of peace and security from his silent presence. She follows him as passively as a 'tired child'. 'She had always thought of him . . . as of someone hateful and obstructive, but whom she could outwit and dominate when she chose to make the effort. . .' (*S*, p. 240). Now she has a sense of their nearness. Yet she goes through the marriage service in a kind of passive terror: 'All her soul was gathered up in one sick sense of coming down.' In her marriage bed, she wonders, ' "What have I done? Oh, what have I done?" she whispered, shuddering to her pillow . . .' (*S*, p. 244). She sees Royall sitting in a chair by the bed: he sat there in the darkness to show that she was safe with him: 'A stir of something deeper than she had ever felt in thinking of him flitted through her tired brain . . .' (*S*, p. 245). In the morning, 'It was as if all the dark spirits had done out of him.'

Royall gives her two twenty-dollar bills. Charity goes to Dr. Merkle, who cheats and blackmails her of both bills, in order to redeem the blue brooch that she means to be a link between Harney's child and its unknown father. She writes to Harney: 'I'm married to Mr. Royall. I'll always remember you. CHARITY' (*S*, p. 247). She is enclosed in Royall's kindness, and the novel ends hopefully.

> 'You're a good girl, Charity.' Their eyes met, and something rose in his throat that she had never seen there: a look that made her feel ashamed and yet secure.
>
> 'I guess you're good, too,' she said, shyly and quickly. He smiled without answering. (*S*, p. 248)

We do not feel that the marriage will be catastrophic. Charity would not have been a suitable wife for Lucius Harney; it is better for her to be with this small-town champion of law and values—at the mundane level—than up the Mountain. She had had her moment of rapture, and has the memories of that: she has the blue pin, and the baby; and it seems unlikely that Royall will bother her. She has had her summer.

Again, I feel, we have to rescue the novel from misrepresentation: Wolff, for example, calls it 'a hymn to generativity and marriage'! In the end, Charity is saved from the appalling consequences of her recklessness by the essential decency of old Royall; but by no means does her submission to the man's kindness represent a good marriage, though it may provide a reasonable chance for her child.

It is a *faute de mieux*; Charity's first impulse when she saw Royall's buggy was to hide:

> Her first impulse was to crouch under the ledge till he had passed: but the instinct of concealment was overruled by the relief of feeling that someone was near her in the awful emptiness. She stood up and walked towards the buggy. (*S*, p. 235)

The story is written out of an ambiguity, which recognizes on the one hand that marriage is the true fulfilment ('Oh, the poverty, of any love that lies outside marriage, of any love that is not a living together, a sharing of all'—Edith Wharton to Charles Du Bos), and on the other that marriage without sexual fulfilment and mutual sharing is less than a free illicit sexual encounter. Inevitably, however, the 'free' encounter involves duplicity, an inadequacy in being related to the rest of the world, and probably ultimate termination, and so failure. But, again, simply to accord to the claims of the world of society can be a disaster, too.

It is perhaps worth going back over the gravest moments of this story, to examine its existential message or 'upshot' in this respect, for, as a woman, Edith Wharton is aware that the claims of a relationship to have meaning must be seen in terms of the procreation of the child and the obligations of a mother.

At the moment she became Fullerton's lover ('I will go with him once before we separate') Edith Wharton wrote:

> How strange to feel one's self all at once *'Jehnseits von Gut and Böse'* ['Beyond God and Evil']. . . . It would hurt no-one—and it would give me my first last draught of life . . . why not? I have always laughed at the *'mala prohibita'*—'bug-bears to frighten children'. The anti-social act is the only one that is harmful 'per se'. And, as you told me the other day—*and as I needed no telling!*—what I have given you is far, far more. (R. W. B. Lewis, p. 221)

Lewis speaks of a 'lingering puritanical strain in her that gave the issue its transcendant importance'; and she is a novelist within the Anglo-Saxon puritan tradition as much as George Eliot was (a woman who also braved out unconventional sexual liaisons).

In *Ethan Frome* the yearning of Ethan to have 'a last draught of life' ends in misery. The symbolic sexual act brings not death, but something worse—a living hell.

In *Summer* she confronts more realistically the question of whether a love relationship can be 'beyond good and evil'. Leaving aside the 'bugs' of religious objections, can a love relationship be an anti-social act? Or if not, what other objections can there be to it? In pursuing these questions, the novelist takes over. First there is the question of trust, and of duplicity. What does Harney mean in his letter:

> DEAR CHARITY
>
> I have your letter, and it touches me more than I can say. Won't you trust me, in return, to do my best? There are things it is hard to explain, much less to justify: but your generosity makes everything easier. All I can do now is to thank you from my soul for understanding. Your telling me that you wanted me to do right has helped me beyond expression. If ever there is a hope of realising what we dreamed of you will see me back on the instant; and I haven't yet lost that hope. (*S*, p. 216)

Charity finds it 'beautifully expressed'. But she detects the man's radical insincerity, despite his urging her to trust him:

'He was not trying to evade an importunate claim; he was honestly and contritely struggling between opposing duties' (*S*, p. 216). But can we believe this? Edith Wharton surely shows herself still to be hypnotized by Fullerton's capacity to maintain several relationships at once, with no sense that one was incompatible with another? The novelist's recognition is in the misery she portrays in Charity, who suffers those 'great waves of anguish'.

But the scene up the Mountain provides a deeper and graver context for Charity's rumination on her *affaire*: the dimension of being-unto-death.

> They stood before a mattress on the floor in a corner of the room. A woman lay on it, but she did not look like a dead woman; she seemed to have fallen across her squalid bed in a drunken sleep, and to have been left lying where she fell, in her ragged disordered clothes. One arm was flung above her head, one leg drawn up under a torn skirt that left the other bare to the knee: a swollen glistening leg with a ragged stocking rolled down about the ankle. (*S*, p. 226)

There is no coffin. Charity remains on her knees by the mattress:

> . . . now that her mother's face was covered it was easier to stay near her, and avoid the sight of the living faces which too horribly showed by what stages hers had lapsed into death. (*S*, p. 228)

The clergyman begins the service: 'Though after my skin worms destroy my body, yet in my flesh shall I see God. . . .'

> *In my flesh shall I see God!* Charity thought of the gaping mouth and stony eyes under the handkerchief, and of the glistening leg over which she had drawn the stocking.
>
> 'We brought nothing into this world and we brought nothing out of it—'. (*S*, p. 228)

We feel the girl's desolation: this is the mother's face that should have reflected her, but did not; her emotions are dead. And the dreadful reality of one's existence, and the fact that one only exists as a being, between the reflection of the mother's eyes and their final starriness, impresses itself upon her. What has she made of that moment of living?

The mighty words fall on Charity's head, as the others there bicker and fight, drunkenly. They leave the body 'in its helpless misery' and lower the creature into the earth, as the earth is shovelled over the corpse:

> 'Through our Lord Jesus Christ, who shall change our vile body that it may be like unto His glorious body. . . .' The last spadeful of earth fell on the vile body of Mary Hyatt. . . . (*S*, p. 230)

The preacher, with a tone of authority Charity has never heard, orders them all to kneel to say the Lord's Prayer; it is a deeply moving scene which presents to us, and to Charity, the tragic predicament. 'Charity lay on the floor, as her dead mother's body had lain' (*S*, p. 231). She tries to imagine her links with her mother, but finds this impossible. She dimly thinks what mother would not want to save her child from such a life? 'Charity thought of the future of her own child, and tears welled into her aching eyes. . .' (*S*, p. 232). She has an impulse to run away, thinking that to save her child from its fate among the Mountain people, 'she would find strength to travel any distance, and bear any burden life might put on her.' She walks off, to find her way to the village and feels herself a mere speck in the lonely circle of the sky. Harney's image fades and 'she thought of him as so remote from her that he seemed hardly more than a memory.' She sees the buggy and 'knew at once that the driver was in search of her' and her impulse to hide was 'overruled by the relief of feeling that someone was near her in the awful emptiness'.

The juxtaposition of birth and death exposes the recklessness of the lovers, Harney and Charity, and offers an answer to 'Beyond Good and Evil'. Charity is aware of the goodness that is in Lawyer Royall. He tells her it was a day like this when he came up to fetch her first:

> Then, as if fearing that she might take his remark as a reminder of past benefits, he added quickly: 'I dunno's you think it was such a good job, either.'
>
> 'Yes, I do,' she murmured. . . . (*S*, p. 236)

The closing pages make it clear that we must see our liaisons in a historical context—in the complex of the one unique life. Certainly, when a woman is fertile, this perspective is starkly revealed. Recognition of this affects Charity more deeply than summer or lover. In her abandoned dismay, she is glad to have the old man to take care of her for her child's sake.

Yet behind this magnificent scene is a deep feeling at the unconscious level that only the father is satisfactory among men. All other men are weak, undependable and duplicitous, with little capacity for that ultimate commitment that can bring meaning to life. They are capable only of the passion of the moment, and their casual promiscuity destroys and menaces the commitment that alone can establish, in the face of our being-unto-death, a sense of having meaningfully existed.

# 5

# *The Age of Innocence*

Newland Archer is another of Edith Wharton's unsatisfactory men. He enters a conventional marriage to one of the old New York families, and the family ensures that the relationship is false, and that he cannot escape it:

> He pulled the sash down and turned back. 'Catch my death!' he echoed; and he felt like adding: 'But I've caught it already. I *am* dead—I've been dead for months and months.'
>
> And suddenly the play of the word flashed up a wild suggestion. What if it were *she* who was dead! If she were going to die—to die soon—and leave him free! The sensation of standing there, in that warm familiar room, and looking at her, and wishing her dead, was so strange, so fascinating and overmastering, that its enormity did not immediately strike him. (*AI*, p. 247)*

By contrast, the Countess Olenska defies the American conventions, and has taken up a European attitude of independence. Yet she has been persuaded to accept the conventional view of the American family that scenes and publicity are better avoided; indeed, Newland Archer himself has persuaded her to this view, as is made plain in the scene in which he first reveals his love for Ellen.

> 'May guessed the truth,' he said. 'There is another woman—but not the one she thinks.'
>
> . . .
>
> '. . . you are the woman I would have married if it had been possible for either of us.'
>
> 'Possible for either of us!' She looked at him with unfeigned

* References are to the Penguin Edition of 1981.

astonishment. 'And you say that—when it's you who've made it impossible?'

He stared at her, groping in blackness through which a single arrow of light tore its blinding way.

'*I've* made it impossible—?'

'You, you, *you*!' she cried, her lip trembling like a child's on the verge of tears. 'Isn't it you who made me give up divorcing—give it up because you showed me how selfish and wicked it was, how one must sacrifice oneself to preserve the dignity of marriage . . . and to spare one's family the publicity, the scandal? . . . I did what you told me, what you proved to me that I ought to do. Ah . . . I've made no secret of having done it for you!' (*AI*, p. 143)

He is crushed by this, but then declares:

'At least I loved you—' he brought out.

On the other side of the hearth from the sofa-corner where he supposed she still crouched, he heard a faint stifled crying like a child's. . . . (*AI*, p. 144)

He cries, after their kiss, 'Do you see me marrying May after this?'—but that is exactly what he goes on to do.

Ellen Olenska declares that he has given her a new perspective on everything: 'you understood . . . you hated happiness bought by disloyalty and cruelty and indifference. That was what I'd never known before—and it's better than anything I've known.' But the logical conclusion of this is her outburst: ' "Ah, don't let us undo what you've done!" she cried. "I can't go back now to that other way of thinking. *I can't love you unless I give you up*" ' (*AI*, p. 146; my italics). One might say this was Jamesian; but it does represent a dilemma: and this dilemma means that, out of their respect for the values of the traditional rich American family, and through the wiles of May Welland's family, they are prevented from ever consummating their love.

In the end, Ellen promises to allow him to sleep with her once, before she leaves for Europe. But May makes a final plea, and tells Olenska that she is pregnant. Ellen sends him her key, but it is too late. The family believe, however, that Newland and Ellen have been lovers, and draw them into a separation ritual—a dinner especially laid on for Ellen's departure.

> . . . then it came over him, in a vast flash made up of many broken gleams, that to all of them he and Madame Olenska were lovers, lovers in the extreme sense peculiar to 'foreign' vocabularies. He guessed himself to have been, for months, the centre of countlessly silently observing eyes and patiently listening ears, he understood that, by means as yet unknown to him, the separation between himself and the partner of his guilt had been achieved, and now that the whole tribe had rallied about his wife on the tacit assumption that nobody knew anything, or had ever imagined anything, and that the occasion of the entertainment was simply May Archer's natural desire to take an affectionate leave of her friend and cousin.
>
> It was the old New York way, of taking life 'without effusion of blood': the way of people who dreaded scandal more than disease, who placed decency above courage, and who considered that nothing was more ill-bred than 'scenes', except the behaviour of those who gave us to them. (*AI*, pp. 279–80)

Archer feels 'like a prisoner in the centre of an armed camp': 'It's to show me . . . what would happen to *me*. . . .' '. . . and a deathly sense of the superiority of implication and analogy over direct action . . . closed in on him like the doors of the family vault' (*AI*, p. 280).

'Deathly' it is, and the family vault swallows everything—swallows, especially, the possibilities of sexual passion and that meeting of true minds that can give meaning to lives. This is the 'family' background which surrounded Edith Wharton, through her earlier trials, as with her first engagement to Harry Stevens, which gave her no knowledge of sexual passion, and which led to her disastrous marriage with Teddy.

But yet Newland Archer's romantic attachment to Ellen Olenska remains at the level of fantasy, and he fails dismally to fulfil this hope. Even at the end, when May has died, and Archer is in Paris with his grown-up son, he shrinks from even meeting Ellen:

> 'It's more real to me here than if I went up,' he suddenly heard himself say: and the fear lest that last shadow of reality should lose its edge kept him rooted to his seat as the minutes succeeded each other. (*AI*, p. 301)

'There was nothing now to keep her and Archer apart'—but Archer cannot face the probability. He goes to an art gallery before seeking her out:

> For an hour or more he wandered from gallery to gallery through the dazzle of the afternoon light, and one by one the pictures burst on him in their half-forgotten splendour, filling his soul with the long echoes of beauty. *After all, his life had been too starved*. . . . (*AI*, p. 298; my italics)

He pauses before an 'effulgent Titian':

> . . . he found himself saying: 'But I'm only fifty-seven—' and then he turned away. For such summer dreams it was too late; but surely not for a quiet harvest of friendship, of comradeship in the blessed hush of her newness. (*AI*, p. 298)

It is terribly poignant, and yet infuriating—because of the cowardice of the man, in the face of the promptings of his own authenticity. The cowardice may be related to that of Laurence Selden, who could have interposed, again and again, to save Lily Bart's life, but who withdrew into a self-defensive neatness, a studied egocentricity, which shrinks from all the complications of giving (and receiving) in love. Archer's final failure to come up to scratch is logically inevitable, if one traces his reasons for failing in commitment to Ellen throughout the novel.

He is a deplorably unsatisfactory man—but his creation seems appropriate for Edith Wharton, who herself must have felt such bitterness about her own cruel fate. She married Teddy, and, after a thoroughly unsatisfactory introduction to sexuality with him, seems to have given sex up. She loved Walter Berry, but Berry, being a confirmed bachelor, seems to have been incapable of passionate sexual commitment. And then, for three years only, she enjoyed a passionate affair with the strangely uncommitted Morton Fullerton, who was incapable of complete committal and of any relationship lasting any length of time, and who was also bisexual.

Why *The Age of Innocence*? That the latter word is heavily imbued with irony is made clear when Archer is talking to May's mother, who has asked, about Ellen, 'what her fate will be?'

> 'What we've all contrived to make it,' he felt like answering. 'If you'd all of you rather she should be Beaufort's mistress than some decent fellow's wife you've certainly gone the right way about it.'
>
> He wondered what Mrs. Welland would have said if he had uttered the words instead of merely thinking them. He could picture the sudden decomposure of her firm placid features, to which a life-long mastery of trifles had given an air of factitious authority. Traces still lingered on them of fresh beauty like her daughter's, and he asked himself if May's face was doomed to thicken into the same middle-aged image of *invincible innocence.*
>
> Ah, no, he did not want May to have that kind of innocence, *the innocence that seals the mind against imagination and the heart against experience*! (*AI*, p. 123; my italics)

Newland Archer has imagination, but it is limited to invention. Contemplating May, 'with a thrill of possessiveness' at the beginning of the book, 'in which pride in his own masculine initiation was mingled with a tender reverence for her *abysmal purity*' (my italics), he is 'hazily confusing the scene of his projected honeymoon with the masterpieces of literature which it would be his manly privilege to reveal to his bride' (*AI*, p. 10).

He has had a previous affair—there has been a married lady 'whose charms had held his fancy through two mildly agitated years'; and Edith Wharton hints at 'the frailty which had so nearly marred that unhappy being's life, and had disarranged his own plans for a whole winter' (*AI*, p. 10). Newland may have 'read more, thought more, and even seen a good deal more of the world' than the men surrounding him in the audience of the opera, but

> grouped together they represented 'New York', and the habit of masculine solidarity made him accept their doctrine in all the issues called moral. He instinctively felt that in this respect it would be troublesome—and also rather bad form—to strike out for himself. (*AI*, p. 111)

So, Archer may not subscribe to the lofty moral pronouncements of Mr. Fullerton Jackson, but he is inhibited enough by hard feeling and lethargy from being truly independent. At first he is appalled that his fiancée May should be 'exposed to the influence of a woman so careless of the dictates of taste'.

Ellen is not accepted by New York society, and May, with trained tact, defends her: when Newland asks why she is not coming to the ball, May replies that 'she made up her mind her dress wasn't smart enough.'

> 'Oh, well—' said Archer with happy indifference. Nothing about his betrothed pleased him more than her resolute determination to carry to its utmost limit that ritual of ignoring the 'unpleasant' in which they had both been brought up. (*AI*, p. 25)

Archer is thus shown to be deeply compromised by the hypocrisy of New York society. Archer seeks to challenge their respectability, but his challenge is only skin deep; when Jackson informs him that the secretary who helped Ellen Olenska to leave her husband was still living with her a year later,

> Newland reddened, 'living together? Well, why not?' Who had the right to make her life over if she hadn't? I'm sick of the hypocrisy that would bury alive a woman of her age if her husband prefers to live with harlots.'
>
> He stopped and turned away angrily to light his cigar.
>
> 'Women ought to be free—as free as we are,' he declared, making a discovery *of which he was too irritated to measure the terrific consequences.* (*AI*, p. 34; my italics)

The slightly sardonic phrase I have italicized makes plain Edith Wharton's position: she is fully aware of the gulf between Archer's statement and the reality of what this freedom would mean, and of how far short he would fall of his assertion if women became free.

By such subtle placings, she shows Archer and May trapped in the hypocrisy of their social milieu, while Archer (who has had a 'silly business' with Mrs. Rushworth which he once regarded as his 'tragedy') develops a romantic yearning for Ellen Olenska. He looks at the portrait of his fiancée and sees 'the gay innocent mouth of the young creature whose soul's custodian he used to be': 'That terrifying product of the social system he belonged to and believed in, the young girl who knew nothing and expected everything, looked back at him like a stranger' (*AI*, p. 39). He reflects that 'marriage was not the safe anchorage he had been taught to think, but a voyage on uncharted seas.' He sees with a 'shiver of foreboding' his marriage becoming what most of the other marriages about him were: 'a dull association of material and social interests held together by ignorance on the one side and hypocrisy on the other' (*AI*, p. 40). Bitter memories of her mother's evasion of all questions to do with sexuality obviously lie behind Edith Wharton's delineation of Archer's view of his bride-to-be:

> She was frank, poor darling, because she had nothing to conceal, assured because she knew of nothing to be on her guard against; and with no better preparation than this, she was to be plunged overnight into what people evasively called 'the facts of life'. (*AI*, p. 41)

All this 'frankness' and 'innocence' was an 'artificial product', 'so cunningly manufactured by a conspiracy of mothers and aunts and grandmothers. . . .' These uncomfortable reflections are prompted in Archer by the 'inopportune arrival of the Countess Olenska'.

The latter is the subject of a snub, which she overcomes, and at last the Countess enters the Van der Luyden drawing room, where Archer is impressed by her 'mysterious authority of beauty': 'It frightened him to think what must have gone to the making of her eyes.' Ellen is not conscious of breaking any rules (though she *is*) when she sits at Newland Archer's side, where she rests with perfect ease. This idiosyncratic poise leads the Countess to behave invitingly to Archer: she touches his knee with her fan, which 'thrilled him like a caress', while she suddenly says, 'Tomorrow, then, after five—I shall expect you'—though there has been no such agreement between them.

Archer is something of a fugitive from his own wedding preparations ('Twelve dozen of everything—hand embroidered') when he enters the mysterious apartment of Ellen Olenska, who returns home there in the brougham of Julius Beaufort. As he tries to urge her to take notice of the Welland mothers and others, she declares suddenly, '. . . The real loneliness is living among all these kind people who only ask one to pretend. . .' (*AI*, p. 68), and is shaken by a sob.

In comforting her he calls her 'Ellen!' Calling at a florist, to send his daily bouquet of lilies of the valley to May, he sees a bunch of red roses which he arranges to be sent to the Countess. . . .

Newland continues to believe that 'presently' it would be his task to 'take the bandage from this young woman's eyes' and 'bid her look forth on the world'. But he recalls the Kentucky cave-fish, and how they ceased to develop eyes because they had no use for them: 'What if, when he had bidden May Welland to open hers, they could only look out blankly at blankness?' (*AI*, p. 72). The self-delusion of his confidence in assuming himself to be such a liberator is made clear, step by step, as he hovers between turning sullen about the niceties of whom Ellen Olenska may call on and feeling distress over the possibility of being asked to advise on her divorce: he hates divorce. He feels a 'wave of compassion' for his cousin and believes he must save her 'at all costs from further wounding herself in her mad plunges against fate'.

He ponders his own morality, and asks, 'Are we only Pharisees after all?' He is 'puzzled by the efforts to reconcile his instinctive disgust at human vileness with his equally instinctive pity for human frailty' (*AI*, p. 83). He ponders his affair with 'poor, silly' Mrs. Rushworth, who had been attracted by the secrecy and peril of the liaison as much as by his charm; he had emerged from it 'with an undisturbed belief in *the abysmal distinction between the woman one loved and respected and those one enjoyed—and pitied*' (my italics). In this view he had been abetted by his female relatives who shared the belief that when 'such things happened' it was 'undoubtedly foolish of the man, but *somehow always criminal of the woman*' (my italics).

He is aware of the difference between the Anglo-Saxon, Protestant, position over such matters, and of what tended to happen in 'rich and idle and ornamental societies' such as those in Europe, where a woman might be drawn into 'a tie inexcusable by conventional standards' by 'force of circumstances'.

So, Archer is firmly embedded in conventional (chauvinistic, as we would call them today) views, and when discussing divorce with Ellen, he finds her saying to him, 'But my freedom—is that nothing?' Yet she is pliable, and agrees with him: 'Very well; I will do what you wish.' She is persuaded into the New York view of what is *fair* and *just*. Beneath the surface, Newland Archer is more drawn to Ellen Olenska than he is conscious of, while she is attracted to him and aware of the seductive influence she exerts over him: by her sudden reference to the two occasions on which he has sent her roses, she causes in him an 'agitated pleasure'; her colour rises 'reluctantly and duskily' and she asks, 'What do you do while May is away?'—a question that 'faintly annoys' him.

Ellen runs away and sends him a note: he thinks, 'what has Madame Olenska been running away from, and why did she feel the need to be safe?' It seems clear she is falling in love with Archer; she tells him, 'I can't feel unhappy when you're here', and 'I live in the moment when I'm happy': 'The words stole through him like a temptation. . . . Archer's heart was beating insubordinately. What if it were from him that she had been running away. . .' (*AI*, p. 114). She anticipates her 'stealing up behind him to throw her light arms about his neck', but Beaufort arrives—the vulgar rich adventurer who is pursuing Ellen.

Again we may reflect on the degree to which Edith Wharton has the advantage over Henry James. She knows how passionate need can creep up on a man or a woman unawares, as James did not, despite his interest in the morality of passion. She is aware of the subtleties of feminine intuition: for example, when May Welland, by a supreme effort, detects how differently Newland Archer has behaved to her since the announcement of their engagement, which happened to coincide with his interest in Ellen Olenska. May deduces that it is because of his regret over Mrs. Rushworth—and offers him his freedom, with tragic fortitude!

In a later exchange with Ellen, Archer confesses (I have already quoted from the scene) that there is another woman, in his life, but it is she, Ellen. Although she cries, 'Ah, don't make love to me! Too many people have done that. . .', she is evidently deeply affected—and admits that she has, through Archer, accepted the New York emphasis on fairness and justice. The scene is one of subtle complexity, since it is clear that Countess Olenska is playing a powerful game, in contradistinction to Archer's betrothed, who is an 'innocent' as she is sophisticated—and Ellen is reckless:

> He had her in his arms, her face like a wet flower at his lips, and all their vain terrors shrivelling up like ghosts at sunrise. The one thing that astonished him now was that he should have stood for five minutes arguing with her across the width of the room, when just touching her made everything so simple. (AI, p. 144)

This subtle and intense scene is written from a perception Henry James could not quite have:

> She gave him back all his kiss, but after a moment he felt her stiffening in his arms, and she put him aside and stood up.
> 'Ah, my poor Newland—I suppose this had to be. But it doesn't in the least alter things. . . .'
> 'It alters the whole of life for me.'
> 'No, no—it mustn't, it can't. You're engaged to May Welland; and I'm married.' (*AI*, p. 144)

She looks 'haggard and almost old'.

Archer says, 'It's too late to do anything else' other than to tell May; but she knows—as a woman knows—he is only saying this because it is the easiest thing to say: 'In reality it's too late to do anything but what we've both decided on.' She cannot go back to 'that other way of thinking', and she cannot love (him) unless she gives him up.

She is satisfied, because she loves him, and so possesses him: and this is enough (we may recall Sophy Viner's experience of Darrow):

> I *was* lonely; I *was* afraid. But the emptiness and darkness are gone; when I turn back into myself now I'm like a child going at night into a room where there's always a light. (*AI*, p. 146)

This sense of *having been loved,* and therefore enriched, whatever happens, is something that had happened to Edith Wharton; our only problem is perhaps that we may doubt whether Newland Archer is capable of understanding the subtlety of the woman's view.

Book Two begins with the wedding rite, which Edith Wharton presents with subtle irony:

> All the old ladies in both families had got out their faded sables and yellowing ermines, and the smell of camphor from the front pews almost smothered the faint spring scent of the lilies banking the altar. (*AI*, p. 151)

The panoply of received convention smothers all hope of life; behind it all is the horror indicated by hints: 'concealment of the spot in which the bridal night was to be spent being one of the most sacred taboos of the prehistoric ritual'. The deity is 'Good Form'—and Beaufort is seen among the congregation 'scrutinizing the women with an arrogant stare'. Archer goes through the ceremony with duplicitous reflections: 'he too had once thought such questions important.' (There has been a heated debate on whether the wedding presents should be displayed; there is much discussion as to whether the pews should be dismantled to accommodate the vast form in a bath chair of Mrs. Manson Mingott.) The vision of ceremony is superbly given:

> The music, the scent of the lilies on the altar, the vision of the cloud of tulle and orange-blossoms floating nearer and nearer, the sight of Mrs. Archer's face suddenly convulsed with happy sobs, the low benedictory murmur of the Rector's voice, the ordered evolutions of the eight pink bridesmaids and the eight black ushers: all these sights, sounds and sensations, so familiar in themselves, so unutterably strange and meaningless in his new relationship to them, were confusedly mingled in his brain. (*AI*, p. 156)

Underneath it all 'the same black abyss yawned before him and he felt himself sinking into it, deeper and deeper': the comic portrayal of the social event is based on the author's awareness of the essential utter unauthenticity of the marriage for Archer.

Aware of the approaching defloration, Edith Wharton touches in subtly the essence of May:

> The blood that ran so close to her fair skin might have been a preserving fluid rather than a ravaging element; yet her lack of indestructible youthfulness made her seem neither hard nor dull, but only primitive and pure. (*AI*, p. 159)

The resonances of the sentence are imbued with Edith

Wharton's deep feelings for this girl as the 'terrifying product' of the social system, who is schooled to be in a state in which she 'knew nothing and expected everything'. Archer has now 'reverted to all his old inherited ideas about marriage'; as for new ideas: 'There was no use in trying to emancipate a wife who had not the dimmest notion that she was not free. . .' (AI, p. 164). 'Whatever happened, he knew she would always be loyal, gallant and unresentful: and that pledged him to the practice of the same virtues' (AI, p. 165). May becomes 'the tutelary divinity of all his old traditions and reverences'.

But it is not long before Archer begins to realize that 'in future many problems would be thus negatively solved for him', and that May's pressure was already 'bearing on the very angles whose sharpness he most wanted to keep'. Yet he is contented, 'for she had fulfilled all that he had expected.' 'As for the momentary madness which had fallen upon him on the eve of his marriage, he had trained himself to regard it as the last of his discarded experiments' (*AI*, p. 174). 'The Countess Olenska remained in his memory simply as the most plaintive and poignant of a love of ghosts.'

Chapter 21 begins with an archery contest in which May triumphs; whereupon Archer overhears Beaufort declare, 'Yes, but that's the only kind of target she'll ever hit'—which words send a faint shiver through his heart: 'What if "niceness" carried to that superb degree were only a negation, the curtain dropped before an emptiness?' He feels that he has 'never lifted that curtain' in May.

Edith Wharton's central theme is surely one that concerns individuals like herself who have been cheated of fulfilment by convention, by 'received ideas', by their family training, so that an emptiness remains at the heart of their being. With Newland Archer this problem is never solved.

We have a foretaste of the end when, at this stage, he re-encounters the Countess Olenska.

> From the willow walk projected a slight wooden pier hiding in a sort of pagoda-like summer-house; and in the pagoda a lady stood, leaning against the rail, her back to the shore. (*AI*, p. 181)

Archer 'stopped at the sight as if he had waked from sleep'. 'That vision of the past was a dream'; the reality was to return to the house 'which one always knew exactly what is happening at a given hour'.

Ellen Olenska, we learn later, is aware of his presence, but he turns and walks up the hill. May declares she is sorry he did not find Ellen, who, she goes on to declare, might have been better off with her husband. Archer remarks he has never heard May say a cruel thing before. The exchange, and the romantic appearance of Ellen, lead to a 'curious reversal of mood' in Archer:

> The heavy carpets, the watchful servants, the perpetual reminding tick of disciplined clocks, the perpetually renewed stack of cards and invitations on the hall table . . . made any less systematized and affluent existence seem unreal and precarious. . . . But now it was the Welland house, and the life he was expected to lead in it, that had become unreal and irrelevant, and the brief scene of the shore . . . was a dose to him as the blood in his veins. (*AI*, p. 183)

In an acutely comic and poignant scene Archer is portrayed as drifting to the house where he believes Ellen Olenska to be; it is not that he is conscious of any wish to speak to her or to hear her voice, but

> she simply felt that if he could carry away the vision of the spot of earth she walked on, and the way the sky and sea enclosed it, the rest of the world might seem less empty. (*AI*, p. 189)

He reaches a summerhouse in the garden, where there is a pink parasol, and lifts the handle of it to his lips: 'He heard the rustle of skirts against the box . . . letting the rustle come nearer without lifting his eyes. He had always known that this must happen. . .' (*AI*, p. 193)—but the woman under the sunshade turns out to be the youngest and largest of the Blenker girls, who prattles at him.

From now on, Archer seems to be sleep-walking, caught up in a dream. Olenska, for her part, when he does catch up with her, seems 'listless'. As soon as Archer appears, her startled look 'gives way to a slow smile of wonder and *contentment*' (my italics). For his part, 'he felt as if he were shouting at her across endless distances, and she might vanish again before he could overtake her' (*AI*, p. 193). When she tells him 'you're not changed', he feels like answering, 'I was, till I saw you again.' Proposing a trip on a steamboat, he suddenly breaks out, 'Haven't we done all we could?' to which she replies, 'You mustn't say things like that to me.' 'Oh, don't calculate!' he exclaims, as she looks at her watch: 'Give me the day!'

Presumably, he means by 'Haven't we done all we could' that they have fallen in as much as they have been able, with what 'society' requires—to overcome their attraction to one another, to meet as beings. It is an extraordinary outburst, and speaks of such a yearning within the man that he falls into a state of drifting abandon, once he re-encounters Ellen. They sit side by side on a bench on the boat, and find

> that they had hardly anything to say to each other, or rather that what they had to say communicated itself best in the blessed silence of their release and their isolation. (*AI*, p. 199)

He feels 'the old familiar world of habit' is receding; surprisingly, we learn:

> There had been days and nights when the memory of their kiss had burned and burned on his lips . . . the thought of her had run through him like fire . . . they seemed to have reached the kind of deeper nearness that a touch may sunder. . . . (*AI*, p. 199)

Ellen Olenska, of course, would have been seen by Edith Wharton's readers as behaving with an extraordinary freedom, in so taking such an excursion with a newly-married man. However, 'She seemed to take their adventure as a matter of course, and to be neither in fear of unexpected encounters, nor (what was worse) unduly elated by their possibility' (*AI*, p. 200). (It is possible, I believe, that just as the archery scene comes from *Daniel Deronda*, so the symbolism of drifting here was taken, possibly unconsciously, from *The Mill on the Floss*.)

During lunch he asks her why she has not left New York, and is startled by her reply: 'I believe it's because of you.' What she means is that he has 'made' her. The exchange is very Jamesian and thus difficult to follow, consisting as it does of obliquities. At the centre of it is his confidence:

> '. . . You sure gave me my first glimpse of a real life, and at the same moment you asked me to go on with a sham one. It's beyond human endearing—that's all.'
>
> 'Oh, don't say that; when I'm enduring it!' she burst out, her eyes filling. (*AI*, p. 203)

She sits with her face abandoned to his gaze 'as if in the recklessness of a desperate peril'.

> The face exposed her as much of it had been her whole person, with the soul behind it. . . .
>
> . . .
>
> 'You too—oh, all this time, you too?' For answer, she let the tears on her lids overflow and run slowly down. (*AI*, p. 203)

It is a meeting at a very deep level, and the power to present it surely comes from Edith Wharton's own most poignant predicament; he remembers once fixing his eyes on her hand so as not to look at her face:

> . . . his imagination spun about the hand as about the edge of a vortex. . . . He had known that love that is fed on caresses and feeds them; but this passion that was closer than his bones was not to be superficially satisfied. His one terror was to do anything which might efface the sand and impression of her words; his one thought, that he should never again feel quite alone.
>
> But after a moment the sense of waste and ruin overcome him. . . . (*AI*, p. 204)

They were 'chained to their separate destinies'. He expresses his wish that she should not go back to the 'abominations' and the 'temptations you half guess':

> 'What a life for you!—' he groaned.
> 'Oh—as long as it's a part of yours.'
> 'And mine a part of yours?'
> She nodded.
> 'And that's to be all—for either of us.'
> 'Well: it *is* all: isn't it? (*AI*, p. 205)

On the boat going back, he feels a 'tranquillity of spirit'. It fills him with a 'tender awe', although he has not even so much as touched her hand with his lips.

From a meeting with the envoy sent by Ellen's husband, he comes to realize that his response to May's reference to her being better off with him has been reported to the family, and in consequence he has been excluded from family discussions of her future. May is aware that her husband takes a special interest in Olenska, and is in opposition to her return to her husband; she is beginning to play a subtle game over the issue. Watching her closely, Archer thinks:

> 'How young she is! For what endless years this life will have to go on!'
>
> He felt, with a kind of horror, his own strong youth and the bounding blood in his veins. (*AI*, p. 222)

Immediately, he announces a trip to Washington, and his wife replies, 'you must be sure to go and see Ellen'—a coded message which Edith Wharton takes half a page to elucidate in full.

When he fetches Ellen from the train to visit 'poor Granny', he declares that *'Each time you happen to me all over again.'* But he is seized by an inability to say anything to her: he could 'only helplessly brood on the mystery of their remoteness and their proximity.' She asks her whether it was M. Rivière who helped her leave her husband, and she admits frankly that it was (we learned earlier that they had been living together). When the carriage lurches, 'suddenly she turned, flung her arms round him and pressed her lips to his.'

He tells her 'a stolen kiss isn't what I want. . . . What I want of you is much more than an hour or two every now and then. . . .' But she declares, 'we'll look not at visions, but at realities.' ' "Is it your idea, then, that I should live with you as your mistress—since I can't be your wife?", she asked' (*AI*, p. 242).

And now the contrast between the imaginative fantasies in which he conceives her and the reality becomes clear:

> 'I want—I want somehow to get away with you into a world where words like that—categories like that—won't exist.

> Where we shall be simply two human beings who love each other, who are the whole of life to each other; and nothing else on earth will matter.'
>
> She drew a deep sigh that ended in another laugh. 'Oh, my dear—where is that country? Have you ever been there?' (*AI*, p. 242)

She goes on 'I know so many who've tried to find it' . . . 'and it wasn't at all different from the old world they'd left, but only rather smaller and dingier and more promiscuous.' She had, one might say, the realism of an Anna Karenina. The Gorgon has opened her eyes:

> . . . it's a delusion to say that she blinds people. What she does is just the contrary—she fastens their eyelids open, so that they're never again in the blessed darkness. Isn't there a Chinese torture like that? There ought to be. Ah, believe me, it's a miserable little country. (*AI*, p. 243)

'What is your plan for us?' asks Archer, but she declares there is no '*us*'. He proclaims himself 'beyond that'—'trying to be happy behind the backs of the people who trust them'. But she declares: 'No, you're not! You've never been beyond. And *I* have . . . and I know what it looks like there. . .' (*AI*, p. 243). He gets out, and walks away. You could say he meets the reality of the situation as Edith Wharton has known it. Though Ellen is in love with him, she is aware they can only have momentary meetings of the soul; theirs is a hard case—and it is his fault, for giving in to the falsifications of the family and Good Form. He has been a coward in the face of life, and there is now no solution, by whatever principles they are guided—least of all, by his, and by what he has taught her. The exchange, again, has a deep bitterness behind its conception, and is drawn from Edith Wharton's own experience of being sacrificed to the conventions and trying to find herself in an adulterous affair.

Newland Archer seems to be groping towards a decision: 'He had so definitely decided on the course he meant to pursue. . .', 'his path was clear, before him.' He contemplates Japan: 'At any rate she would understand that, wherever she went, he was going.' He was 'not only nerved for this plunge but eager to take it'. But he develops a 'growing distaste for what lay before him'. Now he sees the matter in a new light, and recollects his experience with Mrs. Rushworth and the game she had played to deceive a fond and unperceiving husband.

> . . . a smiling, bantering, humouring, watchful and incessant lie. A lie by day, a lie by night, a lie in every touch and every look; a lie in every caress and every quarrel; a lie in every world and every silence. (*AI*, p. 255)

In Archer's little world, a woman's standard of truthfulness was tacitly held to be lower than that of a man; no one, however, laughed at a wife deceived, 'and a certain measure of contempt was attached to one who continued their philandering after marriage.' When he meets Ellen in the street, he feels:

> he had been speaking not to the woman he loved but to another, a woman he was indebted to for pleasure already wearied of: it was hateful to find himself the prisoner of this hackneyed vocabulary. (*AI*, p. 257)

They meet in the Metropolitan Museum and have another Jamesian exchange, trying to determine not to be like all the others. But then she hazards, 'Shall I—once come to you: and then go home?' (*AI*, p. 260). 'It seemed as if he held his heart in his hands, like a full cup that the least motion might overbrim.' She means to go home to her husband; she cannot remain and lie to the people who have been so good to them, or destroy their lives, when they have helped to remake hers. Archer is appalled by the thought of losing her—but agrees:

> for a moment they continued to hold each other's eyes, and he saw that her face, which had grown very pale, was flooded with a deep inner radiance. His heart beat with awe: he felt that he had never before beheld love visible. (*AI*, p. 261)

When he gets home he contemplates the agreement: 'This was what had to be, then . . . this is what had to be.' 'What he had dreamed of had been so different that there was a *mortal chill* in his rapture' (*AI*, p. 262; my italics). His wife comes in, with a deep blush on her cheeks, and announces that she has had a 'really good talk' with Ellen. Archer perceives she has been making a great effort to reach out towards something 'beyond the usual range of her vision'. It is a complex scene: at one point Archer almost throws himself on her mercy. But she reports on an error of Ellen's that has outraged the respectability of the family and 'the open door had closed between them again.' His wife's eyes are of 'the same swimming blue' as when he left her to drive to Jersey City; she flings her arms round him, and he feels her tremble in his.

Archer begins to feel pity for his wife, and recalls her remark before they were married, when she alluded to Mrs. Rushworth, 'I couldn't have my happiness made out of a wrong—a wrong to someone else', and he has again an urge to ask her for the freedom he had once refused.

But 'Newland Archer was a quiet and self-controlled young man.' 'Conformity to the discipline of a small society had become almost his second nature' (*AI*, p. 268). He tries to unburden himself to his wife: 'There's something I've got to tell you . . . about myself.' In response,

> She was extremely pale, but her face had a curious tranquillity of expression that seemed drawn from some inner source.
> . . .
> 'Madame Olenska—' he said: but at the name his wife raised her right hand as if to silence him. (*AI*, p. 270)

May has a note from Ellen to say that Granny has arranged for her to return to Europe, to be independent. She added: 'If any of my friends wish to urge me to change my mind, please tell them it would be utterly useless.' May adds:

> I knew you'd been the one friend she could always count on: and I wanted her to know that you and I were the same—in all our feelings . . . I think she understands everything. (*AI*, p. 272)

Archer receives a key wrapped in tissue paper, which has been sent to his office. He interprets this as a sign that 'Nothing . . . was to prevent his following her' to Europe: 'once he had taken the irrevocable step, and had proved to her that it was irrevocable, he believed she would not send him away.' He believes he still has the trumps in his hands.

But the Archers give a dinner, and Archer perceives this is a ritual *rite de passage*. The Wellands have assumed that he and Ellen have been lovers and the occasion was to mark the end of the *affaire*. He feels 'like a prisoner in the centre of an armed camp', and

> all the harmless-looking people engaged upon May's canvas-backs as a band of dumb conspirators, and himself and the pale woman on his right at the centre of their conspiracy. (*AI*, p. 279)

Afterwards, Archer tries again to reveal his problem to his wife: 'There's something I must tell you. I tried to the other night. . . .' He declares he wants to get away from everything. But she declares he cannot, 'unless you take me with you':

> And then, as he was silent, she went on, in tones so clear and evenly pitched that each separate syllable tapped like a little hammer on his brain. 'That is, if the doctors will let me go . . . but I'm afraid they won't. For you see, Newland, I've been sure since this morning of something I've been so longing and hoping for. . . .' (*AI*, p. 285)

There is a long pause, 'which the inner devils filled with strident laughter'. She then tells him she has told Ellen: 'Did you *mind* my telling her first, Newland?'

> 'But that was a fortnight ago, wasn't it? I thought you said you weren't sure till today?'
>
> Her colour burned deeper, but she held her gaze. 'No, I wasn't sure then—but I told her I was. And you see I was right!' she exclaimed, her blue eyes wet with victory. (*AI*, p. 286)

In the next chapter, May is dead, and Archer is with his grown-up children. Archer has become 'a good citizen', but 'Something he had missed: the flower of life.' He thought of Ellen Olenska 'as one might think of some imaginary beloved in a book or picture: she had become the composite vision of all that he had missed' (AI, p. 289). He has settled for marriage as a 'dull duty': 'this did not so much matter so long as it kept the dignity of a duty'. The thought of Ellen has kept him from unfaithfulness: 'lapsing from that . . . it became a mere battle of ugly appetites'. (*AI*, p. 289)

Newland Archer feels his heart beating with the confusion

and eagerness of youth in Paris. His son announces that 'the Countess Olenska expects us both at half past five.' Fanny Beaumont, to whom the son is engaged, had urged him to look her up. May told her son the day before she died that she had once asked her husband to give up the thing he most wanted: 'She never asked me', is the father's rejoinder.

Ellen never went back to her husband, who has since died. There is nothing now to keep her and Archer apart. When the time comes, however, he prefers to sit outside on a bench and lets his son go up to Ellen's flat alone.

'I believe I'll sit there a moment,' he said. What shall the boy say? 'Say I'm old-fashioned: that's enough.' He imagines the boy going up, and the lady rising to meet him.

> 'It's more real to me here than if I went up,' he suddenly heard himself say; and the fear lest that last shadow of reality should lose its edge to kept him rooted to his seat as the minutes succeeded each other. He sat for a long time on the bench in the thickening dusk, his eyes never turning from the balcony. At length a light shone through the windows, and a moment later a man-servant came out on the balcony, drew up the awnings and closed the shutters.
>
> At that, as if it had been the signal he waited for, Newland Archer got up slowly and walked back alone to his hotel. (*AI*, p. 301)

It is a bitterly sad moment, but perfect in its inevitability: the unsatisfactory man whose opposition to the deathly conventionalities has never been strong enough for him to provoke a crisis is finally exposed: and now it is too late.

*The Age of Innocence* is a superb novel, spun out of Edith Wharton's own deepest experience. It has greater depths of the understanding of passion than any novel by Henry James, it abounds with profoundly feminine insights, and it possesses the penetration into social *moeurs* of the author of *Anna Karenina*. We finish reading the novel in a state of miserable ambivalence. We wish that Newland and Ellen could have consummated their love; yet we have to recognize that, since Archer proved unable to extricate himself from his engagement, the only course open to them was one which would deceive and wound others—and involve them in an impossibility of finding harmony within society—with the possibility only of being brought, as with Vronsky and Anna, to increasing despair and frustration. And while the conventions of society are deadening, one cannot but have respect for the dogged courage of May Welland, who defends her marriage with such tact and resolution. But to point out these complexities is only to pay tribute to the life in the art.

# 6

# *Hudson River Bracketted; The Gods Arrive*

The last two complete novels, *Hudson River Bracketted* and *The Gods Arrive,* are deeply disappointing, despite some remarkable passages. Halo Spear (later Halo Tarrant) is a lovely girl of great integrity, and she displays a responsive intelligence akin to Edith Wharton's own. She is caught in the toils of New York's rich families and sacrifices herself in return for Lewis Tarrant's generosity towards her family. The way she becomes an ideal object for Vance is superbly done. But both books reveal that Edith Wharton's acute judgement of women is not matched by an equal capacity to present and judge men. What is most disappointing about Vance is that his 'genius' remains unrealized; it is extraordinary that a woman writer of such intelligence should offer such a romantic view of the artistic process. On the one hand Vance utters purple passages about the natural world, while on the other he swoons about rather conventional pieces of verse, about which both he and Halo display a vague mysticism, with nothing of the quality of understanding of (say) a Dorothy Wordsworth. He is not *driven* sufficiently to be a genius: he hardly ever seems to finish anything, he is hardly ever depicted working, and his concepts of what writing involves, and of what a novel requires in the creation, are banal. Edith Wharton is good, of course, about the New York literary scene—but is one to believe, despite her own extraordinary luck in that respect, that having published one short story or one novel can lead to such acclaim that her hero comes to be pursued by publishers?

These two novels represent a brave attempt, after all, to relate the creative process to personal relationships. There are superb scenes in them. But what dogs both is a strangely conventional concept of a creative genius. It is, indeed, incredible that such a sensitive and intelligent writer should fall so short of depicting creative power, when she knew genius herself intimately in Henry James, and had such great creative power herself. In a sense these books fail because they are *romans à thèse*—that is, they can only allow the personal drama to develop within the confines of a debilitating concept, of the artist as one *who must be indulged, for the sake of his art.* The hero thus suffers from the limitations which Dickens so devastatingly delineated in Harold Skimpole, who, in the end, is exposed as a simple egoist, dangerous and malign. Alas, Edith Wharton cannot bring herself to blame her Skimpole creature, or even to place his feelings and self-delusions, because as an artist Vance Weston must be given the allowances due to a spoilt child—on the grounds, presumably, that the artist is one who can preserve the child in himself. We need, however, only remind ourselves of (say) Blake, Charles Dickens or Mark Twain to realize that preserving access to the child in oneself may not necessarily mean retaining the selfish egoism of infancy. These novels, in their courageous attempt to relate love to creativity are spoiled by an over-valuation of the child-man, just as many male works are spoilt by the idolized image of a child-wife. And while we appreciate Edith Wharton because she knew passion as Henry James did not, we must have serious doubts about her wisdom on the subject of the dynamics of sexual love in its relationship to creative genius in the man (would the novels have been more successful if the protagonist had been a woman?).

Both novels are serious works and are deeply felt. The first is the much more satisfying book, though its title is absurd—*Hudson River Bracketted.* In that book we have a man writer who is grappling with what might be called the traditional obstacles to fulfilment—his own provinciality, the philistinism of American small-town life, a conventional marriage to a girl whose spirit and sensibility are limited. In the meantime he discovers Halo, a woman who is a potential soulmate, beautiful, inspiring, sensitive. At last, in *The Gods Arrive*, we hope to have fulfilment delineated, despite the obstacles of being refused divorce and the strain of the protagonists trying to live as man and wife, when in fact they are living 'in sin', as Anna and Vronsky live in sin. Certain aspects of Halo's predicament when she is Vance's mistress seem to be influenced by Tolstoy's novel, for Halo, too, comes to ponder that her only 'hold' over her lover is passion, and this is a limiting and falsifying reflection. The very passion itself could sicken the appetite that feeds on it, if the false strains of needing to 'hold' a man are perceived.

But having said that, we may notice another theme, which may also be related to Tolstoy's preoccupations. To both Vance and Halo sexual love seems to have a diminishing effect which undermines the creative drive, and in some way is associated with a demeaning influence. This is not only a question of sex but also of sexuality and involves matters of gender: of male and female. In the end, Vance is a most unsatisfactory man. Despite accounts of certain romantic feelings about nature and certain effervescent effusions, Vance seems seriously deficient in intelligence and understanding, while at the same time he shows no sign of being driven by a daemon, of being compelled to struggle with destiny, with his art, with his own authenticity. He is exasperating, because of the great stretches of time during which, given every advantage, and with everything and everyone offering him what one might suppose to be inspiring and enriching, he fails to seize his opportunity. Instead, he develops this or that kind of writer's block, avoids his work,—is even so foolish as to run out of paper—is restless and acts according to feeble whims and petty forms of egoism.

In personal relationships he is mean and despicable. He is weak, and stupid: could such a man return to the duplicitous blandishments of a Floss Delaney? Or, rather, given the evidence of the awfulness of the woman, again and again, who would not develop some hesitation, some doubt, over her temptations and his own involvement? Even in terms of sheer self-interest, Vance is a fool—and we cannot respect a fool, however much we are assured that he is a distinguished novelist.

The moment when Vance becomes intolerable for most readers, I suspect, is when he is unfaithful to Halo with Floss Delaney in *The Gods Arrive*. It is not so much that the liaison happens; it would be true to life to accept that such extra-marital betrayals occur. But what strikes a false note is that Vance shows not one iota of remorse or regret at having betrayed Halo. The reader, who is aware of what the Halo of *Hudson River Bracketted* did for Vance, and how she has borne his vagaries and maintained her devotion to him without even taking into account her pregnancy (of which he is unaware), must surely find his escapade unutterably despicable—not least in the man's failure, even when the scales fall from his eyes, to see how treacherous he has been to a woman of greatly superior worth, to love itself and to his own judgement. But there is no element of self-awareness or self-reproach in his response, and we cannot believe that a man supposed to be so distinguished a writer would be such a blockhead. He does not even display the shifty unease of Oblonsky, and has none of the deep distress of a Levin, or a Pierre, over his sexual lapses.

How could Edith Wharton be so blind? The reason appears later in the novel. Frenside is talking to Halo, and he feels Vance Webster ought to know she is pregnant. Halo is agitated and says, 'If it's not Floss Delaney it will be some other woman.' Frenside, who is the representative of kindly, humanistic wisdom, replies:

> *Dichterliebe*, eh? Well, you're probably right. Most artists are incurably polygamous. When they're not it's because they die young—and their books generally do too. But I don't know that their loving so lavishly matters as much in itself as in what it makes of them: what sort of stuff they turn it into. . . . (*GA*, p. 433).*

One cannot but feel that the author endorses this view, and with a sinking heart one deplores the author's failure to convince us that Vance Weston is capable of making anything out of any of his experiences, he is so unintelligent. Who could suppose that what he feels for Floss Delaney may be called 'loving so lavishly'? Edith Wharton is here still under

* References are to the Virago editions of both novels.

the influence of Morton Fullerton's propaganda, for the adventurer's sensuality.

It is true that Edith Wharton says of Vance's fascination with Floss, 'There was a dumb subterranean power in her that corresponded with his own sense of the forces of which his inventive faculties were fed. . .' (*GA*, p. 385), and that 'certain obscure fibres in both their natures seemed inextricably tangled' (*GA*, p. 385). But, like Undine, the beautiful Floss is all surface: she uses her charms, with patent obviousness to the reader and (surely) to Vance, to advance her own ambitions calculatedly and cruelly, while offering Vance nothing but false promises, like a nervous schoolgirl promising him sex, but then dodging and excusing herself, with cold-blooded manoeuvres; and he can only be seen as a ridiculous ass to continue to fall for this, as 'love'. There is thus something seriously wrong with Edith Wharton's conception of love in relation to creativity, and her judgement of male involvement, in this novel. This cannot but reflect on her whole *oeuvre* and her treatment of sexuality.

Earlier, she has said of the relationship between Vance and Halo, 'That the veil of passion must wear through was life's inescapable lesson. . .' (*GA*, p. 345), and this is but one of a number of give-away moments in the book. Of course, the failure of fulfilment is an archetypal theme in the novel—as in Dickens, Hardy, Henry James, and Edith Wharton herself. Non-fulfilment, one might say, dominates the novel until D. H. Lawrence.

Supposing fulfilment were possible? What would it feel like? It was this that we might have hoped for in *The Gods Arrive*, not least because of the title. Perhaps in the end, in the final reconciliation, there is something that points to possible fulfilment. The culmination of the central relationships in these two novels, however, must surely be reported to be disappointing.

There are hints throughout that Edith Wharton feels that sexual love has the effect of undermining and spoiling the civilized sensibility—and to see why we must return to the original trauma that Vance suffers.

Floss Delaney's fascination for Vance Weston has to do with his original experience of seeing her have an assignation, when little more than a child, with his grandfather. Here again we encounter the feelings of Edith Wharton for her father, emerging as an obsession with transgenerational sex.

The moment of revelation is perhaps one of the most startling in Edith Wharton: it is strangely 'modern' because it is so voyeuristic.

Early on in *Hudson River Bracketted* the idealistic Vance discovers that Grandpa has a vicious side; when he sees Grandpa sliding down to the orchard to Floss, he is reminded of an earlier incident:

> Something at once dashing and furtive about his air made Vance remember an occasion when, as a small boy, he had gone Christmas shopping with his mother, and they had run into Grandpa, mopping his forehead in the same way, and hurrying toward them round the corner of a certain street that Vance and his schoolmates were always forbidden to play in. The little boy had instantly guessed that something was wrong when his mother, instead of exclaiming, 'Why, there's Grandpa!' had abruptly remembered that, good gracious, she'd never ordered the yeast from Sproul's Bakery, and had jerked Vance back there without seeming to notice Mr. Scrimser. Such subterfuges are signposts on the road to enlightenment. (*HRB*, p. 22)

Grandpa had presumably been on his way to or from a brothel, and the boy and his schoolmates had been forbidden to play there because it was the red light district.

So, in the life of his elders Vance Weston has gradually come to apprehend a degree of viciousness. However, it appals him to believe that the embraces of Floss—

> remembering how he used to go and hide down by the river, and spy out through the bushes for Floss. Or, oftener, she'd be there first, and her strong young arms would pull him down to her. . . . . . . he remembered her kisses and forgave her. . . . (*HRB*, pp. 21)

—were now being shared by Mr. Scrimser:

> Vance continued to smile sardonically at the remembrance of this episode [that is the encounter in the brothel street] and the thought of how far behind him his guileless infancy lay. For a moment he felt inclined to hail his grandfather, then

> something about the old man's air and movements made him decide to turn away. 'Guess it's about time to step round to Sproul's for the yeast,' he chuckled to himself; but as he averted his glance it was arrested by the approach of another figure. . . . (*HRB*, p. 22)

The response of Vance is subtly done: presumably Grandpa is making lustful gestures or postures, and at first Vance is sardonic in his new knowledgeable state. But he is not prepared to see Floss greeting Grandpa with as much libidinal fervour as she greeted him:

> The light was failing fast and Vance was a good hundred yards from the river; but in the thickest dusk, and at a greater distance, he would have known the quick movements, the light outline, of the girl slipping through the trees towards Mr. Scrimser . . .' But he isn't here . . . She isn't here . . . I know she isn't!' stormed through the boy in a rush of useless denial. He stood rooted to the earth while everything she had ever been to him, every look and intonation, every scent and breath and touch that had bound him to her, and made them one, flooded over him in fiery remembrance. He had never been able to imagine what excruciating physical pain was like, the kind you felt when you were smashed under a train, or torn by a whirling engine in a factory—but he knew, he found out in the glare of that blinding instant, that when the soul is smitten deeply enough it seems to become one with the body, to share all the body's capacity for suffering a distinct and different anguish in every nerve and muscle. He saw—or thought he saw—the two figures come together in the dimness, just where, so often, he had caught Floss Delaney to his first embrace; then he stumbled away, unseeing. (*HRB*, p. 23)

This is obviously a moment of great significance, and the rendering of the pain of youthful jealousy is superbly written—we recognize it as authentic. Yet when we read the second novel in this sequence, there is no delineation of such an agony in Halo when Vance is unfaithful to her. Of course, the situations are different: Vance here is young and full of adolescent romantic idealism and is learning that Floss is promiscuous, that his idealization of her is false. But when he betrays Halo, we remember that it is for this same Floss, who becomes vastly more brazen and vicious in later life, that he forsakes Halo, while Halo is not shown to suffer to the degree that a mature lover of such a man must surely suffer. And while, in the light of the boy's ordeal, we despise both Grandpa and Floss, we find it hard to identify with Vance, or even to feel sympathy for him when, smitten with vestiges of his old idealization of this trollop, he persists in doggedly seeking sexual union with her, despite every evidence of her emotional emptiness.

Behind both these novels, thus, we may detect a confusion over questions of male and female sexuality. Grandma, we learn, had been beautiful but cold: of Grandpa she writes that 'while his wife was young her beauty might have served to circumscribe his yearnings if only she had chosen to make use of it.' Perhaps this derives from Edith's feelings about her father? In consequence Grandma had become a Perfectionist (with a capital 'P'): 'Perfection was Grandma's passion—ladies were Grandpa's.' They were, however, in great demand in tableaux representing the Old Folks at Home, and the marriage was accounted a happy one.

The social setting at the beginning of *Hudson River Bracketted* is written about with intelligence and wit. Harrison Delaney— Floss's father—is in the real estate business, and we are clearly in the Apex world again. Vance meets Floss on his way to his grandparents' house—she has fallen off her bicycle. Of course, she is going 'out with another fellow all the time . . . he *knew* it . . . and how she'd lie to him!' But:

> His body and soul still glowed with the memory of it . . . he used to hang about after dark till she came out. On summer evenings they would go down to the maples by the river; there was a clump of bushes where you could lie hidden, breast to breast, to watch the moon and the white cloud reflections sail by, and the constellations march across the sky on their invisible bridges. . . . (*HRB*, p. 15)

Mrs. Scrimser is always on about God; Vance is appalled by the mundanity of her view ('This familiar way of talking about "Jesus" as if He were somebody waiting round the corner at Mondel's grocery . . .'), when he wants to seek the Infinite. He used to think heaven was 'down there' among the maples; but now he realizes he was not the 'only fellow to meet a girl down under those bushes'. It appals him, however, at 19 and still in a state of adolescent idealism, to find he shares his source of heavenly feelings with his evangelical grandmother's disreputable husband. However else we respond to the striking episode, we cannot avoid an undercurrent of disgust; and it is this disgust that so often lurks under the surface of Edith Wharton's novels.

What is disappointing about both *Hudson River Bracketted* and *The Gods Arrive* is that Edith Wharton is unable to offer the illumination she promises of the problem of merging the intellectual life and the life of artistic creation with the experience of love and relationship. In addition to this there is the question of creative achievement itself: Vance falls so far short of the embodiment of creative endeavour, and we simply cannot believe in his genius. Halo says somewhere that he keeps his psychology for his novels; but it is worse than this: we cannot believe that a man who is so hopeless in so many interpersonal experiences can have the insight and integrity of a great artist—or, indeed, of an artist as subtle as Edith Wharton herself.

His antecedents in literature are perhaps Will Ladislaw and some of Dickens's men—Pip and David Copperfield. One passage seems evidently drawn from Dickens, when Vance tells Halo she is the whole earth to him; at first Edith Wharton seems to be bringing a woman's realism to the matter (we may perhaps recall the conversation between Gerald and Birkin in *Women in Love* in which Gerald expresses scepticism about man wanting woman to be God):

> 'There'd be your genius left to you,' she said, still motionless in her corner.
>
> He laughed. 'I sometimes think my genius is a phantasm we've manufactured between us. When I'm not with you I don't believe in it—I don't believe in anything when I'm not with you.'
>
> 'Oh, Vance don't—don't blaspheme!'
>
> 'Blaspheme! The only blasphemy would be to say you're not the whole earth to me!'
>
> Still she did not move: and her immobility held him spellbound on the hearth. 'That's too much to be to anyone,'

> he heard her murmur, and immediately afterward: 'All I've wanted was to help you with your books. . . .' (*HRB*, p. 419)

But then Vance bursts out in terms that seem clearly derived from *Great Expectations*:

> 'My books? My books?' He moved a step or two nearer to her, and then stood checked again by her immobility. 'What do you suppose books are made of?' he cried. 'Paper and ink, or the marrow of a man's bones, and the blood of his brain? But you're *in* my books, you're part of them, whether you want to be or not, whether you believe in them or despise them, whether you believe in me or despise me; and you're in me, in my body and blood, just as you're in my books, and just as fatally. It's done now and you can't get away from me, and you can't undo what you've done: you're the thoughts I think, and the visions I see, and the air I breathe, and the food I eat—and everything, everything, in the earth and over it. . . .' (*HRB*, p. 419)

We may compare that passage with this:

> Out of my thoughts! You are part of my existence, part of myself. You have been in every line I have ever read, since I first came here. . . . You have been in every prospect I have ever seen since—on the river, on the sails of the ships, on the marshes, in the clouds, in the light, in the darkness, in the wind, in the woods, in the sea, in the streets. . . . Estella, to the last hour of my life, you cannot chose but remain part of my character, part of the little good in me, part of the evil. . . . (*Great Expectations*, Ch. CLIV)

Perhaps the epitome of this sense of taking another into oneself, in this Romantic perspective, is Cathy's 'Nelly, I am Heathcliffe.'

What is interesting about these two novels by Edith Wharton is that she is dealing with a male phenomenon of finding woman as an inspiration. But her women are characteristically more realistic: Halo is uncertain about taking on the inspirational rôle; Floss simply calculates coldly, and has no interest in Vance's books at all—even as he persists in trying to find spiritual inspiration in some instinctive liaison with her. Being a woman, Edith Wharton has some sense of woman's mystery, of the *mysterium tremendum*, even though, as several commentators have declared, woman does not always know how mysterious she is, or where the mystery lies. But at the same time, she is firmly realistic about women, knowing them from the inside, as George Eliot does. Halo continually ponders how she will 'keep' Vance, despite his fascination with her. And on the other hand, her men, like Vance, fail to be able to merge the ideal with the real, while sexual passion seems doomed to undermine the oceanic feeling of union, rather than enrich it. This, we suspect, is not only Vance's problem, it is that of his creator.

We can concur, when Edith Wharton tells us of Halo's marriage to Lewis, that 'Habit had wound its benumbing web about her, and she was no more the girl she had been than he was the man she had imagined. . .' (*HRB*, p. 174). But later there is a strange note when Vance is contemplating the possibility of a union with Halo, and finding a more adequate satisfaction than with his wife Lou:

> It was curious, though, how some substitution of values of which she held the secret caused this spiritual communion to bring them nearer then the embraces he had hungered for at the Willows. Or perhaps his recoil from the idea of combining physical endearments with such a communion was due to Laura Lou's persistent suspicion. He would have to dissociate sexual passion from all that had debased and cheapened it before it could blend with his vision of this woman who had understood and pitied him. . . . (*HRB*, p. 394)

The last sentence is puzzling. We know of no debasement or cheapening quality in Vance's sexual passion for Laura Lou; to where does this preoccupation come from? There is a suggestion in the paragraph that Laura Lou's suspicions might sully any physical union he might contemplate with Halo. But the words are strange—'debased and cheapened'—and they do not seem right in the context. It is as if Edith Wharton is revealing in herself a sense that sexual passion can debase and cheapen, of its very nature.

Halo, of course, is the ideal in *Hudson River Bracketted*: 'the quietness of that head supported statuelike on her smooth bare arm' (*HRB*, p. 394); 'She was the woman his arms longed for, but she was also the goddess, the miracle, the *unattainable being* who haunted the peaks of his imagination' (*HRB*, p. 421; my italics). In this novel, Halo resists his advances because she is married to another: 'Because I won't take a lover while I have a husband—or while my lover has a wife,' she said precipitately.

> A moment before his thoughts had enveloped her in a million caressing touches, soul had seemed to clasp soul as body would presently embrace body . . . now the other crowded grimacing world had pushed itself in, and between them stood Laura Lou and the sordid boarding house room. . . . (*HRB*, p. 423)

On Halo's part, she idealizes Vance in *Hudson River Bracketted;* she longs to bring Vance to the fruition of his genius: 'She could almost picture him, in some glorious phase of future achievement, flinging down his pen to cry out like a great predecessor, "My God, but this is genius—!" ' She is aware that her interest in him is intellectual:

> Her sympathy with him, she told herself again and again, was all intellectual; she was passionately in love with his mind. It was a pity that he had not understood this; had tried to mix up 'the other thing' with their intellectual ardours. (*HRB*, p. 463)

The phrase 'the other thing' is a strange way of referring to sex—somewhat childish, and this indicates something about Halo throughout both these novels and, indeed, also about Vance. The notions of inspiration and of love here, although written by a mature woman artist, have something childish about them.

Except, of course, for the touches of cynicism that show through, from time to time, when it is the elderly Edith Wharton talking directly to us:

> The intellectual divorce between them was increasingly bitter to Halo. *That the veil of passion must wear through was life's inescapable lesson*; but if no deeper understanding underlay it, what was left? (*GA*, p. 345; my italics)

> Don't we all make each other unhappy, sooner or later— often without knowing it? I sometimes think I've got beyond happiness or unhappiness—I don't feel as if I were made for them any more. I have nothing to complain of—or to regret. But I want to

> be alone; to go my own way, without depending on anybody. I want to be Halo Spear again—that's all. (*GA*, p. 368)

> Two women peopled these agitated vigils; the one that his soul rejected and his body yearned for, the other who had once seemed the answer to all he asked of life, but had now faded to a reproach and a torment. *The whole question of woman was the age-long* obstacle to peace of spirit and fruitfulness of mind; to get altogether away from it, contrive a sane and productive life without it, became the obsession of his sleepless midnights. All he wanted was to be himself, solely and totally himself, not tangled up in *the old deadly nets of passion and emotion.* (*GA*, p. 414; my italics)

In the end, of course, Vance comes back to Halo, and accepts dependence on another; and she declares: 'But then I shall have two children to take care of instead of one' (p. 439). So, it seems, to Edith Wharton, the committed love relationship is like that of mother to child: she fails to find the possibility of a mature and mutual adult relationship, between free individuals. Around Vance, it is as if she believes that the artist, who keeps open the child in himself, demands allowances appropriate only to a child.

Perhaps this is what Edith Wharton wanted to show, in her portrayal of Vance's relationship with Floss Delaney—'the one that his soul rejected and his body yearned for.' That account of the relationship, however, is not adequate either, because Vance has more than a sensual yearning for Floss; his soul is fascinated, too, and the author seeks to persuade us that what Vance hungers for in her is a deep instinctive vibration that will nourish his creativity. It is in this that the portrayal is confused.

With Halo, the predominance of emphasis is on her intelligence, her capacity to understand literature and creativity, and on her authenticity and loyalty. Insofar as Halo and Vance, like Anna and Vronsky, have to sustain an illicit relationship by passion, the woman is at a disadvantage because she has to rely on passion, and the anxiety affects the passion. Right at the beginning (*GA*, p. 63) she thinks, 'Whatever happens, I must keep him now.' '. . . would he weary of her, or would she be able to hold him?' (p. 85). Vance thinks,

'How did two people who had once filled each other's universe manage to hold together as the tide receded' (*GA*, p. 120).

> Why, by the world-old compulsion of marriage, he supposed. Marriage was a trick, a sham, if you looked at it in one way; but it was the only means man had yet devised for defending himself against his own frivolity. (*GA*, p. 120)

While Edith Wharton may be 'placing' Vance's inadequate attitudes, one suspects the low view is affected by her own experiences, not least the affair with Morton Fullerton.

At this moment Vance reflects on how one of his moody absences may have hurt Halo:

> There swept back upon him the physical and mental torture of his jealousy of Floss Delaney, the girl who had taught him the extremes of joy and pain, and he was oppressed by the thought that he might have made Halo suffer in the same way. (*GA*, p. 120)

Such thoughts, however, do not torment him enough as he becomes involved with Floss again.

Vance, we are told, displays 'the fine edge of a trained intelligence'. But in his being besotted with Floss there is no sign of this intelligence at work. The episode is one of deep moral interest. Halo, for example, feels sure that, in any encounter with Floss, 'the Vance she loved would have recoiled.' She is reading gossip columns, and is stunned to learn that he is associating with such people, while 'she, who had given him her life, sat alone, forgotten. . .' (p. 328).

Not only has Halo's inspiration flagged under the effects of habitual passion, however: 'communion with Halo had once been the completion of his dreams . . . now . . . she was the obstacle that arrested them. . . .'

Edith Wharton may have intended to deepen her enigma, by giving us a woman to tempt Vance who would be merely sensual. Floss, indeed, is totally uninterested in Vance's work: 'I never was much on books.' She says to him, 'I came to see you and not your book'—but all she is interested in is his réclame, if, that is, it can be of use to her.

But where Edith Wharton goes seriously wrong is in making Floss a woman who (to Vance) embodies the *participation mystique*: she is not merely beautiful and seductive, she is a source of spiritual inspiration for Vance. And this is bound up with his mixed feelings of worship and looking for her:

> She had appeared, in that opulent environment, neither rarer nor lovelier than when, as a raw boy, he had worshipped and loathed her in the maple-grove at Crampton. . . . (*GA*, p. 264)

> . . . the common unimaginative girl who had captivated the untried boy exercised the same spell over the young man from whom a world of experience divided her. That was the dangerpoint. (*GA*, p. 264)

It is this fixation, surely, that must make us feel that we cannot accept Vance's 'fine intelligence'. After his experience of the sad marriage with Laura Lou, her death, and his commitment to Halo, he seems to have learned nothing, in that he continues to behave still like the 'untried boy'? Well, it is true that people do behave so: but can we believe that Vance would still be so *spiritually* besotted? We can accept a man who felt that 'The sound of any name connected with Floss Delaney's set all his wires humming' (*GA*, p. 282).

But can we continue to sympathize, or even take a continuing interest, in a man who, even after so many evidences of the hardheartedness of Floss ('in her hardening eyes and narrowed lips he detected the reflection of the lean years at Crampton. . .'), continues to see Floss as 'the archway to the Infinite' (p. 210)?

The weaknesses here are manifest in the lapse of language, the decline into what we may call Scott Fitzgeraldese:

> In the days when Floss Delaney had so enraptured and tortured him, she had never had any real identity to his untaught heart and senses: she had been simply undifferentiated woman: now for the first time he saw her as an individual, *and perceived her peculiar loveliness.* (*GA*, p. 210; my italics)

We can accept that Undine Spragg is *beautiful*, but no one could call her *lovely*. Although Floss is seen through Vance's eyes, in the account the author gives, as with Fitzgerald's view of the world 'through' Gatsby, the language takes on the conventionalities of the ad man's glitz. It seems to be a strange thing to say about Edith Wharton, but in Vance she seems to become involved in a fascination with 'glamour':

> After all her face had not changed: it had the same mid-summer afternoon look, as though her penthouse hair were the shade of a forest, her eyes its secret pools. A still windless face, suggesting the note of stock-doves, the hum of summer insects . . . her body had grown slenderer yet rounder. . . . (*GA*, p. 212)

The author even allows her hero to make unflattering comparisons with Halo:

> Halo had fine lines, but was too thin, the bones in her neck were too visible; this girl, who must have been about the same age, and had the same Diana-like curve from shoulder to hip, was more rounded, and her hands were smaller and plumper than Halo's, though not so subtle and expressive.
>
> Vance was glad that he could take note of all this, could even calmly compare Floss Delaney's appearance with that of the woman he loved; it proved his emotional detachment, and made him feel safe and at his ease. (*GA*, p. 212)

—but it does not put the reader at his ease, for here Vance is clearly not in a state of disturbed infatuation but coldly and coolly exercising his 'fine intelligence' to discriminate against the woman who loves him and to whom he is committed, while the author seems to have lost her capacity to discriminate between one woman and another.

It is true that, when the fireworks go off over the Casino around the moon, it is Halo's face he sees in the sky:

> he saw that she too changed colour with the change of lights, turning now blush-red, now gold, now pearl, like a goddess who reddens and pales because Acteon has looked at her. . . . Somehow that wondering moon, going her cool way alone, yet blushing and faltering in the tangle of earth lights, suddenly reminded him of Halo. (*GA*, p. 225)

The words 'wondering moon' perhaps recall Coleridge's 'wandering moon' from the *Ancient Mariner*, so that Halo here is symbolically the Earth Mother.

But, by contrast, it is the very bitterness he associates with Floss Delaney that fascinates Vance. She is obviously having liaisons, or conducting tempting escapades, with several men, and Vance is jealous:

> A wave of jealousy buzzed in Vance's ears. Jealousy could outlive love, the, cling to it like a beast of prey to a carcase for which it no longer hungered? He have never loved Floss, in the sense in which he now understood loving: and he imagined that his fugitive passion had long since turned to loathing. . . . (*GA*, p. 230)

Yet he cannot shake off the torment, even though 'she was less than nothing to him.' 'But the idea that other men coveted her made his flesh burn though his heart was cold' (*GA*, p. 230).

There is certainly something very strange about Vance's fascination with Floss, for (as we have seen) the powerful theme which flows throughout the book is that she offered him at first a promiscuous adolescent adventure at the Willows, in which experience he found he was sharing her with his grandfather. Yet even to recall this painful and horrible experience at a later moment of intimacy brings 'the old glory' flooding in.

> 'Van, don't be cross. I was the first, wasn't I? Say you remember.'
>
> 'I remember well enough the day I saw you down there with—somebody else,' he said in a choking voice.
>
> 'Oh, Van—' she swung suddenly round on him. 'All I remember is the days I was there with you. . . . Those first days.' . . . Her bare arms were about him, her lips on his. The old glory flooded him, and everything was full of bells chiming, and stars dancing through wind-swayed trees. . . . (*GA*, p. 238)

She promises 'tomorrow', but tomorrow fobs him off. She is evasive, and lies. She is promiscuous still, a whore, really. And Vance feels disgust.

> The residue of it all was a sick disgust, a revolt from life such as he felt when he had seen her down by the river with his grandfather. *She seemed to distil a poison such as no other woman secreted*: his veins were so heavy with it that he felt like a man recovering from a long illness. (*GA*, p. 244)

But the depiction has something *corrupt* about it: Floss's brown shoulders flash 'like a Dryad's in the Fontainbleu woods. . . .' '. . . whenever he shut his eyes there was her bare arm, like amber in the moonlight: the touch of it burned in him.'

And so, despite indication after indication that Floss is calculating, unscrupulous, duplicitous and poisonous, Vance continues to pursue her. When Vance reflects on his experiences of the two women the account is strangely loaded against Halo:

> He merely felt that, in Laura Lou's case, the irritating friction of familiarity had made separation impossible, while in regard to himself and Halo, their perpetual mutual insistence on not being a burden to each other, on scrupulously respecting each other's freedom, had somehow worn the tie thin instead of strengthening it. This was certainly the case as far as he was concerned, and Halo appeared to share his view. Splendid and generous as she had been when he had come to her with his unhappy confession, their last weeks at Oubli seemed to have made it as clear to her as to him that their experiment had reached its term. . . . (*GA*, p. 375)

And so, back to Floss, in Euphoria, where (significantly) he meets her on the very *divan where he had seen his grandfather lying after a stroke*. She is conducting a deal with 'young Shunts', but promises Vance something, and Vance actually thinks of *proposing* to Floss.

> With Floss Delaney it would be different. Certain obscure fibres in both their natures seemed inextricably entangled. There was a dumb subterranean power in her that corresponded with his own sense of *the forces by which his inventive faculty was fed*. (*GA*, p. 385; my italics)

And at last he is unfaithful with Floss; again, we have a language like Scott Fitzgerald at his most *New-Yorker-ish*:

> And after that everything melted again into a golden blur of heat and wine and crowding, out of which Floss Delaney detached herself, firm and vivid, and while Mrs. Alsop's guests scattered in a sudden snow-fall, and the Dakin Blackbirds scuttled away with raised coat-collars under the leafless elms, Vance had found himself in a motor at her side, twisting down the new road from the height, crossing the bridge, gliding through the snow-white streets to the hotel, and descending there at a mysterious side-door ('I gave the reception clerk my ticket for the lecture—and here's his private key', she said with a little laugh'). (*GA*, p. 388)

Their hours are of 'tormenting ecstasy': 'Everything drew him on to a dark future shot with wild lightnings of hope.' 'New York was all she wanted now', and she is sure of it if only she could pull off her deal. She is calculating on the social value of his young celebrity. But Vance persists in trying to make with her a 'turning point in his life, a meeting on which his whole future depended'.

He has, as I have said, little or no remorse over Halo, or regret that what has come to pass must cause her pain.

> It was as if he could justify his break with Halo only by creating for himself a new tie, more binding, more unescapable. He would have felt ashamed to admit that anything but the need to stabilize his life, to be in harmony again with himself and his work, could have forced him to such a step. (*GA*, p. 389)

He surely sinks at this point well beyond any reader's sympathy: a 'fine intelligence', indeed, not to see what hands he has put himself in, not to see the difference between Halo and Floss, to actually expect Halo to understand:

> Halo had seen that, he ws sure: she had understood it. If he was to follow his calling *he must be protected from the sterile agitation of these last years.* Marriage and a home: normal conditions: that was what he craved. . . . (*GA*, p. 389; my italics)

Vance is not a philanderer; but he is surely craven, for nothing could be more despicable than pleading one's 'calling' when acting in such craven ways, a betrayal of himself and the woman who truly loves him—and has given her life for him.

To our incredulous eyes, Edith Wharton pursues a justification which is not (alas) only her character's:

> Floss Delaney seemed to personify the strong emotional stimulant on which his intellectual life must feed. *Intellectual companionship between lovers was unattainable; that was not the service women could render to men.* (*GA*, p. 390; my italics)

For Edith Wharton, of all people to tell us that!—And it is not *placed.*

> But the old mysterious bond of blood which seemed to exist between certain human beings, which youth sought for blindly, and maturity continued restlessly to crave—that must be the secret soil in which alone the artist's faculty could ripen. . . . (*GA*, p. 390)

Yet he *knows* what Floss is like:

> He knew that Floss would always be what she was—he could no more influence or shape her than he could bend or shape a marble statue. But he needed her . . . and out of that double need there might come a union so deep rooted and instinctive that neither, having once known it, could do without it. *Perhaps that was what his grandmother had in mind when she said marriage made people sacred to one another.* . . . (*GA*, p. 390; my italics)

—yet his grandmother had been cuckolded by Floss Delaney herself!

In such connections, surely, we must find a strange confusion in these two novels. Is she speaking from herself, or showing Vance's distortions, when she writes: 'Intellectual comradeship between lovers was unattainable: *that was not the service women could render to men*'? (*GA*, p. 390; my italics). She is at pains to make Vance's attraction to Floss out a mere matter of superficial adventurism:

> He saw it all now, looked on it *with the wide-open eyes of passion and disillusionment.* A few years ago he would have plunged into the adventure blindly, craving only the repetition of its dark raptures. But not it seemed to him that *while his senses flamed his intelligence remained cool.* (*GA*, p. 390; my italics)

> He must make her see that they belonged to one another, that they were necessary to one another. . . . He meant to plead with her, reason with her, *dominate her with the full strength of his will.* (p. 390–91; my italics)

While Edith Wharton intended to place Vance's aberration, she surely confuses us here, because Vance's intelligence is not shown to be engaged in his perception of Floss, and his eyes are not opened, by doubt or disillusionment or anything else. When he is continually played like a stupid fish by this monstrous and cold-blooded woman, how could he suppose he could 'dominate her with the full strength of his will'?

She fails, that is, to 'realise' the inner state of a man. Of course, men do suffer from delusions, as (say) in Thomas Hardy's *The Well-Beloved,* that mysterious novel about idealizing projections. Or we may take *Othello*—but it may perhaps be said that there is in this novel, by contrast with *Othello,* a failure to penetrate to the problem of vulnerable dependence: 'When I love thee not, chaos is come again'.

> Alas that we may call these delicate creatures ours
> But not their appetites.

Supposed to be a genius with a fine intelligence, Vance has none of Othello's sensitivity and vulnerability, despite the monstrous delusion into which the Moor is ensnared. Vance remains an adolescent: 'there were moments when the mere fact of being in the same room with Floss, of watching her enjoyment and the admiration she excited, was enough to satisfy him' (*GA*, p. 395). She speaks of 'when I'm married'; he replies 'Have you decided on the man?'—'his heart giving a thump'. Her reply is coldly calculating: 'Do you suppose I'm going to risk having to hang around some day and whine for alimony. . .' (*GA*, p. 396).

'I wish your new novel wasn't so dreadfully long', she goes on. She is now 'impatient of his tenderness' and is 'on the verge of being bored by his importunities'—so, it seems, after the secret tryst in the hotel, they no longer have sexual relations. What man, then, would still hang around such a woman like a servile dog? Even if we accept that 'most artists are incurably polygamous' and that Vance is caught in the 'deadly net of passion and emotion'. The scales do not fall from Vance's eyes until (like Peter Van Degan in *The Custom of the Country*) he perceives in unmistakable clarity that this woman is ruthlessly immoral and virtually criminal in her fraudulent manipulations.

She is determined to outwit the Shuntses and 'make them buy her out at her own price' (*GA*, p. 399). We are back in the harsh world of Euphoria real-estate dealing. She is trying to gain her end by captivating young Shunts: 'they were even reported to be engaged.' (Vance, though troubled by this, tries to believe that 'he was sure to cut out so poor a creature as young Shunts.') Vance still hopes to marry her!

He meets Frenside, who asks him if he has any message for Halo (Frenside knows Halo is pregnant and is waiting for Vance). The encounter brings 'Halo back to him as a living suffering creature', when his memories of Halo 'had taken on the mournful serenity of death'. His response, again, is childish:

> For months he had been trying to shut his eyes and ears . . . as sometimes, in camp as a boy, when he heard a trapped animal crying at night far off in the woods, he would bury his head under the blankets and try to think the wail had ceased because he had closed his ears against it. . . . *Ah, well, no use going back to all that now.* (*GA*, p. 402; my italics)

The last lame phrase is the kind of flabby response Edith Wharton attributes to her hero which makes it impossible for us to sympathize with him.

Vance becomes jealous, when Floss does not turn up to a dinner party. So, he seeks her out.

> She lay curled up on a lounge, in a soft velvet wrapper, her hair tossed back, her feet in gossamer stockings and heelless sandals, peeping out . . . her fur cloak, a withered cluster of orchids pinned to it, had been flung across the piano beside an unwatered and half-dead azalea from which the donor's card still dangled. . . . (*GA*, p. 403)

The scene ('squalid in its luxury') is written with pointed irony, revealing that Floss's voluptuousness is directed at cupidity and power. 'Floss had none of Halo Tarrant's gift for making a room seem a part of herself—unless indeed this cold disorder did reflect something akin to her own character' (*GA*, p. 403). She greets Vance with a happy purr, all the same; she lies 'brooding, a faint tremor on lips and eyelids'. She almost supposed Vance is a co-conspirator, as if he would share her excitement at overcoming others, in which she finds passionate satisfaction; 'there was a veiled radiance in her face which he had seen in it only once or twice, in momento of passionate surrender' (*GA*, p. 403). 'Vance,' she tells him, 'I've pulled it off. The cheque's locked up in my bank.' The Shuntses have paid her price, and she waits for his approval, 'which was her due'. We have an appalling sense that in giving himself to Floss, in betrayal of Halo, he has conspired in the evil spirit of concupisence. Floss has never met him in any way, except in the conspiracy of squalid luxury and indulgent excitement, in which lust and acquisitiveness are combined.

He even supposes that now she is free—has his moment come? He sees she wants to exult in her triumph.

She is busy for 'that poor boy', Honoré Shunts. She has asked him back after going out to dinner with him: 'he wouldn't listen to reason: but he had to. I never saw anybody cry so I told him I couldn't stand it—it was unmanly of him. . .' (*GA*, p. 404). But Honoré has not been crying because she has refused his advances. Floss has used his letters to blackmail the family, into accepting her price.

> She had held the socially ambitious Shuntses through the boy's letters: she had forced them to buy up her land at her own price through their dread lest the heir to their millions should marry her. . . . (*GA*, p. 405)

There had been nothing difficult about it but the boy's crying: 'She had thought that unmanly; an obvious warning to Vance not to repeat the same mistake. . .' (*GA*, p. 405).

She is, that is, a whore—or, really, worse than a whore, since her price is not one exacted for sexual services, but a gain achieved by hard-bitten bitchery, whereby she employs her seductive powers and blackmail, using the foulest emotional duplicity, to acquire property. Yet she cannot bear the signs of the distress she causes. 'Floss always liked the people about her to be cheerful, he knew that. *And after all perhaps she was right*. . .' (*GA*, p. 405; my italics). The italicized phrase, must surely lower our estimation of Vance: he only gradually comes to find a moral indignation in himself because he 'seemed to feel those tears in his own throat'. Like Van Degan, he now thinks, 'she might do this to me!'—but she *has* been doing it to him all along and he has not understood the implications.

'He's just a spoilt baby and I told him so': this is Floss's only response to the heir's distress.

> 'Ah—you told him so.' He stood looking down on her, remarking for the first time that her cheek-bones were too high, that they gave her a drawn and grimacing look he had never before noticed. He thought: 'This is the way she talked about me to the fellow who kept her at Dakin.' (*GA*, p. 405)

Vance continues to resist the recognition that she is 'like that':

> She was not really like that—he couldn't endure the thought that she was like that. She must constantly do something to disprove it, to drag him up out of the *black nightmare of his contempt for her*. (*GA*, p. 406; my italics)

Her response is petulant and repulsive in the contempt it reveals for 'men'—again, the response of the whore: 'I did my duty, that's all. It isn't always a pleasant job—*and you men don't generally make it easier for us*. . .' (*GA*, p. 406; my italics). She brushes him away, like a tired whore: 'You can come back tomorrow, if you'll try to treat me a little more politely. . . . So long, dear' (*GA*, p. 406). But we can only feel he is seriously bewitched, not to have divined, ages before, that Floss's beautiful mask hid a cruel and corrupt harpy. But (as the next page reminds us), this is the same woman whose earliest duplicities in his sexual life had nearly brought him to shoot himself with his father's revolver. 'Nothing mattered—nothing would ever again matter. . .' (p. 407).

He is in a state of 'moral wreckage', and now the presence of Halo begins to seem to haunt him, as if he were 'watching her between closed lids, like a sick man'. Our response, I believe, is to feel that Vance is even more unsatisfactory as he turns now for comfort to the Halo he has so stupidly betrayed.

Grandmother Scrimser is dying; her last message to him is, 'Maybe we haven't made enough of pain—been too afraid of it. . . .' He goes off to a camp at Bel Air: such vagaries are too often, in these books, presented as the restless signs of 'genius'. He returns to the Willows, which (unknown to him) is being restored by Halo for herself.

Vance seems to her as if he were dead when Frenside reminds her of him. But 'The first weeks after Vance had gone to America had been a dark blur of pain' (*GA*, p. 429). She had attained a degree of equinamity because of her child, which is the future. She wants her child born at the Willows. We are reminded that Halo is unmarried, and so the arrival of the baby will represent a 'fling at society'.

Frenside speaks to Halo about Vance, in the above-quoted reference to *Dichterliebe* ('Most artists are incurably polygamous'):

> When they're not it's because they die young—and their books generally do too. But I don't know that their loving so lavishly matters as much in itself as in what it makes of them; what sort of stuff they turn into. I don't pretend to know yet what Weston's going to turn into. (*GA*, p. 433)

Perhaps this speech gives us the clue to what is wrong with the two books under consideration—an absurd idea of 'genius' and what is due to it. Are we to believe that Edith Wharton really found this view satisfactory? Frenside is surely an embodiment of 'liberal wisdom' close to hers? She may have been thinking of Dostoevsky, with his succession of loves; but if one reads biographical material on Dostoevsky, there is nothing like the stupid fascination of Vance with Floss Delaney, only a sense of him growing in spiritual stature with each devotion. It is difficult to believe that Vance Weston learns anything from any of his liaisons.

If only we could feel that Vance would turn into anything new, by his experiences. No sooner have we thought that than he appears in the hallway of the Willows, thin and changed: his face with 'All its boyishness . . . gone; it was drawn and stern, like that of a man who has been through some inward ordeal which makes everything else remote' (*GA*, p. 434).

He wants to tell her he is never coming back.

> 'I must pull myself together first, make something out of myself, be worth something. . . .'
>
> 'I've got no will and purpose. . . . I wanted to come back some day, though I didn't know whether you'd ever have me. . . . I'm burnt out; I'm just cinders. (*GA*, p. 436)

Halo's scruples are 'borne down by a fresh wave of solicitude'. He says, 'I've been down in hell, and I wanted to see the stars again. . .' (*GA*, p. 437). There seems an impenetrable barrier between them. But Halo is not capable (as was Floss) of subterfuge, or women's tricks. Boldly she asks him: '. . . when you say you're not sure of yourself, are you thinking of Floss Delaney? I've got a right to ask that, you know' (*GA*, p. 437).

She wonders whether she has committed a folly in touching on this wound, as 'a painful contraction passed over his face'. She tells him Floss is married: he did not know, and he turns pale at the news, then 'it's nothing to me . . . I said goodbye to her long before.' A great weight lifts from Halo's heart, 'but in another moment it descended on her again, this time with a more intolerable oppression. . . . "A real goodbye, Vance? Are you sure?" ' (*GA*, p. 438). The exchange is superficial and fails to be realized, bedevilled as it is by that spurious concept of 'genius' and its need to be indulged. Halo is presented with a little more spirit at this moment, but she is not as tormented by bitter jealousy and hatred as she would be in reality. He is not repentant and seems insufficiently imbued with the contempt and loathing which the discovery of Floss Delany's revolting unscrupulousness should have generated in him, had he the integrity and intelligence claimed for him. Instead, what matters, it seems, is the harm her unmasking has done to his *Weltanschauung*: 'She took something with her; my belief in things, my old reasons for living and working. It's as if my mainspring was broken. I've got to get it mended first. . .' (*GA*, p. 438). Again, he is too feeble: the reader must surely feel outraged, for Halo in the past did everything to provide the callow uncultivated writer with a mainspring. Yet now, after his disloyal infatuation, he is leaning towards her to 'mend' him, on the grounds that Floss has let him down!

With a gesture of passionate entreaty he turns to her: 'Don't you see, Halo—*can't* you see? I can't come back to you just because I'm at the end of everything. To any other woman—not to you. . .' (*GA*, p. 438). At least he says 'the only strength left to me is the strength not to pretend, or to invent lying reasons.' But then she challenges him: 'if you say no, it must be because I'm less to you than any other woman, and not more. . .' (*GA*, p. 438). All Vance can say is 'you're different.' And the book ends with painfully inept banalities:

> I read something up there in the woods about God . . . or experience . . . it's the same thing . . . being the food of the full grown. . . . That seemed to explain a lot to me. I'm not fit for you Halo; I'm only just learning how to walk. . . . (*GA*, p. 439)

It is, almost, Hollywood. Perhaps there is hope in his humility. Perhaps there is strength in their mutual recognition of their dependence on one another, for an 'instinct' has drawn him home to her. She indicates her pregnancy by saying, 'But then I shall have two children to take care of instead of one!' But, to be realistic, we all find it hard to believe that the pregnancy will solve any problems in this relationship, while to suppose it will unite them is an overworked convention of sentimental literature.

> 'You see we belong to each other after all,' she said; but as her arms sank about his neck he bent his head and put his lips to the fold of her loose dress. (*GA*, p. 439)

This is simple and touching, and indicates presumably a new respect and even adoration in him. But for the reader there is something repugnant in the way he so belatedly makes up to the woman he has so grossly failed to appreciate and value, and accepts the rôle of being her 'child'.

So, overall, one respects Edith Wharton for attempting to show the conflict in a creative artist between his need of the spiritual in woman and the sensual. But the course of the novel becomes confused, for it seems Vance's relationship with Halo goes dead because of her very devotion on the one hand and the habitual passion of cohabitation on the other hand, while the attraction of Floss Delaney is not her beauty and sensuality but her very failure as a woman: her cold evil and bitch-like behaviour, even her history as one who committed adultery, disgustingly, with Vance's grandfather. Her inspirational effect on Vance is described in terms of some transcendent magic rather than of the misuse of charm; and while Edith Wharton strives to 'place' Vance's weaknesses, the same proclivity for glamour that she shares at times with Scott Fitzgerald undermines her insights, and as a result she cannot make her 'genius' hero into anything than a fool and a blockhead. He loses inspirational status himself: one cannot but feel his novels must be awful, since he displays nothing of the sensitive and subtle intelligence of Halo and remains a weak, stupid and irresponsible man—like, alas, so many of Edith Wharton's men do. If Vance is the best she can do, we cannot help feeling that it was characteristic that she can never have encountered a man worthy of respect, as a sexual partner.

The scenes in both these novels between men and women are bedevilled by Edith Wharton's preconceptions about 'woman's rôle' on the one hand and her strangely romantic concept of a 'creative genius' on the other. At times, however, she continues to display her powers as an artist. There is one scene, in Chapter XIV of *The Gods Arrive,* between men, which is superb and is truly 'Jamesian' in its power.

Vance wants to talk to Halo's husband Tarrant, to plead with him to divorce her. He accosts him by chance in the street; he looks 'paler and older'.

> 'Tarrant!' he said. 'I—I want to speak to you . . . I must.'
> Tarrant turned under his umbrella, and surveyed him with astonishment. 'I don't—' he began: then Vance saw the colour rush to his pale face. '*You*?' he said. 'I've nothing to say to you.' (*GA*, p. 142)

Nothing is clear-cut: it is a muddle, as the two men stand confronting each other in the rain. Vance is even capable of pity for the man and admiration for the way he pulls himself together to take hold of the situation.

> Vance felt a secret admiration for the man whose worldly training had given him this discipline: he knew what mental and physical distress Tarrant underwent after such an effort of the will. 'Poor devil,' he thought . . . 'we're all poor devils. . . .' (*GA*, p. 144)

The movements of the men are clearly and exactly delineated, and for once we can believe that Vance has sensitivity and intelligence: he is aware of Tarrant's 'moral disarray'. Come to think of it, the scene has the same quality of rivetting the reader's attention to the suffering of the characters that Saul Bellow often achieves in his unhappy novel *Herzog*.

Vance notices that the edge of Tarrant's thinly cut nostril is 'white and drawn up, like that of a man in pain': ' "After all, I suppose he did love her once," Vance thought' (*GA*, p. 146). There is a feeling that the men are united by their suffering: 'You're wet through,' says Tarrant, who gradually becomes aware of the reality of the man.

Vance sees that Tarrant is trying to preserve his 'real self'. And, as so often with George Eliot, the characters reach the theme of suffering. Vance declares it is 'hell' to see a woman suffering, '. . . because you can't give her the place in your life that she ought to have. . . . That's what I came here to tell you. . .' (*GA*, p. 149). Tarrant replies:

> 'In my opinion she ought to suffer. . . .'
> 'Why—because you do?'
> Tarrant was silent, and Vance pressed on: 'There's such a lot of suffering everywhere; what's the use of adding to it? . . .' (*GA*, p. 149)

Vance for once is aware of the moral subtleties of the confrontation—'Here they stood, he reflected, two poor devils caught in the toil of human incomprehension. . .' (*GA*, p. 150)—and he is aware how awful Tarrant will feel when he leaves him. When Tarrant continues to refuse a divorce, Vance reflects, 'I can remember when I used to think he was a great fellow.'

And the final line of the scene is very Jamesian: ' "Ah—you poor man," Vance thought, as he turned and left him' (*GA*, p. 151). This is the essence of the novel as an art form, and it has a choric quality of being portrayed by a sensitive and insightful intelligence; it comes to life, as the characters interact, as art. And in this Vance's musings on what is happening show a novelist insights, such as he disastrously does not display, in his interactions with the women of the novel. So, it is in delineating man in his dealings with woman that Edith Wharton seems to fall short in this novel.

Another great scene in these two novels is the death of Laura Lou, in which the man she was once destined to marry plays a prominent part—Bunty Hayes, who actually closes her eyes, and afterwards kneels to pray, 'Oh God, yes, I do forgive her!' Vance takes his hand, and they walk out of the room together. The attraction between Hayes and Vance is not unlike the relationship so strikingly achieved by D. H. Lawrence in *Sons and Lovers*, between Paul Morel and Baxter Dawes. Again, where men are in conflict over woman, Edith Wharton can find her creative strength. Strangely, where she seems to become confused is when her man of 'genius' is trying to find a satisfactory woman to inspire and guide him.

Here she is continually undermined by a belief that her hero cannot merge mind and sensuality. Vance, in *Hudson River Bracketted*, goes to Halo as 'the one confidante of his literary projects', and at one point (*HRB*, p. 394) surpasses himself by bursting out at her about his private life. But he feels a *recoil* at the idea of mingling their shared intellectual interests with passion:

> It was curious, though, how some substitution of values of which she held the secret caused this spiritual communion to bring them nearer than the embraces he had hungered for at the Willows. Or perhaps his recoil from the idea of combining physical endearment with such a communion was due to Laura Lou's persistent suspicion. (*HRB*, p. 394)

Halo is a statuesque *unattainable* woman: 'the quietness of that head supported statue-like on her smooth bare arm' . . . 'she was also the goddess, the miracle, the unattainable being who haunted the peaks of his imagination' (*HRB*, p. 421).

Associated with this problem of the emotional and sexual life, in these late novels is a characteristic American idea of what literary creativity is—a literary idea with a capital 'L'. It appears in this passage:

> Vance raised himself on his elbow. 'See here,' he broke out, 'what I really want is to write poetry. From the very first I've always felt inside of myself that for me it was that or nothing. All the rest is just pot-boiling. Using words to tell stories is like paving the kitchen floor with diamonds. God! Words are too beautiful to be walked over in that way, with muddy feet, like the hall oilcloth. Supposing Keats had used *his* words to write best-sellers with. Don't it strike you like turning a knights of Pythias picnic loose down there in the cathedral? Words ought to be renewed at the door of the mind with lighted torches and incense and things—like one of the big church ceremonies you described to me. See here, Halo—when did you say they danced before the altar at Seville? I wish I could get that into poetry.' (*GA*, p. 40)

Edith Wharton goes on to speak of 'the bright confusion of his mind', and makes Halo see his impulses as 'capricious': so, Edith Wharton is placing this uneducated genius from Euphoria. But yet her own attitudes to Keats and poetry come through and show themselves to be limited by a characteristic 'great writers of the world' mentality, just as later she throws together 'Chartres, the Parthenon and the

Pyramids'. With her immense experience of places, and the wide range of her interests in architecture and gardens, it is extraordinary how naïve she could be, in her account of the creative life, in these last two novels.

# 7

# *The Mother's Recompense*; *The Fruit of the Tree*; *Twilight Sleep*; *The Buccaneers*; *The Children*

We now come to a number of works in which the incest theme is strong. *The Mother's Recompense* is a bitter story with a theme that is close to incest and most revealing. Kate Clephane, a mother of 45, is shown to be living in a third-rate hotel in the South of France. She left an unsatisfactory marriage some eighteen years before, when her daughter was aged 3. After taking a trip on a yacht with one Hylton Davies, she later had an affair with Chris Trenno, who seems a somewhat ambivalent man, her relationship with whom broke up after a few years. She is now living alone, and receives a telegram declaring 'Mrs. Clephane dead . . .' and inviting her to go to New York to live with her daughter, who is now 21. She gradually realizes that 'Mrs. Clephane' refers to her late husband's second wife, although there is a resonance that begins to sound in her mind that she herself is dead or, rather, lives on the verge of being nothing.

She goes to New York and establishes a close and tender relationship with her daughter Anne, and with some of the middle-aged people she used to know as the wife of John Clephane. These include Fred Landers, who seems fond of her.

But by degrees she discovers that Chris Trenno, who lives

in Baltimore, has established a relationship with her own daughter. He did not know, when he embarked upon this affair, who Anne was, and he tries to resist his inclinations when he does find out; but now the liaison seems irrevocable, as Anne loves him deeply.

The whole story thus revolves round the question of how Kate Clephane can oppose the marriage, and whether or not she can tell her daughter. In the end she compromises, gives her daughter away in marriage, and flees from New York, even from Fred Landers, who would have married her—even though she tells him she has been the lover of her daughter's bridegroom. She flees back to the little English–American colony in the South of France.

This is the story. But the intensity of feeling behind it has obvious connections with the author's life. Trenno is, in one respect, Morton Fullerton; this man brought sexual meaning into Kate's life, as Fullerton did into Edith's:

> For the first time, when she met him, her soul's lungs seemed full of air. Life still dated for her from that day—in spite of the way he had hurt her, of his having inflicted on her the bitterest pain she had ever suffered, he had given her more than he could take away. *At thirty-nine her real self had been born; without him she would never have had a self.* . . . And yet, at what a cost she had bought it. (*MR*, p. 18; my italics)*

But the book is dominated by a greater horror, the horror of the mother being faced with the daughter's sexual knowledge of a man who is in the father's position since he has in the past been the mother's passionate partner. If we are realistic, we could suppose such a situation would be one with which an individual might well come to terms. But with Edith Wharton there is a tendency for her to become obsessed with themes in which there is an unspeakable relationship—as between Lawyer Royall and Charity, or between Martin Boyne and Judith, or between the father in *Twilight Sleep* and his daughter-in-law:

> She seemed hardly to be suffering more than she had suffered then. It had seemed unbearable, impossible, at the moment that Christ Trenno should enter, even so episodically, so

* References are to the Virago edition.

> remotely, into her new life; and here he was, esconced in its very centre, in complete possession of it. . . .
>
> Every one to whom she had tried to communicate her secret without betraying it had had the same instantaneous revulsion. 'Not that—don't tell me that!' their averted eyes, their shrinking voices seemed to say. *It was too horrible for any ears. (MR, pp. 268–69; my italics)*

If I am correct in my conjectures, this was the horror that Edith Wharton lived with. When Kate Clephane sees Chris and Anne looking at the white virginal wedding gown, she is overcome:

> Jealous? Was she jealous of her daughter? Was she physically jealous? Was that the real secret of her repugnance, her instinctive revulsion? *Was that why she had felt from the first as if some incestuous horror hung between them?* (*MR*, p. 279; my italics)

In truth, there is nothing incestuous about the relationship between Chris Trenno and Anne. He is a man of 31 and she is 21; they are not related and the only obstacle could be that he has had a brief affair with the girl's mother. But the dread and horror, the scruples about telling, the agony of mind of Kate Clephane have, I believe, roots in Edith Wharton's secret dread of her own relationship, as a child, with her own father. She is imagining what it might have been like for her own mother had she known:

> She did not know—it was impossible to analyse her anguish. She only knew she must fly from it, fly as far as she could from the setting of these last indelible impressions. . . . She must put the world between them—the whole width of the world was not enough. The very grave, she thought, would be hardly black enough to blot out that scene. (*MR*, p. 279)

Such intensity of dread and horror is surely superfluous to the real situation of the novel, and has its roots in Edith Wharton's own agony.

*The Fruit of the Tree* has some good moments, but overall fails as a novel. Like Bessy, the mill-owner's wife, Edith Wharton finds herself out of her depth in trying to present working-class life or, even, the life of the nurse, Justine. The novel is, however, extremely painful to read and is, in the end, disquieting. Throughout, John Amherst's idealism is thwarted, and his attempt to join together his ambitions for the mill and his love for his woman never comes to fruition. Bessy turns out to be unrealistic when it comes to paying for the reforms he seeks to introduce, and does not expect to reduce her life-style to meet his radical aims. She is not as interested in the welfare of the workers who provide her income as John Amherst is—and, indeed, we cannot help seeing his proposed reforms as inadequate, in the face of the 'system'.

All the same, the reader is unhappy when the couple become estranged, and more so when, in a fit of defiance of her husband's prohibitions on riding, Bessy is thrown by her horse and suffers a lingering and painful death from damage to her spine. Throughout the novel a continuity of detachment is given by a somewhat Jamesian pair, Mrs. Ansell and Mr. Longhope, Bessy's lawyer, who discuss the affair with what seems to be almost villainous pragmatism.

Bessy's suffering is relieved by Justine who eventually deliberately gives her an overdose of morphine. Then, by degrees, Justine herself becomes the object of John Amherst's attentions, and marries him. However, one Dr. Wyant, who is a drug addict and also attracted to Justine, knows that she is guilty of euthanasia and blackmails her. By degrees the story, that John Amherst and Justine were lovers before Bessy's accident, comes out and is compounded by people's suspicions. Bessy decides to go away, after promising Bessy's father that she will do so, but she goes without telling her husband. But when he learns of her renunciation of him, he searches for her and they are reunited.

But at the end of the book, when he is speaking at the opening of a new gymnasium for the workers, he speaks of the degree of support for these new projects that he had obtained from his previous wife—which misrepresentation appalls Justine. She, however, finds she cannot speak out against the lie and compromises, thus totally falsifying her relationship with her husband and herself. They opt to live on a plane of compromise hereafter.

Behind this clever plot we can surely see that there is an unconscious undercurrent in this novel—of getting rid of Mother, so that the protagonist can marry the youthful figure who is nearer to the author. In its preoccupation with financial lack of realism and with compromise in marriage, this novel would seem also to draw on Edith Wharton's experience of Teddy and his adventurism, while the painful development of events conveys the author's disillusionment with life.

Throughout her work Edith Wharton has a particular attitude to the father and to incest by the father which is astonishingly endorsing of that kind of act. We may even, I believe, detect that in her own childhood, at the moment when a growing human being learns moral values from the parent, she was taught by her own experience that, even though guilty of such abuse, the father must be 'right'; she must, that is, preserve the 'good father' in spite of his offence—an effort that must distort all her views of sexuality.

In *Twilight Sleep,* we have I believe a glimpse of this process at work. The anti-heroine is the mother Pauline, who is devoted to ignoring and denying pain, and who pursues endless trivial obsessions to avoid reality. She falsifies everything, even by coming to believe her own fantasies, and by seeking to make everything seem good and proper, when it is not. She seems clearly to be based on Edith's own mother. She has a first husband, Arthur (called by the family 'Exhibit A'), and they have a son, Jim. Jim is married to Lita, and much in love with her. Lita however is bored by Jim. Pauline asks her to stay, to try to help overcome the crisis.

Pauline has a 'serious' daughter, Nona, by her second husband, Dexter Manford, and he, apparently starved of affection and fulfilment, begins an affair with his stepson's wife Lita. In an absurd moment of melodrama Arthur appears at night with a pistol, to avenge the family honour, and by mistake shoots Nona, whose arm is broken. Afterwards, while she is recovering her father calls on her.

For a moment she lay and looked up at Manford without being

> clearly conscious that he was there, and without knowing what to say if he were.
>
> It appeared that he did not know either. Perhaps he had been led to her side, almost in spite of himself, by a vague craving to be alone with her just once before they parted; or perhaps he had come because he suspected she might think he was afraid to. (*TS*, pp. 368–69)*

There is very little indication earlier in the novel that Manford is fond of Nona, so what are we to make of that 'vague craving'?

> . . . Nona was aware of the presence at her side only as a shadowy bulk. After a while her father put out his hand and laid it on hers . . .
>
> . . .
>
> She wound her fingers into his, and then sat silent again. She liked to have him near her in this way, but she was glad, for his sake and her own, that the twilight made his face indistinct. (*TS*, p. 369)

There is a sense of shame between them: she does not want to see his face—yet she likes to have him near.

> She hoped their silence might be unbroken. As long as she neither saw nor heard him there was an unaccountable comfort in feeling him near—as if the living warmth he impacted were something they shared indissolubly. . . . (*TS*, p. 369)

That is, she enjoys the warm presence of her father, so long as nothing is seen outwardly, or spoken, of his guilt. Surely, here, we have Edith Wharton re-living her feelings when her father abused her as a child?

> 'In a couple of hours now—' he began, with an attempt at briskness. She was silent, and he went on: 'I wanted to be with you alone for a minute like this. I wanted to say—'
>
> 'Father—'
>
> He turned suddenly in his chair, and bending down over her pressed his forehead against the coverlet. She freed her hand and passed it through the thin hair on his temples. (*TS*, p. 369)

It is utterly unlike what we expect. From the woman, suffering because of her father's infidelity and philandering, we

* References are to the New York Appleton edition of 1927.

would have expected a cooler response, but she seems even more affectionately drawn to him; they are closer than ever:

> 'Don't. There's nothing to say.' She felt a tremor of his shoulders as they pressed against her, and the tremor ran through her own body and *seemed to loosen the fibres of her heart.*
>
> 'Old dad.'
>
> 'Nona.'
>
> After that they remained again without speaking till a clock chimed out from somewhere in the shadows. (*TS*, p. 370; my italics)

The moment is one of intense intimacy, at a deep bodily level, quite out of line with the rest of the story.

> Manford got up. He gave himself one of his impatient shakes, and stooped to kiss his daughter on the forehead.
>
> 'I don't believe I'll come up again before we go.'
>
> 'No.'
>
> 'It's no use—'
>
> 'No.'
>
> 'I'll look after your mother—do all I can . . . Goodbye, dear.'
>
> 'Goodbye, father.'
>
> He groped for her forehead again, and went out of the room; and she closed her eyes and lay in the darkness, *her heart folded like two hands around the thought of him.* (*B*, p. 370; my italics)

The affection is so intense it would seem that she has been the subject of his incestuous love (and, of course, we do not know why she received the bullet intended for Manford—the melodramatic scene of the shooting is so confused); she may be said to have been, in the fantasy, substituted for Lita. But nothing in the novel would seem to justify the intense erotic closeness (with its emphasis on hands) of the last phrase.

Edith Wharton involves the reader in her presentation of such cases; even such an astute critic as Geoffrey Walton cannot extricate himself. He points out the 'ominous undertones' in passages in which Lita's entanglement with Dexter Manford, 'with its suggestion of lover, father and straying husband combined', makes an ominous atmosphere, in which these characters are found 'displaying further stretches of egotism and silliness'. Yet he sees Nona as embodying the 'intuitions' Edith Wharton drew from many 'frank conversations' with young people in her later years.

> Young as she is, and appropriately young, she represents a combination of free intelligence and human sympathy, which Edith Wharton seems to have felt were needed to recreate a genuine society in which the individual could find fulfilment. . . . (Walton, p. 159)

Surely Walton has been seduced by Edith Wharton's own persuasions, to find such positives in a passage condoning an almost incestuous act of adultery on the part of her father!

*The Children* is a novel in which Edith Wharton actually set out to vindicate and justify a seductive appeal by a child girl to a man old enough to be her father.

In *The Children* we have yet another triangular situation: Martin Boyne's intention is to take up with a mature woman who is free after her marriage, and after a number of easy and free sexual encounters he looks forward to a real relationship. But, again, on the way to Mrs. Sellars, he encounters Judith—a child of 15 in charge of a heterogenous group of children who are refugees from their promiscuous parents. Becoming involved in preventing this group of children from being returned to their uncaring parents, Boyne takes a growing interest in Judith—in a relationship in which he has all the fatherly involvements, but none of the sexual ones; Judith herself finds the idea of a married relationship with Martin simply comic. However, his fascination with her destroys his interest in the true object of his affections. We can say that in this novel Edith Wharton fantasies a young daughter figure destroying the father's relationship with the mother, even though she cannot have him for herself.

Judith is seen by many critics as a heroine, with a deep sense of moral responsibility, intelligence and open-mindedness, with a profoundly critical view of the awfulness of her parents and their set. But the presentation is strangely distorted by the author's needs: since she is a child, Judith is given all the 'goodness' of an incestuous, father-claiming daughter, with none of the culpability that might follow such sexual involvement—while Martin Boyne is portrayed as bewitched by her—also, of course, preserved as 'good', but then hived off to be a lonely, disappointed man, who has given up everything for her.

In the original eight-page typed outline (February 1927),

the novel ends with Martin Boyne marrying Judith Wheater. The conclusion

> would be made up of the struggle on Judith's part to keep her children together, of Boyne's struggle against his growing love for a girl who might be his daughter, and of Mrs. Sellar's struggle to keep Boyne, and detach him from Judith. . . . The heart-break is terrible for Judith, and she turns in despair to Boyne's sheltering and understanding love. She is now nearly 17, and she agrees to marry Boyne if he will let her adopt [the other children]. He sees the folly of the marriage, and yet is so frightened by her loneliness . . . that, having obtained the consent of her parents, Boyne marries her—but *as if he were taking a little sister home*. . . . (Wolff, p. 381)

(This is from the 1924–28 notebook, Wharton Archives, Beinecke Library.) After the death of Walter Berry, however, the more serious aspects of the novelist took over, and the book ends bleakly, with Martin Boyne losing both women and going off into loneliness.

What the perceptive novelist sees is that, to Judith, Boyne's sexual love has no meaning. His attraction to the child at the end is seen as being devoted to a mysterious phantom:

> '*Judith*!' Boyne thought, as if her being Judith, her being herself, were impossible to believe, yet too sweet for anything else in the world to be true. . . . It was one of her moments of beauty—that fitful beauty which is so much more enchanting and perilous than the kind that gets up and lies down every day with its wearer. This might be—Boyne said to himself—literally the only day, the only hour, in which the queer quarrelling elements that composed her would ever join hands in a celestial harmony. It did not matter what had brought the miracle about. . . . (C, p. 347)*

The passage is sentimental, written in that somewhat brittle language of the ad man such as we find in Scott Fitzgerald: 'sweet', 'fitful beauty', 'enchanting', 'celestial harmony'. But one word to be noted is 'perilous': this alone indicates the clue to Edith Wharton's fascination with incestuous enchantment.

So, we have a middle-aged man caught in a spell 'as if he were taking a little sister home': 'he had climbed the same

* References are to the Virago edition.

path, and his feet had seemed winged, and the air elixir, because a girl's shoulder brushed his own, and he listened to unpremeditated laughter' (*C*, p. 254). As the spell takes hold, his adult partner becomes 'the lovely shadow': 'she was now a shadow irrevocably, whereas before he had always believed she might become substantial' (p. 259).

In an outburst against Judith, he declares at one point, 'There's no harm done . . . *only don't try meddling with grown up things* . . .' (*C*, p. 268; my italics). This is at a moment when he had flung his boots into the cradle that the children had given him—a gesture that reveals his indifference to the potential sexual relationships with Mrs. Sellars. Then,

> She was still looking up at him, her face full of compunction and perplexity, and suddenly he put his arm about her and bent his head to her lips. They looked round and glowing, as they did in laughter or emotion; they drew him irresistably. But he turned his head aside and his kiss fell *harmlessly* on her cheek, near the tear-hung lashes. . . . (*C*, p. 269; my italics)

We may note the word 'harmlessly' and associate it with the word 'perilous' above. The feeling behind the word is that if Boyne kissed her on the lips, there would be sexual feelings, and these would be terribly dangerous. And yet when the children write (in a game) what they want to be, Judith writes 'an explorer', and 'At the reading of that, something darted through Boyne like a whirr of wings' (*C*, p. 296). That is, he is excited by the possibility of her exploring his body; the dangers are considerable. He shows a marked reluctance to make physical love to Mrs. Sellars, too, even though Edith Wharton says early on in the book that

> In the course of his life so much easy love had come his way, he had grown so weary of nights without a woman, that he needed to feel there was one woman in the world he was half-afraid to make love to. (*C*, p. 84)

He had found her 'far more intelligent and adaptable than he had guessed when their relation had been obscured by his passion and her resistance'. 'Now there was no resistance—and his passion lay with folded wings. It was perfect' (*C*, p. 85). We have to make allowances for a very different period, when a woman was fearful of becoming pregnant, and when all kinds of considerations would govern her and make it essential that she was married before she embarked on sexual relationships; but even so, the careful reluctance of this pair to consummate their engagement seems strange. It reads rather as a romance that ought to have been written by a *child author who wants to keep her father for herself.* I cannot myself believe that a man who has had so much 'easy love' could live in the same house with a woman to whom he is engaged and not make love to her.

But this is a general feature of Edith Wharton's novels: despite her knowledge of passion, her 'good' male characters, such as Newland Archer and Lawrence Selden, are so often reluctant to commit themselves to sexual encounter. Elsewhere there are significant barriers. Amherst in *The Fruit of the Tree* can only possess Justine after she has killed his wife; Darrow is prevented from a fulfilled marriage by his affair with Sophy Viner. (An exception is that impossible story *Glimpses of the Moon* in which Nick and Susy Lansing are so much in love that they become bored and appalled by their own foolish and cynical plans to marry rich partners—and manage to avoid sexual contact with them in favour of their own marriage.)

The moment for Boyne to commit himself to Judith comes at the end of Chapter XXVIII; they are seeking a way to 'keep us all together': 'If he could have kept her there, not speaking, only answering her with endearments, how exquisite it would have been. . .' (C, p. 308).

Speaking and not-speaking are crucial in this novel; in the end Boyne cannot speak to Mrs. Sellars at all, and withdraws confusedly. But what is he to say to Judith?

> 'I don't belong to any one but you—for as long as ever you'll have me. . . .'
>
> Her eyes still bathed him in their radiance. 'My darling, my darling.' She leaned close as she said it, and he dared not move, in his new awe of her nearness—so subtly had she changed from the child of his familiar endearments to the woman he passionately longed for. . . . (C, pp. 308–9)

What lies under the surface is the recognition that this is a father-daughter relationship, in which they are committed one to another in love forever, but also one in which sexual relationships are dangerous and forbidden. 'Boyne felt like a man who has blundered along in the dark to the edge of a precipice' (C, p. 310).

> . . . he shrank from her touch . . . from everything about her which he had to think back into terms of childhood and comradeship, while every vein in his body still ached for her.

It is like a father awakening from an incestuous fantasy: 'there was nothing he would have dreaded as much as her detecting the least trace of what he was feeling.'

> His first care must be to hide the break in their perfect communion—the fact that for a moment she had been for him the woman she would some day be for another man, in a future he could never share. (C, p. 310)

He has told her he has a plan, but in the face of her incomprehension he has to relinquish it: 'Could she have such a power of awaking passion without any inkling of its meaning? He hated himself for doubting it' (C, p. 311). We have to say, I believe, that a girl who was not aware of her seductiveness and its implications could not exist, and a man who was so unaware of where he had brought himself is impossible, too. What Edith Wharton is doing is trying to *vindicate* incest; she is trying to keep her father 'good' and to pretend that although he seduced her, her sexual awareness did not play a part.

A few minutes before he had thought it a 'profanation' to 'brush her with the thought of his love'; now, 'He shrank not so much from the possibility of hurting her as from the sudden fear of her hurting him beyond endurance' (C, p. 312). Boyne edges towards discussing marriage. She mentions the word and then says,

> 'If things went wrong, and you were very lonely, and a fellow asked I'd marry him—'
>
> 'Who asked me?'
>
> He laughed again. 'If I did.' (C, p. 313)

She laughs at him: her laughter seems 'to bubble up, froth and limpid, from the very depth of her *little girlhood*' (C, pp. 313–14; my italics).

> 'Well, that would be funny!' she said.
>
> There was a bottomless silence. (C, p. 314)

He walks away from her disconsolate figure, 'as if to put himself out of its reach for ever'.

Of course, we need to gloss, the little daughter cannot marry her Daddy; but Edith Wharton has written a convincing idealization of two people as innocent of the involvement and its incestuous implications as they could never ever have been. Adult sexuality, by contrast with the father-daughter kind of relationship, is felt to be intensely dangerous. In *The Children*, as Geoffrey Walton points out, 'there is more animus against Rose Sellars' than the book intends, in the following passage: 'His eyes rested on her profile, so thin, drawn, bloodless, that a fresh pang shot through him' (*C*, p. 235). He sees himself as Rose Sellars's Great Adventure; she had been married for twenty years, but

> the thought of Boyne was storing up treasures for her which she could one day put out her hand and take—no matter how long she might have to wait. Her patience, Boyne knew, was endless—*it was as long as her hair*. . . . (*C*, p. 235; my italics)

She is like 'a tireless animal waiting for its prey. . .'. 'It was terrible, it was hideous, to be picturing her distress as *something grasping and predatory*. . .' (*C*, p. 235; my italics).

There is something of Wharton herself in this woman, as there is in Anna Leath in *The Reef* who is 'not a denier but a chooser'. And in her self-criticism we may see perhaps her anger at her own sheltered and carefully controlled life. But we can also see how, in taking her mother into herself, Edith Wharton was also embracing the mature femininity she rejected in the mother—because of her induced preference for a childhood relationship with the father. So, she is unable to identify fully with the mature sexual woman on the one hand—and discriminates against her as *hungry* and *predatory*—while her men, in relation to such women, are themselves castrated by her: unable to advance their passionate causes, because they are locked in incestuous temptations.

*The Buccaneers* is a much inferior novel, despite attempts by various critics to generate interest in the work. Of course, those who enjoy Edith Wharton's writing will find interesting moments, but in general this novel falls below expectations. The much applauded Miss Testvalley does not emerge as a character of independence and quality to put on a par with Lily Bart, Sophie Viner or Undine Spragg, while Nan (Annabel St. George, later Lady Tintagel) does not stand out as well even as Anna in *Twilight Sleep* and certainly not as well as Judith in *The Children.*

Of course, it is difficult for us to judge the work, since the novel is unfinished. But for the most part *The Buccaneers* seems to belong to the attempt to write a critical record of the daily antics of high society, but without any controlling theme, which makes *Twilight Sleep* so dull. If there is any underlying preoccupation, it is that of trying to achieve gratitude—the sense of allowing life to go on, with one's blessing. So, the lively young women in this novel, including Mrs. Closson, are the 'buccaneers', while society, both in American high life and British aristocratic life, are deadly and conformist. However, the solutions chosen by Edith Wharton seem wrong and essentially inauthentic, while her picture of the English aristocracy seems wooden and too simple a caricature—as in the case of Lord Tintagel's obsession with clocks and his gradual discovery that women are not 'as simple as clocks'.

Laura Testvalley is made out in the notes towards the end of the novel as being a collaborative organizer of Nan's elopement and escape with Guy Thwarte; and so, governess figure as she is, one cannot but find her a somewhat undermining figure who abuses the trust people put in her—indeed, a slightly corrupt figure. This celebration of corruption seems to have behind it Edith Wharton's own love affair and the incestuous motive in yet a new form; Cynthia Wolff makes this connection in the same footnote:

> This relationship really does not smack of 'incest' in the way that the relationships in the earlier novels of this period did: in fact, this sort of 'incest' seems to have become almost entirely without ominous overtones by the time Wharton was writing *The Buccaneers*. (Wolff, pp. 440–41)

The loss of ominousness could, however, mark a serious loss of the artist's authenticity. And Cynthia Wolff again indicates a confusion in the writer when she says that after the 'old adventurer' Laura Testvalley has seen her heroine through these romantic perils, and into a successful marriage with Guy Thwarte, 'she goes back alone to old age and poverty.' This, as Wolff suggests, is hardly credible: 'it is impossible to believe that the girl would allow her beloved friend to sink into such indignities' (Wolff, p. 441).

It should be noted that Edith Wharton's note speaks only of Nan's 'joining her lover'; there is no suggestion of a marriage, while it is assumed that the English aristocracy never divorce. The reference to *Anna Karenina* is thus apt: the hell of the non-married state of liaison to which Ellen Olenska has so vividly pointed (*The Age of Innocence,* p. 242–43)—is that forgotten here? Was Edith Wharton's gesture towards the new independent woman of America and gratitude for their new freedom merely an acquiescence in their defiance of society and of all obligations—in favour of self-fulfilment? It would seem to be so, and we may well come to feel that in this last book Edith Wharton could no longer summon up any of her penetrating insights into the capacities of her earlier heroines for a genuine sense of inner authenticity, by which to claim their dignity and self-respect in a world that denied these to woman.

It seems to me astonishing that Geoffrey Walton, in his excellent critical study of Edith Wharton, can claim that *The Buccaneers* is 'one of her major works'. He declares that it 'begins where her novels of the 1920s, *Twilight Sleep* and *The Children,* leave off—in social anarchy':

> And, by involving the anarchic spirits in all their free vitality with a social system which is at once very old and very stable, it gradually works toward a vision of social reintegration with moral and intellectual concomitants, a concept of balance between ancient order and dignity and new, sincere, and unconventional individualism. (Walton, p. 185)

Almost significantly, Walton confuses in a subsequent sentence Judith of *The Children* and Nona Manford of *Twilight Sleep* ('There is a strong relationship to Nona Manford of *The*

*Children'*—he writes, discussing Nan St. George).

The claim seems hopeless on all counts. It is true that *Twilight Sleep* and *The Children* do show a great deal of what may be called 'social anarchy'; but Edith Wharton fails to show this is menacing as she does in *The House of Mirth,* in which the expectations of society destroy Lily Bart. Indeed, the failure to hold on to a critical view in *Twilight Sleep* means that the promiscuous antics of the people lose interest for the reader, while the one strong character, Nona, as I have shown, compromises with her father in his absurd in-family *affaire.* In *The Children,* while the behaviour of the adults is implicitly condemned, the diagnosis is done largely without the kind of bitter moral irony that governs Henry James in *What Maisie Knew,* which has its roots in a passionate concern for authenticity.

Walton declares that Edith Wharton's prose 'has lost its epigrammatic tension and much of the vivid figurative language that marks her pre-war books . . . but . . . it has not become dull' (Walton, p. 185). But despite excellent passages, her writing has become thin and lame, as have some of her concepts. Here perhaps the weakest liaison is between the Duke Tintagel, and Nan St. George. Nan is singled out to be a child of unusual independence and promise; she shows herself aware, in a scene with Guy Thwarte, of 'something beyond'. But little or nothing is developed of this, and she does not come into focus. Whatever unusual qualities she may have are never defined and are left vague, as in the comic scene in which Tintagel becomes entranced with her; but this relationship has none of the attentive tension of (say) the relationship between Selden and Lily Bart. Tintagel is an ass, with his defective attitude to women and his stilted conversations with his mother, and the comedy that arises from these are thin.

Guy Thwarte is to go to Brazil, in some large-scale engineering enterprise to make enough money to rescue his estates from his father's mismanagement; all the scions of the English aristocracy seem to do is to spend beyond their means, while expressing only contempt for learning, culture or intellect, and manifesting only narrowmindedness about peoples of other races ('Is she black?' asks the cable sent by Lord Richard's mother about his Brazilian bride; Laura Testvalley replies, 'No, but comely').

The Americans, of course, all have fathers doing deals in business or in Wall Street, so there is no problem over the financial basis of the characters' lives. And while they are mostly portrayed with their 'fantastic arrogance, frequent absurdity, and breath-taking hypocrisy', as Walton declares (Walton, p. 192), where is the contrasting 'new, sincere and unconventional individualism'?

The 'buccaneers' are pretty women, 'happy girls' with a 'collective grace with a vividness almost exempt from envy'; but what do they display in their behaviour except a youthful refusal to conform—while ultimately conforming as Nan so stupidly does by accepting Tintagel?

Close examination exposes severe weaknesses in Edith Wharton's novel. Who are these 'buccaneers'? One does not want to side with the stuffy English aristocracy, but there seems a limited value in a bevy of American girls leading everyone in a dance through the bedrooms and, through this 'openness', becoming selfishly dissatisfied with their lot. Astonishingly the one independent act Nan undertakes in the latter stages of the book is to ask her husband for £500 without telling him what she wants it for; in fact, it is to finance an adulterous escapade by Conchita Marable:

> . . . a lady with tumbled auburn curls, red-heeled slippers, and a pink deshabille with a marked tendency to drop off the shoulders. A headless ghost would have been much less out of keeping with the traditions of the place. (*B*, p. 297)

Conchita uses Annabel to 'strike' and let her order her clothes for her, 'especially . . . underclothes'. When she bursts into tears, Annabel is distressed and Conchita declares:

> What do you know about being over ears in debt, and in love with one man while you're tied to another—tied tight in one of those awful English marriages, that strangle you in a noose when you try to pull away from them? (*B*, p. 300)*

Is the buccaneer spirit, then, supposed to be manifest in Annabel's response: 'might one perhaps not feel less lonely

* References are to the New York Appleton-Century edition of 1938.

with such a sin on one's conscience than in the blameless isolation of an uninhabited heart?' (*B*, p. 301).

Conchita goes on, 'I can't live without affection, and Miles is so understanding, so tender. . . .'

> 'Oh, I know, I know, Conchie—'
> Lady Dick lifted her head quickly, and looked straight into her friend's eyes. 'You know—?'
> 'I mean, I can imagine . . . how hard it must be not to. . . .' (*B*, p. 302)

There follows a conversation in which Annabel declares:

> ''. . . it's all turned out a dreadful mistake, hasn't it?'
> 'A dreadful mistake—you mean my marriage?'
> 'I mean all our marriages. I don't believe we're any of us really made for this English life. . . .' (*B*, p. 303)

But Conchita mocks Annabel's sudden impulse to go back to New York society: she needs £500 to make her a 'free woman'.

> 'Nan,' she said, almost solemnly, 'don't judge me, will you, till you find out for yourself what it's like.'
> 'What what is like? What do you mean, Conchita?'
> 'Happiness, darling,' Lady Dick whispered. (*B*, p. 307)

This is surely as close as you can get to the women's magazine story? The simple-mindedness of the incident is absurd—but, of course, there lies behind the bland assurance of Edith Wharton's *affaire* with Morton Fullerton which awakened her true self, or so she thought. We are given, however, too little of the details of Conchita's entrapment, her relationship with her lover and Annabel's consideration of the problem for us to endorse her impulse to dispense this 'private charity'.

Of course, Edith Wharton resents the patronizing air of the male: Guy Thwarte thinks of Annabel and addresses her as a child ('Poor little thing!') and she rebukes him. But in her callowness Nan is as much of a child as Judith in *The Children*. There is the scene in which they go to look at the Correggios after the dance: 'She was only a child, he reminded himself—she didn't measure what she was saying. . .' (*B*, p. 284). This is, of course, the endearing aspect of several of Edith Wharton's heroines—that they speak in an open unconventional way, often unaware, seemingly, of the implications of their utterances. Their discontent thus emerges, as Annabel's now does, in spite of herself, and tears come into her eyes; he responds: ' "My dear child—" he began: and then, half-embarrassed: "For you *are* a child, still, you know. Have you any idea how awfully young you are?" ' (*B*, p. 286).

She is surely not too young to realize the degree to which she is compromising her marriage? Of course, Edith Wharton wants to portray that marriage as dead; but there remains the question that Nan, as we might say, was in her own shoes when she married, and continues to enjoy the advantages, even if she spurns them. Something more powerful and insightful would be needed by the reader for him to sympathize with her quest for authenticity: something, one might say, more like George Eliot on Gwendolen Harleth. In this novel, how are we to know Nan will not act with equal impulsiveness in order to land herself in yet another prison of relationship? The 'buccaneer' spirit, that is, would require more than mere dissatisfaction as its impulse to gain our intelligent sympathy.

> As soon as he had spoken he reflected that she was too young not to resent any allusion to her inexperience. She laughed. 'Please don't send me back to the nursery.'
>
> 'Little girls shouldn't ask questions. You'll understand better when you're grown up. How much longer am I to be talked to like that?' (*B*, p. 286)

—but this actually fizzles out into a discussion of the difference between the climate of New York and England, while she goes on:

> Somehow it seems as if this were wrong—my being here. . . . If you knew what I'd give to be able to try again . . . somewhere where I could be myself, you understand, not just an unsuccessful Duchess. . . . (*B*, p. 287)

Geoffrey Walton actually quotes this scene and speaks of Nan's 'intelligence and personal poise'. But surely her determination to quit her situation must seem like Judith's attempt to rescue the children, a mere childish fantasy, desperate and impossible? It would indeed have been interesting to see how Edith Wharton might have realized her flight in a future with Guy; even Geoffrey Walton cannot stomach the idea of this pair becoming 'white settlers'. Yet he sums up the 'social criticism' of *The Buccaneers* in glowing terms of a fusion of the 'ancient obligations and courtesies of his class' with 'a new managerial efficiency'; but, surely, there are no substantial signs that Guy Thwarte embodies either, nor that Nan would be able to share in embracing any such 'obligations'.

Walton may tell us that 'the sensitive and independent girl is becoming a lively and thoughtful woman who cannot conform to any social pattern unless she understands it and believes in it' (Walton, p. 200); but her proclamations that she feels not herself as an 'unsuccessful Duchess' and that she would like to 'try again' seem merely callow. Though she protests that she does not want to be 'sent back to the nursery', we find ourselves asking—wasn't her original sense of 'something beyond' childish, too? What is it in her that Edith Wharton values? Has not this ageing author, in her elderly yearning to be on the side of the young, come to overvalue a childish kind of wilfulness and resentment of social ties and an equally immature celebration of the impulse to throw such obligations off?

Edith Wharton in this novel may be struggling heroically with her envy of the young but fails to resolve her envy into gratitude. After so much encounter with real life and real people—with real suffering—it seems strange that she should turn, in this '20s' novel, to the world of vapid and manic rich American girls, whose chief manifestations of independence are smoking cigars, dancing Virginian reels, chasing and then deserting husbands, and celebrate this as freedom—even as their impact on an English aristocracy remains at the level of a concern merely to relish their 'old stones'.

Towards the end, Guy Thwarte, who has returned from Brazil, and Nan 'drift out again to the wide terrace', after visiting the 'old house' and lingering over 'each piece of rare old furniture or tapestry'. She says:

'. . . when my spirits were always jumping up and down Miss Testvalley used to call me Clärchen, just to tease me.'

'And doesn't she any longer? I mean, don't your spirits jump up and down any more?'

'Well, I'm afraid they do sometimes. Miss Testvalley says things are never as bad as I think, or as good as I expect—but I'd rather have the bad hours than not believe in the good ones, wouldn't you? What really frightens me is not caring for anything any more. Don't you think that's worse? . . .' (*B*, p. 346)

This is an old woman's comment and shows Edith Wharton's degree of identification with Nan. She goes on:

. . . sometimes life seems like a match between oneself and one's gaolers. The gaolers, of course, are one's mistakes: and the question is, who'll hold out longest. When I think of that, life, instead of being too long, seems as short as a winter's day. . . . (*B*, p. 346)

This is a poignant comment made through Nan's mouth by the author herself, who is trying to find a position from which she can feel glad to have existed, but is yet haunted by being imprisoned in the 'mistakes' of her society and upbringing. But would the end of her novel, as she conceived it—Guy and Nan going off to a 'deep and abiding love', aided by Laura Testvalley, who then retreats into solitary poverty and old age—have solved the problem of existence? Where in this is the 'social reintegration with moral and intellectual concomitants' that Geoffrey Walton promises us?

# Conclusions

It would seem that while once she required rescuing from neglect, today Edith Wharton requires rescuing from misinterpretation. Even Q. D. Leavis tells us that in *The Custom of the County* Undine Spragg is 'no monster'—when she must surely be the most monstrous woman ever depicted in a novel. But recent feminist writers seem to work from an ideological basis which is concerned with woman's rôle and how 'society' imposes submission on them, and this leads to further misrepresentation. For instance, discussing *The Age of Innocence* Cynthia Wolff declares that Newland Archer 'achieves genuine maturity' when, at the end of the book, he fails to go up to Ellen's apartments in Paris: 'The drama is over, and Newland is free to go.' She speaks of the 'infantilizing' force of 'the mutilating image of women that society fosters'—that affects Lily Bart (Wolff, p. 130). But did not Lawrence Selden offer her a way out? Here we may detect the same errors as the feminists fall into over Sylvia Plath, when they take her feeling of being a false self to be a product of 'society' rather than of a breakdown of her relationship with her mother. Cynthia Wolff considers Sophy Viner to be the heroine of *The Reef*, while at the same time she persistently reports that book as a failure: 'the technique that had worked so brilliantly in *Ethan Frome* fails utterly here' (Wolff, p. 208); it is 'an interesting and necessary failure'. She speaks of Sophy's 'open sensual nature', and declares that 'Anna eventually decides she cannot marry Darrow', thus failing to allow herself to encounter the essential ambiguity of the end of the novel, which must surely be the greatest of Edith Wharton's achievements.

The way to resist such misrepresentation, I believe, is to invoke the findings of psychoanalysis, to try to estimate the degree of human truth in the novels. The artist is always searching for the truth about human nature, and so is the psychotherapist in his consulting room. Cynthia Wolff tries to make an estimation of Edith Wharton on the basis of her reading of Erik Erikson, and she even refers to works by R. D. Laing and D. W. Winnicott, but she seems to me very seldom to offer insights based on these works of psychotherapy, in trying to indicate the unconscious factors in her work. It is true that she reflects on Edith Wharton's fear of animals and reports an intense, wolf-like hunger in her as a child, whose unsatisfied hunger for affection was 'converted into an insatiable hunger for aural beauty'. I am not convinced that Edith Wharton suffered unduly from an intensity of oral hunger, or that her fear of a wolf under the bed is a clue to her sexual difficulties; she seems to me (by comparison, say, with Sylvia Plath) to have had the child's normal phobias and hungers for affection, and I am not convinced either that she felt 'the deadly fury of her childhood rage' (p. 135). There is an unsatisfied infant within Edith Wharton, and this becomes clear, as I have shown, in the symbolism of the end of the novel *The House of Mirth* when she is dealing with the death of Lily Bart.

But what we still have to explain is the sense Edith Wharton had of 'some dark and indefinable menace':

> Fear of '*what*? I cannot say—and even at the time, I was never able to formulate my terror. It was like some dark undefinable menace, forever dogging my steps, lurking and threatening: I was conscious of it wherever I went by day, and at night it made sleep impossible, unless a light and nursemaid were in the room. But whatever it was, it was most formidable and pressing when I was returning from my daily walk (which I always took with a maid or governess, or with my father). During the last few yards, and while I waited on the doorstep for the door to be opened, I could feel it behind me, upon me; and if there was any delay in the opening of the door I was seized by a choking agony of terror. It did not matter who was with me, for no one could protect me. . . . ('Life and I', pp. 16–18; quoted in Wolff, p. 23)

Edith was also tortured by moral scruples: she speaks of the 'darkness of horror' that weighed on her childhood in respect of the vexed problem of truth-telling, and of 'the impossibility of reconciling God's standard of truthfulness with the conventional obligation to be "polite" and not to hurt anyone's feelings'. She dare not tell anyone of her trouble, 'because I vaguely felt that I *ought* to know what was right, and that it was probably "naughty" not to' (*ibid.*, p. 7, quoted p. 23). Wolff speaks of her 'constant monitoring of speech and thought to protect herself from uttering or even thinking the forbidden thing.' We have seen this sense of an *unspeakable* horror in *The Mother's Recompense*. Her imaginative effort could have been in part an escape from this horror. So, Edith Wharton remembers her imagination as if it were that unborn self: 'My imagination lay there, coiled and sleeping, a mute hibernating creature . . . which needed so little feeding from the outside. . .' ('Life and I', quoted by Wolff, p. 23).

Wolff detects in the child a 'failure of trust and emotional satisfaction':

> The child's trust, betrayed by Lucretia, had been transferred to language as the means by which she may free herself from loneliness and desolation; the unsatisfied hunger for affection and reassurance has been converted into an insatiable, but infinitely rewarding, hunger for visual and aural beauty. The child is a nascent artist. (Wolff, p. 28)

Writing about her experience above, Edith Wharton gives us a sense of having a sleeping self within her, and we may, I believe, link this with the extraordinary attitude that she takes to herself when she is temporarily sexually awakened by Morton Fullerton as her lover in middle-age; it is often as if she is writing of another woman altogether.

But to return for a moment to Wolff's comments above, about the betrayal of trust by Lucretia. Obviously, there were problems with Lucretia, who seems to have been cold and unresponsive. Granted that the period was one of American Victorianism in which 'All girls . . . suffered in an environment that utterly discouraged the healthy development of their emotional lives' (Wolff, p. 37). But could it not have been that the real and heavily suppressed betrayal of trust was by the father? Wolff says, 'His warm presence, like the encompassing touch of his warm hand, must have been a powerful emotional magnet, drawing to it all the child's unsatisfied cravings' (Wolff, p. 19). Edith Wharton says of him:

> I have wondered since what stifled cravings had once germinated in him, and what manner of man he was really meant to be. That he was a lonely one, haunted by something always unexpressed and unattained, I am sure. ('Life and I', quoted by Wolff, p. 19)

Writing of his death, she declares herself 'still haunted by the look in his clear blue eyes, which had followed me so tenderly for nineteen years. . .'. Cynthia Wolff here discusses the child Edith's fear of the wolf under the bed, and writes:

> A little girl whose image of emotional satisfaction would forever more carry with it the lingering fantasy of total incorporation (or total annihilation), a little girl whose yearnings have gradually turned to a generous and affectionate father—how frightened she must have been by the strength of the *almost palpable* fantasies that thronged her imagination. Every little girl of four or five 'falls in love' with her father; and for every little girl, this attachment is a crisis whose resolution is beset with difficulty. (Wolff, p. 20; my italics)

Wolff then relates this to the fear of the incorporating wolf and Edith Wharton's fear of animals: the intensity of the need they represent is fearsome. To avoid the consequences of this terrible need, the child sought her mother or Doyley, to 'act as a restraint of her own competitive sexuality'.

'The mortal desolation is there, will always be there', Edith Wharton wrote, and 'at the heart of her social formalities was an unconquerable expectation of pain', writes Cynthia Wolff. Such an intense expectation of disappointment, together with the pressing sense of horror in her life, seem unlikely to have been created simply by her mother's coldness. I believe it is unlikely that the mere force of her own fantasies about her father could have traumatized her (which is how it appears in Cynthia Wolff's account) and that the only explanation of her fear, and her persistent obsession with incest must be that she was actually abused. With a mother who was remote, disapproving, impatient and unloving, it could seem quite possible (given what we have found out about this problem in recent years) that the respectable Jones household concealed such a horror, such an abuse of trust, such a disaster.

It could have been paternal sexual abuse that caused the sense of being haunted by a horror that Edith Wharton speaks of and the dread of letting something be spoken, or even *thought of*. It could explain the sense she had of something sleeping and hidden within her, and the horror she associated with sexual love. It could explain the sense she expresses, when she experiences a sexual awakening by Morton Fullerton, of this happening to 'someone else'. And it could explain her pervading sense of the unsatisfactory male: all males failing on the one hand to come up to the idolized father, and on the other to commit themselves to her as woman. It could even explain her own maleness, which Cynthia Wolff comments on.

Critics speak of Edith Wharton having 'lived' by her *affaire* with Morton Fullerton, but even supposing she did find some sensual experience thereby, it is surely no solution to the fundamental problem of finding one's fulfilment of being through sexual joy to have a brief sensual experience with an experienced professional seducer? Edith Wharton wrote:

> I have sometimes thought that a woman's nature is like a great house full of rooms: there is the hall, through which everyone passes in going in and out: the drawing room, where one receives formal visits: the sitting room, where the members of the family come and go as they like; but beyond that, far beyond, are other rooms, the handles of whose doors perhaps are never turned; no one knows the way to them, no one knows whither they lead; and in the innermost room, the holy of holies, the soul sits alone. (*Collected Short Stories*, I, 14)

The question for the novelist is what kind of sexual relationship provides a way to penetrate to this 'innermost room': her subject is the degree of being involved in any form of meeting. If it is, as Martin Buber puts it, 'from man to man that the heavenly bread of self-being is passed', then sexual meeting must be one of the deepest sources of authenticity, of meaning, since it is there that, one hopes, true being meets true being, with an absolute mode of reflection that confirms the self, and so provides a feeling that one has meaningfully existed.

How far did Edith Wharton ever achieve this kind of meeting? And what does she show of sexual meeting in her novels? To take the first question, Cynthia Wolff makes a useful point in a footnote:

> The affair with Fullerton served a purpose (perhaps, even, Fullerton himself did little more than serve a purpose): given Edith Wharton's problems with trust, it seems likely that she would find it easier to abandon herself passionately in a relationship in which she felt no real, binding emotional tie and where she unconsciously sensed herself to be superior to her partner in the nonsexual area of their lives; in such a situation, only a part of herself would be vulnerable. (Wolff, p. 433)

Perhaps, indeed, the fondness his women showed for Fullerton, even after the end of a relationship with him, was a recognition of this kind of usefulness to them. (Edith Wharton retained a fondness for Fullerton even into old age: 'But she *loved* Walter Berry', says Wolff.)

The astonishing thing about Edith Wharton's relationship with Morton Fullerton was that, as Cynthia Wolff reports, there was 'An eventual termination . . . implicit in the inception.' 'At the very moment when she and Fullerton first strolled and talked so intently, he was a newly affianced man' (Wolff, p. 199). He was intimidated, however, by the thought of committing himself to one woman for the rest of his life. He always had a compulsion to tell his current lover about his past. And,

> Basking in the spiritual glow of this relationship, Wharton must have been confused, at the very least, when she began to discover the prodigality with which her lover had spread his talent. (Wolff, p. 195)

While Cynthia Wolff is careful (as in the above sentence) not to condemn Fullerton, she cannot avoid revealing her feelings at times, as by speaking of 'the rather more squalid depths of Fullerton's voluptuary past'! We may postulate, I believe, that such a man is like Daddy, because, like Daddy, he has another sexual partner.

Fullerton had arrived in the U.S. in 1890 and 'had dallied in any number of casual sexual intrigues'. There were two serious entanglements, one with Lord Gower and one with a woman old enough to be his mother, Margaret Brooke, the Ranee of Sarawak. The latter gave him up because 'he was unable to stay out of the beds of young women', and it seems that he had many sexual encounters both with men and women, besides those who are named in the biographies. In 1900 he was seriously involved with Henrietta Mirecourt, and yet in 1903 he suddenly married an actress Victoria Camille Chabet, with whom he had a daughter, while still carrying on with Mirecourt. By 1907, when he was developing his relationship with Edith Wharton, Fullerton had divorced Victoria and was being blackmailed by Mirecourt, who had broken into his flat to find papers which revealed the affairs with Lord Gower, Margaret Brooke and many others. By 1909 both Edith Wharton and Henry James were involved in plans to extricate Moreton Fullerton from Henrietta Mirecourt, even to the extent of Edith Wharton putting up £100 which James was to offer to a publisher to pay as part of an advance to Fullerton for a book on Paris, so that he could buy the incriminating letters from Henrietta.

No wonder Edith Wharton's attitudes to sexuality (as, for instance, embodied in the novel which immediately followed, *The Reef*) are ambiguous! Evidently she could hardly sustain the idealized view of love she expressed in her poem 'Terminus'. She was soon to discover Morton's relationship with a woman raised in his house as his sister—actually his first cousin—to whom he had been affianced. He asked Katherine, for that was her name, whether they could not have a platonic relationship, to which she replied: '. . . you've a power, my poor darling, of inflicting pain.' But after a last impassioned letter, she married someone else.

Her knowledge of this relationship evidently raised scruples with Edith Wharton: she recognized that Fullerton's relationship with her must have injured this girl, and 'the matter of individual fulfilment was inextricably linked to larger questions of emotional obligation', as Cynthia Wolff puts it.

Fullerton obviously exercised a technique of seduction to prove something to himself, rather than to love someone sexually for their own sake. Rendering sex into literature was all part of this. Like Edith, Fullerton was given to turning sexual experience into words. His letters are written in a tone of 'hypnotized wonder'—'the voice is of one utterly enraptured by passion'—and he expresses (says Wolff) a 'voluptuous ideal': 'in the very perfection of their love, they shared mystically in the experience of all that preceded them' (Wolff, p. 194). It is this 'doctrine' that emerges in the extraordinary poem 'Terminus'.

We are left with two conundrums concerning Edith Wharton. One is why she was herself attracted by men who were bisexual, bachelors or homosexuals—or who, like Fullerton, disguised their fundamental inadequacy by superior 'techniques' of love, by idolization and by imbuing their seductions with literary references. The second problem is what force sexual intercourse plays in her novels: if it is the focus of being, how does it feature in the symbolism of her art?

The answer to the first question lies in her relationship to her father—whether he abused her, or whether he was merely the focus for her intense erotic (masturbation) fantasies. In either case, the effect was to 'give' sexual intercourse to her father, so that only he had *the right* to it. The father, and incest, must be kept 'good', hence her distorted view of sexuality throughout. Yet sex is somehow demeaning, and can only be enjoyed with those who find the end of a relationship in its inception, or who are limited in their commitment. Any man except the father must be found unsatisfactory: this it would seem, is the inherent guiding principle in Edith Wharton's approach to sex. With most of her men friends her enjoyment is verbal and platonic—she enjoys their company. Several writers urge us to believe she was the lover of Walter Berry, but I retain doubts, except that it is clear that they were fond friends, and she loved him in that way.

Sexual intercourse is for Edith Wharton the most dangerous thing in the world, and maybe this is because its intensity of hunger could lead to mutual incorporation and thus annihilation; she feels this because of the voracious hunger diagnosed by Cynthia Wolff. It is always accompanied by a sense of nameless (schizoid) horror and is liable to lead to catastrophe and death, such as is hinted at in the poem 'Terminus' beneath the surface. There are two accompaniments to this, one of which is that when writing of her relationship with Morton Fullerton, as in 'Terminus', she has a fantasy of being 'another' woman while she establishes a 'literary' existence in which the *affaire* can exist. Her 'love diary' is an indication of the latter; she wrote this as if to him—a curious document:

> For I had no one but myself to talk to, and it is absurd to write down what one says to oneself . . . but now I shall have the illusion that I am talking to you. (Wolff, p. 116)

She develops the sense of another self, or a figure called 'Happiness'—as if the happiness were not 'in' her:

> I thought after all I was mistaken, and poor 'ame close' barred its shutters and bolted its doors again, and the dust gathered and the cobwebs thickened in the empty rooms, where for a moment I heard an echo. . . . Then we went to Herbloy. . . . In the church it was still and dim, and in the shadowy corner where I sat while you talked with the curé, a veiled figure stole up and looked at me a moment. Was its name Happiness? I dared not lift the veil. . . . When you came to dine, two nights afterwards, you said things that distressed me. At first it was exquisite. . . . Why did you spoil it? . . . You hurt me—you disillusioned me—and when you left me I was more deeply yours. . . . Ah, the confused processes within us. (Wolff, p. 149)

Was it part of Fullerton's technique to tell the woman he was seducing about his past *affaires*—to draw out jealousy in them, and thus advance his cause? Whatever the truth of the matter, Edith Wharton develops a problem of identity: the *joy did not seem for herself.*

> I said to myself all the week, 'I have never in my life known what it was to be happy (as a woman understands happiness) even for a single hour—now at last I shall be happy for a whole day talking *à coeur*, saying for once what I feel, and all that I feel as other women do.' (Wolff, p. 149)

Elsewhere she writes:

> . . . it penetrated every sense and every thought . . . and said to myself: 'This must be what happy women feel.' . . . I have known 'what happy women feel'. . . . I feel that what I want is to be in your arms to be held fast there 'like other women'. (Wolff, pp. 149–50)

At least, she feels, 'I have been warmed through and through never to grow quite cold again till the end.' And in a sense the sexual awakening did yield a new perspective:

> Oh, my free, proud, secure soul, where are you? What were you, to escape me like this . . . let us not lose one of the few remaining chances to 'be happy together' . . . strange words!—that I never spoke, or heard spoken to me, before . . . I appear to myself like a new creature opening dazzling eyes on a new world. *C'est l'aube.* (Wolff, p. 150)

It needs to be said that her experience of such happiness was brief, and falls short of that which might have been experienced by a happily married woman all her life. It is clear from everything she writes that, although she knows as much, she withheld herself from any such complete commitment.

In Vance's final reconciliation with Halo in *The Gods Arrive* Edith Wharton comes to the end of a long pursuit of authenticity in personal relationships through the novels. But this, alas, still fails to move beyond a stage in which the man is accepted as a child who is in need of cherishing in the way one cherishes a child. In a sense, she never achieves a satisfactory coming-to-terms with sexual love anywhere in her work, in the context of an on-going committed relationship. The man is nearly always undependable—like Morton Fullerton.

The men in her heroines' lives never come up with the goods. They allow their women to die, and then find bliss over her pure corpse, like Selden; or they try to kill their women and themselves, like Ethan Frome; or they are defeated by the family, like Durham (in *Madame de Treymes*); or they abandon their pursuit of a long-term mature relationship for a brief moment of sensuality with an adventuress, like Darrow; or they shoot themselves on discovering they were not the first man in their wives' lives, like Ralph; or they abandon their women in pregnancy, like Harney; or they hold her in fantasy and fail her in reality, like Newland Archer; or they become fascinated by a child-girl and relinquish a mature relationship, like Martin Boyne; or they are simply to be indulged like selfish, uncommitted, children, like Vance Weston. No doubt many of the men in Edith Wharton's life were like this; but there must have been something in her subjective life that made her seek out men like that: weak, undependable, duplicitous, cowardly, ineffective and incapable of commitment—except, of course, for a few father-figures, like Lawyer Royall and Dexter Manford.

But her women, too, are often over-valued for their 'innocent' and 'open' childishness—their appealing state of *daughter-dom*. This free, critical position adopted by some of her women engages many critics, and it is, of course, preferable to the cunning manipulations of the conventional in May and her family in *The Age of Innocence*. Lily Bart dreams of the child who has not grown up in herself, a revealing moment in her tragedy. But is not that childish impulse not idealized—in Sophy Viner, in Mattie, in Charity, in Ellen Olenska, in Judith, Nan and Nona—and only placed, for its essential voraciousness, in Undine? (Interestingly enough, it is her mature women who suffer life's defeats—Anna Leath, Rose Sellars.)

If we examine the plots of Edith Wharton's novels, as I have done, we can see that she is trying as a novelist to celebrate fulfilment, through various tormented contortions in relationship. But often she has her own distortions, and is impelled by these in her presentation of sex and gender. In all her work a sense of dread adheres to sexuality. After her *affaire* with Morton Fullerton she tries to believe in the fulfilment and renewal brought by passion, and to play down her sense of doom. In *The House of Mirth* and *Ethan Frome* she symbolizes her fear that sexuality is death; in *The Reef* she still dreads the destructiveness of sex, while, again, her mature women like Anna, Ellen Olenska and Rose Sellars evidently feel a deep reluctance to enter into sexual relationships. Even in *Hudson River Bracketted* and *The Gods Arrive* she lets slip the sense that 'the other thing' is essentially demeaning and dangerous, a feeling that surfaces certainly in *The Mother's Recompense*.

Of course, it has to be said that if she had not had these deep perplexities about gender, and dreads about sex, she would not have been the profound novelist she was—an undoubted artist, as Q. D. Leavis insisted. Anyone who writes between the period of Victorian morals and modern life must inevitably confront the problem of sexuality—only Edith Wharton went even deeper, into the sphere of authenticity. We have by no means solved the problem: the sexual explicitness and exploitation of sexual violence and perversion that has overtaken the modern novel is a great false posture and evasion of the real issues; it merely separates sex from the emotional life, as Edith Wharton refused to do.

Edith Wharton's concentration at best is on being true to oneself, and seeking to relate to another in love, in such a way as to have one's true self confirmed: to pursue one's destiny in love, *sub specie aeternitatis*. Her characters at best are involved totally, in their emotional life, their sexual potentialities, their obligations to society on the one hand, and 'the republic of the spirit' on the other. I think she failed to be able to take in the prodigious changes in consciousness that came with the mass suffering of the Great War (her war novel *A Son at the Front* is a failure because she was unable to develop a language capable of dealing with the atrocious new experience of industrialized war: but that is another question). She was in the end, as in *The Buccaneers,* too tolerant of what today we would perhaps call flapperdom and confuses this with freedom. But in her greatest novels, *The House of Mirth, The Reef, The Age of Innocence, The Custom of the Country* and *Summer,* her achievement was very serious and great indeed, while several of her other works are interesting to read and often rewarding—not least for the modern reader pursued by the same crucial problems of being.

# Bibliography

## I Edith Wharton's Works


*Verses* (Newport: C. E. Hammett, Jr., 1878)
*The Decoration of Houses*, with Ogden Codman, Jr. (New York: Scribner's, 1897)
*The Greater Inclination* (New York: Scribner's, 1899)
*The Touchstone* (New York: Scribner's, 1900). Published in England as *A Gift from the Grave* (London: John Murray, 1900)
*Crucial Instances* (New York: Scribner's, 1901)
*The Valley of Decision*, 2 vols. (New York: Scribner's, 1902)
*Sanctuary* (New York: Scribner's, 1903)
*The Descent of Man and Other Stories* (New York: Scribner's, 1904). Published in England under the same title with the addition of one story, 'The Letter' (London: Macmillan, 1904)
*Italian Villas and their Gardens* (New York: Century, 1904)
*Italian Backgrounds* (New York: Scribner's, 1905)
*The House of Mirth* (New York: Scribner's, 1905). World's Classics edition (London: Oxford University Press, 1936) contains the author's Introduction.
*Madame de Treymes* (New York: Scribner's, 1907)
*The Fruit of the Tree* (New York: Scribner's, 1907)
*A Motor-Flight through France* (New York: Scribner's, 1908)
*The Hermit and the Wild Woman and Other Stories* (New York: Scribner's, 1908)
*Artemis to Actaeon and Other Verse* (New York: Scribner's, 1909)
*Tales of Men and Ghosts* (New York: Scribner's, 1910)
*Ethan Frome* (New York: Scribner's, 1911). The Modern Student's Library edition (New York: Scribner's, 1922) contains the author's Introduction.
*The Reef* (New York: Appleton, 1912)
*The Custom of the Country* (New York: Scribner's, 1913)
*Fighting France, from Dunkerque to Belfort* (New York: Scribner's, 1915)
*Xingu and Other Stories* (New York: Scribner's, 1916)
*Summer* (New York: Appleton, 1917)

*The Marne* (New York: Appleton, 1918)
*French Ways and their Meaning* (New York: Appleton, 1919)
*The Age of Innocence* (New York: Appleton, 1920)
*In Morocco* (New York: Scribner's, 1920)
*The Glimpses of the Moon* (New York: Appleton, 1922)
*A Son at the Front* (New York: Scribner's, 1923)
*Old New York: False Dawn, The Old Maid, The Spark, New Year's Day*, 4 vols. (New York: Appleton, 1924)
*The Mother's Recompense* (New York: Appleton, 1925)
*The Writing of Fiction* (New York: Scribner's, 1925)
*Here and Beyond* (New York: Appleton, 1926)
*Twelve Poems* (London: Medici Society, 1926)
*Twilight Sleep* (New York: Appleton, 1927)
*The Children* (New York: Appleton, 1928)
*Hudson River Bracketed* (New York: Appleton, 1929)
*Certain People* (New York: Appleton, 1930)
*The Gods Arrive* (New York: Appleton, 1932)
*Human Nature* (New York: Appleton, 1933)
*A Backward Glance* (New York: Appleton-Century, 1934)
*The World Over* (New York: Appleton-Century, 1936)
*Ghosts* (New York: Appleton-Century, 1937). Stories from other volumes reprinted
*The Buccaneers* (New York: Appleton-Century, 1938)

(For short stories not included in the collections listed above see Geoffrey Walton's study.)

## II Critical and Other Studies

AMMONS, ELIZABETH, *Edith Wharton's Argument with America* (Berkeley: University of California Press, 1980)
AUCHINCLOSS, LOUIS, 'Edith Wharton and her New Yorks', *Partisan Review* 18, July–August 1951, and in *Reflections of a Jacobite* (Boston: Houghton Mifflin, 1961)
———, *Edith Wharton* (Minneapolis: University of Minnesota Press, 1961)
———, *Edith Wharton: A Woman in her Time* (London: Michael Joseph, 1972)
BELL, MILLICENT, *Edith Wharton and Henry James* (London: Peter Owen, 1966)
BERENSON, BERNARD, *Sketch for a Self-Portrait* (London: Constable, 1949)

# *Bibliography*


BEWLEY, MARIUS, *The Eccentric Design* (London: Chatto & Windus, 1959)

BLACKMUR, R. P., *The Lion and the Honeycomb* (London: Methuen, 1956)

BLOOM, HAROLD (Introduction by), *Edith Wharton*, Modern Critical Views Series (Philadelphia: Chelsea House, 1981)

BRENNI, VITO J., *Edith Wharton: A Bibliography* (McClain, 1966)

BROWN, E. K., *Edith Wharton: Etude Critique* (Paris: Librairie E. Droz, 1935)

CHASE, RICHARD, *The American Novel and its Tradition* (London: G. Bell & Son, 1958)

COWLEY, MALCOLM, *Exile's Return* (London: Bodley Head, 1961)

CUNLIFFE, MARCUS, *The Literature of the United States* (London: Penguin, 1954)

DAVIS, LAVINIA, *A Bibliography of the Writings of Edith Wharton* (Portland, Maine: Southwood Press, 1933)

EDEL, LEON, *Henry James: The Untried Years* (London: Hart-Davis, 1953)

———, *Henry James: The Conquest of London* (London: Hart-Davis, 1962)

———, *Henry James: The Middle Years* (London: Hart-Davis, 1963)

———, *Henry James: The Treacherous Years* (London: Hart-Davis, 1969)

———, *Henry James: The Master* (London: Hart-Davis, 1972)

FREYER, JUDITH, *Felicitous Space: The Imaginative Structures of Edith Wharton and Willa Cather* (Chapel Hall: University of North Carolina, 1986)

HOFFMAN, FREDERICK J., *Points of Moral Reference: A Comparative Study of Edith Wharton and F. Scott Fitzgerald*, English Institute Essays (New York: Columbia University Press, 1950)

HOWE, IRVING (ed.), *Edith Wharton* (New York: Prentice Hall, 1962)

JAMES, HENRY, *The American Scene* (including selected *Portraits of Places*), edited by W. H. Auden (New York: Scribner's, 1946)

———, *The Art of the Novel* (New York: Scribner's, 1934)

———, *Hawthorne* (London and New York: Macmillan, 1879)

———, *The Letters*, edited by Percy Lubbock, 2 vols. (London: Macmillan, 1920)

———, *The Art of Fiction* (New York: Oxford University Press, 1948)

———, *Notebooks*, edited by F. O. Mathiessen & K. B. Murdock (New York: Oxford University Press, 1947)

KELLOGG, GRACE, *The Two Lives of Edith Wharton: The Woman and her Work* (New York: Appleton-Century, 1965)

LAWSON, RICHARD H., *Edith Wharton* (New York: Ungar, 1977)

LEAVIS, Q. D., 'Henry James's Heiress: The Importance of Edith Wharton', *Scrutiny* 7, December 1938

LEWIS, R. W. B., *Edith Wharton: A Biography* (London: Constable; New York: Harper & Row, 1975)

LINDBERG, G., *Edith Wharton and the Novel of Manners* (Charlottesville: University Press of Virginia, 1975)

LOVETT, ROBERT MORSS, *Edith Wharton* (New York: McBride, 1925)

LUBBOCK, PERCY, *The Craft of Fiction* (London: Jonathan Cape, 1921)

———, *Portrait of Edith Wharton* (London: Jonathan Cape, 1947)

LYDE, MARILYN JONES, *Edith Wharton: Convention and Morality in the Work of a Novelist* (Norman, Oklahoma: Oklahoma University Press, 1959)

MANSFIELD, KATHERINE, *Novels and Novelists,* edited by J. M. Murry (London: Constable, 1930)

McDOWELL, MARGARET B., *Edith Wharton* (Boston: Twayne, 1976)

MELISH, LAWSON, M., A Bibliography of the Collected Writings of Edith Wharton (New York: E. B. Hackett, 1927)

MENCKEN, H. L., *The American Language,* 4th edn. (New York: Knopf, 1936)

NEVIUS, BLAKE, *Edith Wharton: A Study of her Fiction* (Berkeley: University of California Press, 1953)

QUINN, ARTHUR H., *Edith Wharton* (New York: Appleton-Century, 1938)

SANTAYANA, GEORGE, 'The Genteel Tradition', *Winds of Doctrine* (New York: Scribner's, 1926)

TRILLING, LIONEL, 'The Morality of Inertia', in *Great Moral Dilemmas,* edited by Robert MacIver (New York: Harper & Bros., 1956). Reprinted in Irving Howe (ed.), *Edith Wharton: A Collection of Critical Essays* (Englewood Cliffs, N.J.: Prentice-Hall, 1962), p. 137–46

———, *The Liberal Imagination* (London: Secker & Warburg, 1951)

———, *A Gathering of Fugitives* (London: Secker & Warburg, 1957)

WALTON, GEOFFREY, *Edith Wharton: A Critical Interpretation* (Rutherford, N. J.: Farleigh Dickinson, 1982)

WERSHOVEN, CAROL, *The Female Intruder in the Novels of Edith Wharton* (Cranbury: Farleigh Dickinson, 1982)

WHARTON, EDITH, *The Collected Letters of Edith Wharton* (New York: Scribner's, 1988)

WILSON, EDMUND, *The Wound and the Bow* (London: Secker & Warburg, 1941)

———, *Classics and Commercials* (London: Secker & Warburg, 1950)

WINTERS, IVOR, 'Maule's Curse', reprinted in *In Defence of Reason* (London: Routledge, 1960)

WOLFF, CYNTHIA GRIFFIN, *A Feast of Words: The Triumph of Edith Wharton* (New York: Oxford University Press, 1977)

# Index